Sufi Metaphysics and Qur'ānic Prophets

Sufi Metaphysics and Qur'ānic Prophets

IBN ʿARABĪ'S THOUGHT AND METHOD IN THE *FUṢŪṢ AL-ḤIKAM*

Ronald L. Nettler

THE ISLAMIC TEXTS SOCIETY

This edition published in 2003 by
The Islamic Texts Society
Miller's House
Kings Mill Lane
Great Shelford
Cambridge CB22 5EN, U.K.

Reprint 2012

British Library Cataloguing-in-Publication Data.
A catalogue record for this book is
available from the British Library.

ISBN 978 1903682 05 0 cloth
ISBN 978 1903682 06 7 paper

Earlier versions of some of the chapters in *Sufi Metaphysics and Qur'ānic Prophets* have appeared in the following publications:

'Ibn ʿArabi as a Qur'anic Thinker: Reflections on Adam in the *Fusus al-Hikam*', in *The Scottish Journal of Religious Studies*, Vol. XIII, no. 2, Autumn 1992.

'Prophecy, Qur'ān and Metaphysics in Ibn ʿArabī's Discussion of ʿUzayr (Ezra)', in *Studies in Muslim-Jewish Relations*, Vol. I, ed. R. L. Nettler, Harwood Academic Publishers, Reading, 1993.

'The Wisdom of Divine Unity: Qur'anic Paradoxes and Inversions in Ibn ʿArabi's Gloss on Hud in the *Fusus al-Hikam*', in *Journal of the Muhyiddin Ibn ʿArabi Society*, Vol. 16, 1994.

'Ibn ʿArabi and the Qur'an: Some Passages Concerning Musa in *the Fusus al-Hikam*, in *Journal of the Muhyiddin Ibn ʿArabi Society*, Vol. 20, 1996.

'Ibn ʿArabi's Conception of God's Universal Mercy: The Chapter on Zakariyya in the *Fusus al-Hikam*', in *Consciousness and Reality: Studies in Memory of Toshihiku Izutsu*, Tokyo, Iwanami Shoten Publishers, 1998.

'The Figure and Truth of Abraham in Ibn ʿArabi's *Fusus al-Hikam*: A Scriptural Story Told in Metaphysical Form', in *Journal of the Muhyiddin Ibn ʿArabi Society*, Vol. 24, 1998.

Cover illustration: MS. MARSH 684, fol. 36v, bu permission of
The Bodleian Library, University of Oxford.

For Bonnie and Amir

Contents

Preface

1 Ibn ʿArabī, His Sufi Thought and the *Fuṣūṣ al-Ḥikam* 1

2 The Wisdom of Divinity in the Word of Ādam 17

3 The Wisdom of Exaltedness in the Word of Mūsā 25

4 The Wisdom of Leadership in the Word of Hārūn 38

5 The Wisdom of Ecstatic Love in the Word of Ibrāhīm 69

6 The Wisdom of Divine Unity in the Word of Hūd 102

7 The Wisdom of the Heart in the Word of Shuʿayb 114

8 The Wisdom of Divine Decree in the Word of ʿUzayr 137

9 The Wisdom of Divine Sovereignty in the Word of Zakariyyā 154

10 The Wisdom of Singularity in the Word of Muḥammad 176

11 A Lūṭian Epilogue 204

Bibliography 217

Index 221

Preface

This book is the fruit of many years of studying and teaching Ibn ʿArabī's thought, particularly his *Fuṣūṣ al-Ḥikam*. Some chapters are revised versions of pieces published earlier and others are completely new. The focus is on the text of the *Fuṣūṣ* itself, with no reliance on the standard commentaries or on Ibn ʿArabī's other works. The book is thus conceived as an analytical commentary on the *Fuṣūṣ*, closely following Ibn ʿArabī's arguments in their order and organisation, and referring, where necessary, to other sources and ideas apart from those of Ibn ʿArabī. In elucidating the Qur'ānic/metaphysical synthesis at the heart of the *Fuṣūṣ*, it brings out the main metaphysical points and related Qur'ānic content, showing how Ibn ʿArabī reaches his own metaphysical interpretations of the Qur'ān. The book is not, then, a summary of Ibn ʿArabī's thought, but rather a step-by-step presentation of his own logic and procedure in the *Fuṣūṣ*. Ibn ʿArabī's sufi metaphysical interpretations of the Qur'ān are different from other interpretations. The differences are best shown by allowing Ibn ʿArabī in this way to guide us. This approach reveals the main features of his interpretations, as well as clarifying the paradoxes and 'logical gaps' so central to his method. I have chosen to arrange the chapters differently from their order in the *Fuṣūṣ*, so that the analysis will progress from 'simpler' ideas to more complex ones. This will allow a cumulative approach toward a comprehensive understanding. The *Fuṣūṣ al-Ḥikam*—often translated as 'Bezels of Wisdom'—is organised in twenty-seven chapters (*fuṣūṣ*). Each chapter (*faṣṣ*) is devoted to a particular

Qur'ānic prophet (except in the case of Khālid b. Sinān) whose special 'wisdom', *ḥikma*, as exemplified in the 'word', *kalima*, of that prophet, serves as the theme of the chapter. The present work is concerned with ten chapters of the *Fuṣūṣ*.

I should like to thank the Faculty of Oriental Studies, Oxford University, for a grant toward the cost of copy-editing, the Islamic Texts Society and Fatima Azzam for their encouragement and editorial efforts, and my students at the Oriental Institute, Oxford University, for their diligence and ideas.

Ronald L. Nettler
Oxford

CHAPTER

I

Ibn ᶜArabī, His Sufi Thought and the *Fuṣūṣ al-Ḥikam*

THE MAN

Muḥammad b. ᶜAlī al-ᶜArabī al-Ḥātimī al-Ṭā'ī, commonly known and referred to as Ibn ᶜArabī, was a major figure of Islamic religious thought and of sufism, the mystical tradition of Islam. Ibn ᶜArabī was born in Murcia in al-Andalus, Islamic Spain, on 27 July 1165 (17 Ramaḍān 560). He grew up in a privileged position, as a result of his father's various posts of political importance. Inclining in his later teen years toward a quest for intellectual, religious and spiritual truth, Ibn ᶜArabī spent the rest of his life on this path. From his late twenties, he began his physical journeys outward from Spain, first to the Maghrib several times and, in following years, to various points in the East. In 1223, Ibn ᶜArabī finally settled in Damascus where, now finished with his wanderings, he lived out his remaining years, working assiduously and producing a number of important works; among these was the *Fuṣūṣ al-Ḥīkam*, which Ibn ᶜArabī claimed to have received in a vision from the Prophet Muḥammad in that city.

The long period of travel was for Ibn ᶜArabī the physical correlative and the context of his concomitant intellectual and religious journey. Learning from others, as well as himself teaching them during his wanderings, Ibn ᶜArabī achieved an impressive literary productivity closely linked with his physical movements. Each place, it seems, provided the human and creative resources which made possible the development and refinement of his outlook. The 'arc' of Ibn ʿArabī's life, as Henri Corbin called it, was in this sense truly integrative.[1] The result was an original perspective that in later Islam served to re-orientate religious thought, whether sufi or other, in most profound ways.

IBN ʿARABĪ'S SUFI THOUGHT

Ibn ʿArabī's sufi thought is highly complex and subtle. In both its method and content, Ibn ʿArabī's thought resists any simple and straightforward understanding; it yields itself only to the most strenuous interpretative efforts and then only partially, often leaving unresolved problems and some degree of ambiguity. This is particularly true in the case of the *Fuṣūṣ al-Ḥikam*, but it holds also for Ibn ʿArabī's other works which propound his characteristic sufi metaphysics.

The difficulties derive mainly from conceptual and linguistic ambiguity, and complex, overlapping and multilevelled ideas in an esoteric formulation. Additionally, there is a linguistic complexity borne out of literary richness and nuance, as well as the obfuscation generally associated with esoteric ideas. Then, as with much of the literature of medieval Islamic religious thought, there is here also an oral factor. The texts derived to some extent from an interweaving of discussion and writing. The discussion would be absorbed within the texts and the texts in their final forms would thus reflect and contain the discussion. As in most cases the history of this process obviously cannot be reconstructed, for this reason certain ambiguities will remain in the writings. These cannot easily (if at all) be resolved,

1. Henri Corbin, *Creative Imagination in the Sufism of Ibn ʿArabī*, pp. 38–73, for Corbin's discussion of Ibn ʿArabī's life. The most important biographical study of Ibn ʿArabī thus far is Claude Addas's book *Quest for the Red Sulphur: The Life of Ibn ʿArabī*. This work should be consulted for the detail of Ibn ʿArabī's life and for the historical development of his thought.

because they originally arose in discussion and they remain there. In Ibn ʿArabī's work, however, the complexity of his thought and the subtlety of his expression remain the greater problem.

Despite these barriers, modern scholarship, greatly aided by traditional sources, has achieved a certain comprehension of Ibn ʿArabī's outlook. However provisional and sometimes obviously uncertain, our present understanding does constitute a firm foundation for going forward. I should like now, however briefly, to provide some overview of Ibn ʿArabī's thought, in particular as this is relevant to his *Fuṣūṣ al-Ḥikam*. While the understanding and explication below are my own, they will inevitably reflect also some views of other modern scholars who have contributed to our common base of knowledge. As my purpose here is more general than specific, I may not in all instances cite them, but I remain grateful for their various contributions.[2]

SUFI METAPHYSICS

The main term I use to describe Ibn ʿArabī's mystical thought is that of sufi metaphysics. This term, in my view, incorporates the experiential, personal element and its profound intellectualisation with Ibn ʿArabī in his metaphysics. By metaphysics here I do not mean a full philosophical doctrine, as more narrowly and precisely formulated in the true philosophical traditions; this is rather a far-reaching intellectual expression of intertwined experience and ideas which addresses ultimate transcendent

2. In addition, some of the traditional commentaries on the *Fuṣūṣ* have in some respects aided my attempts to understand this work, as have Professor ʿAfifi's interpretative comments in his edition of the text. ʿAbd al-Razzāq al-Qāshānī's *Sharḥ ʿalā Fuṣūṣ al-Ḥikam* has been particularly helpful. However, for the approach I have been trying to develop, as presented in this book, it was important and necessary to work mainly with the *Fuṣūṣ* itself, in an 'unmediated' way, and even without reference to other of Ibn ʿArabī's works or influences upon him. Translations from the *Fuṣūṣ* are my own.

issues of cosmogony and cosmology, God and man, this world and the next. There is here much that may be drawn from traditional Islamic philosophical and theological thought—especially the problem of the One and the many with its components of classical and post-classical ideas; there are also many elements of the other Islamic religious and secular, intellectual and scientific traditions. Ibn ʿArabī, like many other great medieval Muslim intellectuals, was very much a polymath who brought all he possessed to bear on the issues of his concern. Indeed, it is quite clear even that he saw in his sufi metaphysics a basis for the resolution of the major outstanding problems of Islamic religious thought in his time from a new perspective.

Though sometimes, then, redolent of aspects of philosophical metaphysics, Ibn ʿArabī's outlook goes beyond and differs from the other tradition in its formulations, expressions and content. It is also different in its very reason for being, as an intellectualisation of the earlier tradition of sufism—thus, again, the name 'sufi metaphysics'. For though it would be wrong to deny sufism prior to Ibn ʿArabī, whether 'Western' or 'Eastern', any intellectual attributes or systematisation, the core and focal point of the tradition usually remained decidedly on the side of personal religious experience and its expression. These basic 'mystical' features understandably still remain critical for Ibn ʿArabī and, by his own claim, they define and direct his sufi career; but his sufism must in great part be understood as an intellectualisation of that prior tradition, if it is to be understood at all, and if its significance is to be appreciated. Annemarie Schimmel has put it well:

> But whatever the Spanish-born mystic who soon became known as *ash-shaikh al-akbar* (Magister Magnus) might have intended, there is a world of difference between his approach to religion and the dynamic, personal religion of Hallaj. With Ibn ʿArabī, Islamic mysticism comes close to the mysticism of infinity, and his approach is theosophical or gnostic rather than voluntaristic, for his goal is to lift the veils of ignorance which hide the basic

> identity of man and the Divine, while in early Sufism the element of personal love between man and God was predominant.[3]

Ibn ʿArabī's sufi metaphysics is vast and vastly complex. Its main ideas, style and method, as said above, render it difficult to penetrate. A focused survey of the main ideas, as these are formulated and appear especially in the *Fuṣūṣ*, will give more substance to this general characterisation of the metaphysics; it will also provide a necessary conceptual background for the Qur'ānic analyses of the *Fuṣūṣ* made in the following chapters. Preliminary to this survey, let us briefly consider Ibn ʿArabī's own view of the origin of the *Fuṣūṣ*.

THE ORIGIN OF THE *FUṢŪṢ*

Like most of Ibn ʿArabī's works, the *Fuṣūṣ* on his claim is a product of transcendent inspiration; in this case, indeed, his inspiration seems clear and direct:

> I saw the Messenger of God, peace be upon him, in a vision given me at the end of [the month of] Muḥarram, in the year 627, in Damascus. Thus, he said to me, 'This is the book, *Fuṣūṣ al-Ḥikam*. Take it and reveal it to the people, who would benefit by it.' I then said, 'With fidelity and obedience to God, we shall do exactly as we have been commanded.' Thus did I actualise the demand, purifying intention and directing purpose and resolution toward disseminating this book, just as the Messenger of God, peace be upon him, delineated it for me, without addition or deletion....[4]

3. Annemarie Schimmel, *As Through a Veil: Mystical Poetry in Islam*, 1982, p. 38. Again, I do not mean that sufism prior to Ibn ʿArabī did not possess a developing intellectual expression. It did. Ibn ʿArabī, however, constituted a watershed in that development.

4. *Fuṣūṣ* , p. 47. The word Ibn ʿArabī uses here for his 'vision' is *mubashshira*. For a brief discussion of this term as seen in Islamic religious literature, see Simeon Evstatiev, 'The Khātam al-Nabiyyīn Doctrine in Arabic Historical Thought', pp. 458–461.

All references to the *Fuṣūṣ* will be to the edition of Professor Abū al-ʿAlā ʿAfīfī which includes his introduction and interpretative comments: *Fuṣūṣ al-Ḥikam wa'l-Taʿlīqāt ʿalayhi*, Cairo, Dār al-Fikrī al-ʿArabī, n.d. For a full English translation, R. W. J. Austin's *The Bezels of Wisdom* is standard.

Ibn ʿArabī's claim here that he is merely transmitting in the *Fuṣūṣ* what the Prophet Muḥammad 'revealed' to him is also accompanied by the assertion that the people should therefore have no fear of any 'deception' (*talbīs*) in it. For, he says, he would not 'reveal' to others in 'this writing' (the *Fuṣūṣ*), anything other than what the Prophet had 'revealed' to him.[5] Concerning his personal status in all of this, Ibn ʿArabī says, 'I am neither a prophet nor a messenger, but merely an heir (*wārith*), sowing the seed for my hereafter.'[6] Though here, typically for him, making clear that a *walī* (sufi 'saint') such as himself, can make no pretence to true prophethood, Ibn ʿArabī is also making clear that his own book, the *Fuṣūṣ*, in being 'revealed' to him by the Prophet of Islam who sought its wide dissemination, provides an esoteric correlative to the original Qur'ānic revelation: thus Ibn ʿArabī's use of the Arabic root *n-z-l* in referring to the Prophet's 'revealing' of the *Fuṣūṣ* to him and his particular presentation of the whole 'revelatory' experience. This prophetic visionary origin of the *Fuṣūṣ* serves Ibn ʿArabī as the implicit, ultimate support in his 'Qur'ānic story-telling' in the book, thereby linking Qur'ān with sufi metaphysics in fully integrative fashion. This link is also clear in the very content and structure of the *Fuṣūṣ*, with its organisation in twenty-seven chapters devoted to Qur'ānic prophets.

SUFI METAPHYSICS IN THE *FUṢŪṢ*

Ibn ʿArabī's sufi metaphysics in the *Fuṣūṣ* represents his general metaphysical thought as that is seen in so many of his works, appearing there in various formulations and presentations. The *Fuṣūṣ* presents this metaphysical thought in a particularly distilled fashion and with a sharply defined prophetic theme.

5. *Ibid.*
6. *Ibid.*

While making the *Fuṣūṣ* a 'dense' work (even for Ibn ʿArabī), these features also give it a useful focus for analysis. In my synopsis of some central ideas in Ibn ʿArabī's sufi metaphysics I shall be concise, the goal again being to provide proper background and foundation for the Qur'ānic analysis of the *Fuṣūṣ*, rather than an exhaustive exposition of this thought. Further and more detailed discussion of the metaphysics will figure prominently in the Qur'ānic analysis. Three categories of ideas, then, will be addressed here: the One and the many; the metaphysical and the ethical; the *Fuṣūṣ* and the Qur'ān.

THE ONE AND THE MANY

The issue of the One and the many, unity and diversity, may be seen as the bedrock of Ibn ʿArabī's sufi metaphysics. From here all else issues and to this all returns. Derived ultimately from a synthesis of the religious experience, the philosophical and theological reflection in various Islamic intellectual traditions and his own creative thought, Ibn ʿArabī's single-minded pursuit of a resolution to this issue constitutes a primary intellectual concern for him. The question is how a 'mystical', unitive presence and a correlative theoretical universal oneness may be aligned with an empirical multiplicity. Further, if the ultimate answer is on the side of unity—which it is for Ibn ʿArabī—then what of the Islamic monotheistic notion of God and His creation separated by an unbridgeable gulf? Indeed, how *is* the issue of the One and the many related to traditional ideas of God and His creation and God and His attributes for Ibn ʿArabī? Put simply, all these issues are for him as one, though sometimes expressed in 'different languages' requiring different formulations in different circumstances. Ibn ʿArabī's answer always emphasises the oneness and unity of things, known by way of multiplicity.

Eschewing standard philosophical, theological and traditional views positing God Himself as either the cause of multiplicity, or as a causal intermediate influence, Ibn ʿArabī then chooses to affirm an *identification* of the One and the many, God and His creation. However, though in one sense the 'two' for him *are* as one, in another they are not—and cannot—be reduced to the oneness of total identification. Indeed, Ibn ʿArabī's complete fidelity to the conventional monotheistic pattern of unity (God) and multiplicity (His creation) again is patent *on one level.* But in the context of Ibn ʿArabī's sufi metaphysics, there *is* an identification. Is this not contradictory? I think not—certainly not for Ibn ʿArabī—though it has posed a significant barrier for some in understanding his thought. Ibn ʿArabī's most perceptive and vehement traditional critics within the Islamic world do indeed see the unitive theme in all its complexity; and they see it as the whole of Ibn ʿArabī's outlook, to the exclusion of the more usual Islamic notions of God and His creation. For these critics, Ibn ʿArabī clearly reduces God and man, God and His creation, to one and the same thing, thereby, apart from all else, deifying man and throwing law and ethics into confusion. In my view, these critics correctly identify *one dimension* of the sufi metaphysics, but they also neglect, or fail to see, Ibn ʿArabī's most subtle interweaving of this notion with the other, more usual, conception of the gulf between God and His creation. It is in this subtle interweaving, on different levels and from various perspectives, where Ibn ʿArabī's full meaning is situated and where a dialectical tension between both notions is achieved in a fluid synthesis. An analysis of Ibn ʿArabī's thought must take account of the complexity of this issue; it must not be based on the principle of 'excluded middle', an 'either/or' approach, which Ibn ʿArabī himself so thoroughly denies. We must, then, recognise that while the unitive principle for Ibn ʿArabī provides the most comprehensive meaning for religion, it does not thus negate the notion of God and His creation in strict separation and with creation's total dependency upon its Creator

Ibn ʿArabī's unitive principle—either a 'monism' or 'non-duality', as some would refer to it[7]—is expressed and formulated in various ways, throughout his works. These formulations are usually among the most subtle and difficult passages. I shall discuss some examples here, mainly as they are germane to the thought of the *Fuṣūṣ* and, more narrowly, to our Qur'ānic analyses of the *Fuṣūṣ*.

The basic issue of the One and the many, unity and multiplicity, as Ibn ʿArabī interweaves it with traditional Islamic conceptions of God and the world, is prominent in a particular way in the sufi metaphysics of the *Fuṣūṣ*. Ibn ʿArabī's conceptual foundation is the notion of 'being', *wujūd* (sometimes rendered in English also as 'existence', depending on the context). *Wujūd* serves Ibn ʿArabī as the main concept in the expression and formulation of his metaphysics; in this role, *wujūd* has two faces, that of absolute being (*wujūd muṭlaq*) and that of conditional being (*wujūd muqayyad*). *Wujūd muṭlaq* is the unitive principle, the fundamental undifferentiated oneness of things; it alone represents true being. The differentiated world of multiplicity (*wujūd muqayyad*, conditional being) seems by contrast to indicate a 'less real' realm of being.[8] Posited in this rigorously contrasted way, the formulation here seems one of stark difference between absolute and conditional being. But Ibn ʿArabī's usual aversion to sharp contrasts operates here as well—indeed, the contrast for him, while remaining constant on one level, is ultimately transcended on another. The 'contrast' for him, in fact, serves then

7. I shall not get involved in the difficult (and endless) debate on the proper term to be applied here. There are numerous ideas about this in the scholarly literature on Ibn ʿArabī which are useful. My own views will, I trust, emerge in the context of the analyses presented. In general, I prefer not to use one exclusive term, but to deal with the notion in different ways, as will be seen.

8. For *wujūd mutlaq* and *wujūd muqayyad* see, e.g., *Fuṣūṣ*, p. 132. For extensive references to these and the related notions of *waḥdat al-wujūd* and *waḥdat al-shuhūd*, see Suʿād al-Ḥakīm, *al-Muʿjam al-Ṣūfī*, pp. 1130–1157. It must be noted that the idea expressed in the terms *wujūd muṭlaq* and *wujūd muqayyad* often appears in the *Fuṣūṣ* without the explicit use of this terminology. In these cases, the idea is usually clearly understood.

as the main vehicle of its own overcoming. This leaves absolute being dominant through an 'upgrading' of conditional being.

For Ibn ʿArabī, the issue of absolute being and conditional being is also formulated in a more conventional theological language, as the issue of God as remote and unknowable Essence (*dhāt*) and God in His manifest attributes (*ṣifāt*). The *dhāt* may be seen as representing the One, while the *ṣifāt* are the many. Then again, from a different angle, the contrast is simply between God (unity) and His creation (multiplicity). And sometimes Ibn ʿArabī speaks of multiplicity as the 'God created in the religious doctrines' (*al-Ḥaqq al-makhlūq fī al-iʿtiqādāt*).[9] 'God created' is God as we conceive Him in the religions ('conceived' being perhaps a more correct rendering of *makhlūq* than created). God here is, again, simply God as revealed in the realm of the many, conditional existence, in His attributes.

However, Ibn ʿArabī 'transcends' these distinctions through an ultimate linking and identification of the One with the many, unity with diversity, absolute being with conditional being, the remote God with the manifest God, God as essence and God as manifest ('created') in attributes and names. He effects this linking through a number of bridging concepts, all of which have one main point: the One and the many inevitably meet. This happens in several ways: the One may reveal itself in certain particular forms in the world of the many, thereby showing its omnipresence or 'immanence'. A prime example of this is Ibn ʿArabī's use of the notions of *majālin* and *tajalliyāt* ('manifestations' or 'appearances'), or *maẓāhir* ('sites of manifestation') which may be certain persons, places or things, to indicate the foci of the coalescence of the One/many in the manifestation of the One. Or the whole world of multiplicity may be seen as the shadow (*ẓill*) of the One; therefore, just as the physical body

9. E.g., *Fuṣūṣ* pp. 121 and 178 and in ʿAfīfī's *Taʿliqāt*, p. 250. For discussions of this and related terms in Ibn ʿArabī's thought see: Suʿād al-Ḥakīm *al-Muʿjam al-Ṣūfī*, pp. 87–93, and Henri Corbin, *Creative Imagination in the Sufism of Ibn ʿArabī*, pp. 124-125; 195–200; 265–267.

and the shadow it casts are inseparable, so too are the One and the many. [10] Or, the world of multiplicity in conditional being may be the true God's outward form. Though multiplicity *is* real for Ibn ʿArabī in its seeming opposition to unity, the reality of this opposition is conceptual, while unity is the overriding ontological truth in its ultimate subsuming and absorbing of all diversity. But again, it is the presumed and felt tension between these two 'sides' which provides the rich intellectual core of Ibn ʿArabī's sufi metaphysics in its integration with traditional religion and in its fullest expression.

THE METAPHYSICAL AND THE ETHICAL

One major area of intersection, and integration, of metaphysics and tradition here is in the realm of ethics and the law. From the perspective of an all-embracing unity of the kind mooted by Ibn ʿArabī, the ethical and legal distinctions, both theoretical and practical, are part of the world of multiplicity; as such, they too may be seen in their ontological absorption in the One. But the inevitable effacing of such distinctions would wreak havoc with the traditional ethical codes and legal systems which, in theory and practice, were the very foundation of Islamic tradition and society. For, it might seem, in the all-encompassing unity, the ethical would be assimilated into oblivion. As we shall see in the following chapters, Ibn ʿArabī does indeed subsume the ethical within metaphysical unity, thereby detaching the ethical from its erstwhile moorings and rendering it 'defunct' in a new world of ethical as well as metaphysical oneness. He does this in several ways. One main way is his paradoxical inversion of conventional ethical principles into their opposites, thereby

10. The chapter on Hārūn contains examples of such derivatives of the *j-l-y* root, as does p. 120 of the *Fuṣūṣ*, while for references to and discussion of *ẓill* see Suʿād al-Ḥakīm, *al-Muʿjam al-Ṣūfī*, pp. 747–750. Finally, another bridging concept, though somewhat different than those mentioned here, is that of the 'fixed essences', *al-aʿyān al-thābita*; this will be discussed below in the ethical context.

emptying conventional judgements, commands and prohibitions of their usual meanings and contents. Thus, for example, in the story of the worship of the golden calf in the chapter of Hārūn, Ibn ʿArabī claims this act paradoxically to have been true worship of God who resides in everything, including such images and idols. God, as ontological unity, has here absorbed the particularity of the idol into a realm of oneness, in which good and evil, themselves distinctions of diversity, can no longer be meaningful. It would seem that for Ibn ʿArabī here ethics would actually require this transcendent position in order fully to realise God in His identity as ontological unity.

Another way in which Ibn ʿArabī treats ethics within his metaphysics is through the metaphysical notion of the 'fixed essences' (*al-aʿyān al-thābita*),[11] prefigured patterns of all that will exist in the realm of conditional being, the world of diversity. Human nature and behaviour, like everything else, are thus determined according to their fixed essences, even to the exclusion of God's own ability to affect events and things in the world, including human actions. These actions are thus 'predetermined', but *not directly* by God. God's 'inability' in this respect is in no sense a defect in Him. On the contrary. For fundamental to Ibn ʿArabī's methods in dealing with ethics is the underlying assumption that this world of diversity is in fact an expression of God's very essence, as that essence has become manifest. *God's essence* as absolute being is thus transformed into *God's manifestation* as conditional being or diversity, as mentioned above. The whole realm of ethics thus becomes 'relativised', as part of the phenomenal flux behind which lies the ethical stillness of true reality, undifferentiated oneness. In addition to these most prominent approaches to ethics in Ibn ʿArabī's metaphysics, others are also employed as variations on these themes.

11. Discussed often in the following chapters, this notion is basic to Ibn ʿArabī's sufi metaphysics and also provides a mechanism for ethics with the metaphysics. For reference to and discussion of this notion in Ibn ʿArabī's works, see Suʿād al-Ḥakīm, *al-Muʿjam al-Ṣūfī*, pp. 831–839.

Here, then, good and evil have truly been inverted and transcended in the essence of God as ultimate unity. However, lest one think Ibn ʿArabī was thus a true antinomian, on the evidence of his thinking about ethics within his metaphysics, that would not be true. For though a casual reading of the *Fuṣūṣ* might sometimes give cause for such an assessment, more careful consideration reveals there an absolute fidelity to traditional ethics and law. It is here, as with so much else in Ibn ʿArabī, that his *understanding* and *interpretation* of religion are so dramatically original and challenging, while his adherence to traditional conceptions and upholding of punctilious practice of religion remain constant, if within the context of his original views.

Ibn ʿArabī's adherence to tradition may in one aspect be seen in the Qur'ān-centredness of the *Fuṣūṣ* and of other works. One might even argue that the Qur'ān and, secondarily, other traditional elements of Islam constitute for Ibn ʿArabī the core and foundation of religion through which his sufi metaphysics takes form and achieves its significance. Indeed, on the basis of the origin of the *Fuṣūṣ* as reported by Ibn ʿArabī, it would seem, as I said earlier, that for him the *Fuṣūṣ* represented the truth of the Qur'ān in esoteric, metaphysical form. In the same way, Ibn ʿArabī believed that he was the final and most complete manifestation of the esoteric and metaphysical nature of the Prophet.[12]

THE *FUṢŪṢ* AND THE QUR'ĀN

My basic approach to Ibn ʿArabī's thought in the *Fuṣūṣ* is, then, from a Qur'ānic and traditional Islamic perspective.[13] Such a

12. See M. Chodkiewicz's *The Seal of the Saints: Prophecy and Sainthood in the Doctrine of Ibn ʿArabī* for an excellent discussion of this issue. Particularly relevant to my concerns in the following chapters are the related epistemic issues and the notion of specific prophecy and general spiritual inspiration.

13. Renderings of Qur'ānic passages are my own, but A. Yusuf Ali *The Meaning of the Holy Qur'ān* is an English rendering that is always suggestive and has been helpful to me.

perspective reveals Qur'ānic (and, sometimes, also *ḥadīth*) framework stories as the core round which Ibn ʿArabī builds and explicates his sufi metaphysics. This is effected in the text in different ways, the better to fulfil Ibn ʿArabī's purpose in the various chapters of the *Fuṣūṣ*. He might, for example, take certain elements directly from a Qur'ānic narrative(s) concerning the prophet to whom a particular chapter is dedicated and construct his framework story in this way. Other Qur'ānic passages and selected *ḥadīth* which are not directly related to that prophet might also be incorporated here. Or, he might construct a Qur'ānic 'story' composed of elements which have no overt relation in the Qur'ān to the prophet involved, but which for Ibn ʿArabī exemplify important aspects of that prophet's life and character. Or, again, in yet another, less typical, formulation, Ibn ʿArabī might use a framework story based on a *ḥadīth* narrative not overtly related to the designated prophet and employing some Qur'ānic components. Finally, Ibn ʿArabī might use any or all of these, alone or in combination.

Whichever method Ibn ʿArabī employs, Qur'ānic and traditional elements, in direct citation or in paraphrase, most often serve in the *Fuṣūṣ* as foundation and framework for explicating his metaphysics. Indeed, for him the metaphysics clearly *is* the meaning of the Qur'ān and of some later religious textual traditions. The *Fuṣūṣ* thus combines an earthy narrative literature of scripture and prophetic story with an extremely abstruse 'sufi metaphysics', the latter for him presumably reflecting the inner, essential, truth of the former. This *genre* may be called a form of 'sufi metaphysical story-telling'. It may be considered an Islamic religious literary *genre* in its own right, introduced and refined by Ibn ʿArabī in the *Fuṣūṣ* and perpetuated by later disciples. It is a *genre* in which Islamic 'popular' and 'high culture' come together, thereby providing a base of appeal also for a wide audience, despite the obvious 'high culture' bias of the *Fuṣūṣ* in its abstruse metaphysical message for an esoterically-orientated elite. The 'popular scriptural' part of that base also reflects a continuity of religious culture, from Biblical and post-Biblical, canonical and non-canonical narrative in its many oral and written forms in various times and places, to the Qur'ān and its subsequent interpretations in different Islamic contexts. The figures designated as 'prophets' and 'messengers' in the Qur'ān of course take pride of place here, as most are central in that continuity of religious culture. The *Fuṣūṣ*, with its great prophetic theme, is an important Qur'ānic context of that sort and thereby situates Ibn ʿArabī's thought in an even more comprehensive background.[14]

Ibn ʿArabī's metaphysics, so imposing in its presence and so insistent in its demands on the interpreter, is created and given meaning in the *Fuṣūṣ* through its integration with that scriptural and traditional narrative. The narrative for Ibn ʿArabī is both a religious literary link with the broader tradition of Islamic (and other) prophetic monotheism as well being his ultimate source in pursuing the insights of his sufi metaphysical theory. Ibn ʿArabī's role in Islamic history as the great intellectual theoretician of sufism must here be seen from this broader narrative perspective. The great genius of his sufi worldview, as expressed so impressively in the *Fuṣūṣ*, lies precisely in this integration of religious story and abstract thought.

The present book explicates ten chapters of the *Fuṣūṣ*, informed by this view of the text. Through close and detailed analysis of the chosen sections, Ibn ʿArabī's ideas and methods are delineated and his unique literary *genre* identified. Ibn ʿArabī's achievement in the intellectualisation of sufism may then be seen in its fullness.

Apart from the present one, each chapter of the book is a commentary on and analysis of a chapter of the *Fuṣūṣ*. I have chosen these particular ten chapters of the *Fuṣūṣ* as, in my view, they especially exemplify its ideas, methods and outlook. The

14. In a number of chapters I have discussed some Biblical, Jewish and Christian themes as suggestive commentary on this background. This is not meant to be exhaustive but, again, suggestive.

Fuṣūṣ is, in any case, a work which reiterates its main themes throughout, from different angles in the stories of the different prophets. Though any of its chapters would, therefore, convey these themes, the chapters treated here do this particularly well for my purpose. The book is thus conceived as a concise presentation of the worldview of the entire *Fuṣūṣ* and thereby of Ibn ʿArabī's sufi metaphysics. One hopes the book will serve the needs of newcomers to Ibn ʿArabī as well as those of advanced students and specialists. The Qur'ānic analysis is presented for consideration as a method and interpretation to help us look again at the texts from yet another angle.

CHAPTER

2

The Wisdom of Divinity in the Word of Ādam

ADAM IN THE BIBLICAL TRADITION

For the three prophetic monotheistic religions, Adam has, of course, a central and basic role in their conception of sacred history and the place of humanity in its unfolding. From being the progenitor of the human race created in God's image and representing humanity in general in Genesis I:26–30, to the more varied accounts where God made man (Adam) out of earth, breathed His breath into his nostrils and put him in charge of the Garden of Eden in Genesis 2–3, variations on the Biblical stories of Adam are to be found in the three monotheistic traditions. Christianity often emphasised Adam's fall as indicative of human moral frailty and, even, of original sin, while also, sometimes, seeing in him a sign of spiritual renewal. In later Judaism, particularly in the Kabbalah mysticism, Adam is portrayed as being infused with the divine breath and is conceived as theophany[1]—themes which find prominent associations in the Qur'ān and the *Fuṣūṣ*.

ĀDAM IN THE QUR'ĀN AND THE *FUṢŪṢ*

The Qur'ānic story, in brief compass, portrays Ādam as God's most important creation and His 'successor' (*khalīfa*) on earth, to whom He has taught all the divine names, into whom He has

1. For a good survey of Adam in the Biblical/Judaic and Christian traditions see *The Encyclopedia of Religion*, Volume 1, pp. 27–28.

breathed His divine breath and to whom He commands the angels to bow. Ibn ʿArabī's Ādam in the *Fuṣūṣ* exemplifies 'the wisdom of divinity' (*ḥikma ilāhiyya*), as the title of the chapter on Ādam puts it. In itself, *ḥikma ilāhiyya* is an indeterminate term, never specifically defined by Ibn ʿArabī. These themes, reflecting the Qur'ān, all have to do with Ādam the first human, Ādam as progenitor of the race and Ādam as manifestation of divine perfection in human form. Ādam is here also an 'all-encompassing being' (*kawn jāmiʿ*) and, in another formulation, *al-Insān al-Kāmil*, the Perfect Man. God created Ādam as a divine self-expression in which He could better 'see' and contemplate Himself. As theophany in this sense, Ādam is also a metaphor for the implicit perfectibility of man. This is Ibn ʿArabī's basic sufi metaphysical evocation of the Qur'ānic Ādam, who was generally and popularly known in traditional accounts as Abū al-Bashar, Father of Humanity. Ibn ʿArabī amplifies the metaphysical concept of Ādam, developing along various lines through his integrated Qur'ānic– metaphysical exposition. He does this on the metaphysical plane in a way similar to his treatment of the Qur'ānic notion of God's mercy in the story of Zakariyyā and Qur'ānically by following the basic outlines of the Qur'ānic story of Ādam.[2]

GOD, HIS NAMES AND DIVINE SELF-REVELATION

God, in His Qur'ānic and traditional name of al-Ḥaqq, and qualified by the Qur'ānic formula of praise to Him, *subḥānahu*, is Ibn ʿArabi's point of departure in his discussion of Ādam. In particular, it is God's 'most beautiful names', the Qur'ānic *al-asmā' al-ḥusnā*, which are the most prominent feature in Ibn ʿArabī's opening lines.[3] Thus does Ibn ʿArabī assert that:

2. Qur'ān, 2:30–32; 7:10; 15:31; 18:48; 38:74.

3. *Fuṣūṣ*, p. 48; Qur'ān, *e.g.*, 7:180. Crucially important in Islamic religious thought, God's names have been the subject of much discussion. For a major study of the theological implications of the names, see M. Allard, *Le problème des attributs divins dans la doctrine d'al-Ashʿarī et de ses premiers grands disciples*.

> Al-Ḥaqq, praise be to Him, wanted, through His most beautiful names which are innumerable, to see the essences (*aʿyān*) of the names—or, if you will, to see Himself [or His own *ʿayn*, essence]. He wished to do this through an all-encompassing being (*kawn jāmiʿ*) who embraces the whole matter: a being which embodies the attribute of existence. Through this being, God's secret would then be revealed to Himself.[4]

The Qur'ānic God and His names have become enmeshed here in another vocabulary and outlook, that of Ibn ʿArabī's sufi metaphysics. Thus, God's names have 'essences' which God wants to 'see', and, through these essences, He wishes to see Himself (or 'His essence'). Further, He wants to see Himself and His secret in this way through a *kawn jāmiʿ* who is suited for this role because he embodies being, *wujūd*. This, as we know, is in Ibn ʿArabī's metaphysics the phenomenal expression of the remote, unknown God, in the form of conditional being (*wujūd muqayyad*).

The essences which God's most beautiful names possess here are *al-aʿyān al-thābita*, the fixed essences of Ibn ʿArabī's sufi metaphysics, which from archetypal forms become the things in the world of conditional (phenomenal) being. In giving these essences to God's Qur'ānic names, Ibn ʿArabī has here extended the significance of the names from their meaning as descriptions of God in the Qur'ān to 'things' in the phenomenal world. God's names may then be known, the way other things are known. God will then be able to see Himself in the essences of His names as He so wishes to do. The divine names, embodied through their essences in this way represent for Ibn ʿArabī God's 'projection outward' of Himself, as opposed to His internal 'encapsulated' self, His remote essence, or *dhāt*.[5] God's names from this perspective are God's creation and in this sense they *are* God. He can 'see' Himself in this objectification of His

4. *Fuṣūṣ*, p. 48.

5. Ibn ʿArabī here, as elsewhere, borrows the essences/attributes conception of God from Islamic theology and uses it in a very different way.

names—they *are* He, just as, for Ibn ʿArabī, all creation is He. This is Ibn ʿArabī's sufi metaphysical notion of creation, as metaphysical analogue of the Qur'ānic divine linear creation from nothing. Furthermore, the Qur'ānic names of God serve here conceptually as a 'two-way filter' through which Qur'ānic and metaphysical meanings are enmeshed, pointing towards their ultimate identity in fact. Ādam will play a central role in this organisation and process.

THE LOCUS OF DIVINE SELF-REVELATION

Though for Ibn ʿArabī God (al-Ḥaqq) is all, and all is He, and this 'circular process' is manifested in His names which incorporate and express creation as existence, Ibn ʿArabī also designates a special focal point within this process in which divine self-observation occurs in the essences of God's names. This focal point is the *kawn jāmiʿ*, the 'all-encompassing being',[6] which embraces 'the whole matter' or the (divine) command, *al-amr*. The Qur'ānic *amr* is permeated here by an ambiguity, signifying either (or both) 'the whole matter' or God's existential command to be—'*kun*'. For Ibn ʿArabī, both meanings are relevant and operative, as God's command here is the existential one which creates and thereby it is 'the whole matter'.[7]

A non-Qur'ānic metaphysical term and concept, the *kawn jāmiʿ* thus embraces the Qur'ānic *amr* and serves as a focal point and locus for the totality of the Qur'ānic names in their metaphysical sense. It represents God's manifestation as all of creation. The reason God 'needs' the *kawn jāmiʿ* in which to see Himself, says Ibn ʿArabī, is 'because for something to see itself through itself is not the same as its seeing itself in something else which serves as a mirror for it'.[8] Thus, in this case, 'the self appears to

6. For a survey of Ibn ʿArabī's use of this term, see Suʿād al-Ḥakīm, *al-Muʿjam al-Ṣūfī*, pp. 975–988.

7. See, *e.g.*, Qur'ān, 2:118 and 11:123.

8. *Fuṣūṣ*, p. 48.

itself in a form provided by the special place [mirror] in which it appears'.[9] Such a degree and quality of self-revelation, says Ibn ʿArabī, could not occur 'without the existence of this special place [mirror]'.[10] This *kawn jāmiʿ* is the created world in its most perfect, polished form. For:

> al-Ḥaqq, praise be to Him, had at first created the whole world as a sort of flat, undifferentiated place, devoid of the [divine] spirit, like an unpolished mirror. But the divine determination (*ḥukm*) would never do that without [making certain] that such a place was able to receive the divine spirit to which [God's] determination gives expression by breathing into [that place].[11]

And this whole process of divine breathing, says Ibn ʿArabī, is nothing but:

> Preparation of that flat, undifferentiated, form to receive the eternal divine expression. Nothing then remains but that 'receiver' whose existence comes only from [God's] own holy presence. The whole of the matter, then, its beginning and its end, is from [God]. 'And to Him the whole of the matter returns',[12] just as from Him it began. The divine command necessitates the polishing of the mirror of the world and Ādam is the very polishing of that mirror and the Holy Spirit of that [undifferentiated] form [of creation].[13]

For Ibn ʿArabī, the esoteric meaning of Ādam in the Qur'ān is the *kawn jāmiʿ* and the Perfect Man. However, the exoteric structure of the Qur'ānic Ādam story has thus far been adhered to with great fidelity: Ādam is the pinnacle of creation, God teaches him the Names which become Ādam's unique possession and Ādam receives the infusion of God's breath (*nafkh*). The

9. *Fuṣūṣ*, pp. 48–49.
10. *Fuṣūṣ*, p. 49.
11. *Ibid.*
12. Qur'ān, 11:123.
13. *Fuṣūṣ*, p. 49.

specialness of Ādam is thus incontrovertible, in a distinctively Qur'ānic sense. In the Qur'ān, Ādam's exalted status as a result of these characteristics renders him a unique prophet–person, the 'Father of Humanity'; here the meaning of these traits is conceptually transmuted for Ibn ʿArabī into the metaphysical sense which, in effect, makes Ādam a special manifestation of God Himself and an exemplar of the true nature of all created being.

This esoteric conception of Ādam means that his creation as the polished mirror is the true, inner significance of his high Qur'ānic standing. Ādam's main esoteric features for Ibn ʿArabī, his being a repository of the divine names and a recipient of the divine breath, point toward his metaphysical reality as theophany. In this way does God 'fulfil' Himself in the creation of 'the other' in whom He sees Himself very differently from the perspective of His internal self-reflection. 'Creation' here is, again, a circular process, not a linear one. What exists is not 'created' from nothing; it simply *is*. For Ibn ʿArabī, the multiplicity which is so apparent in the world and the associated conception and reality of the transcendent God who created it from nothing in linear fashion must point metaphysically to the deeper reality of divine immanence and the circularity of ontological unity. The prophets (*anbiyā'*) and great 'saints' (*awliyā'*) manifest this truth in their own being. Each in his own way is a living exemplar of it, a focal point of truth whose very presence is a complete expression of it. Ādam is of particular importance (as is Muḥammad, in another sense), because of his position in the conventional Qur'ānic and exegetical scheme; for Ibn ʿArabī's structural and thematic fidelity to Qur'ān and tradition is, again, of the highest order. Thus is Ādam an ontological point where all is revealed and concentrated. The specialness of the Qur'ānic Ādam now becomes the metaphysical specialness of the ontological Ādam. The nature of being in its circularity expressed here is for Ibn ʿArabī the true meaning of Qur'ān 11:123, which he quotes as proof of that truth: 'To Him the whole matter returns.'

THE ANGELS

One other theme remains to be discussed in Ibn ᶜArabī's treatment of Ādam: the angels. The subject of the angels completes the structure of the Qur'ānic Ādam story in Ibn ᶜArabī's version. The angels in the Qur'ān are, in general, subservient to God and rather limited and weak. More specifically for our purpose here, they are related to Ādam as inferiors to a superior. God orders them to bow to His special creation, Ādam, who is described as God's successor (*khalīfa*) on earth. With some hesitation they accede to God's command, with the exception of Iblīs who haughtily refuses.[14]

Ibn ᶜArabī first raises the subject of the angels immediately after his full portrayal of the metaphysical Ādam. He does this through invoking the notion of the universe as the Great Man (*al-Insān al-Kabīr*) which has as its corollary the conception of Man as the Small Universe (*al-ᶜĀlam al-Ṣaghīr*). Man and universe thereby form a seamless unity of being, each reflecting and incorporating the other. Approaching the issue from the side of the universe as the Great Man, Ibn ᶜArabī likens the angels to 'powers' (*quwā*) which play a subsidiary role in the metaphysics of being in the Great Man–universe, much as human sensory faculties operate in an individual person. Thus each of these powers is 'limited by its own self' and 'unable to see anything greater than itself',[15] just as the power of hearing or vision, for example, is similarly limited for an individual human being. However, Ibn ᶜArabī says that sometimes, in an obvious reference to the renegade Iblīs of the Qur'ānic Ādam story, these angels (powers) think that they are on a higher plane and that they possess the 'divine universality' (*al-jamᶜiyya al-ilāhiyya*) which partakes of 'the truth of truths' (*ḥaqīqat al-ḥaqā'iq*).[16] This divine universality is the metaphysical truth of

14. Qur'ān: 2:33–34.
15. *Fuṣūṣ*, p. 49.
16. *Fuṣūṣ*, p. 50.

the divine names. And this is only for Ādam. For 'the universality of Ādam is not for the angels',[17] as 'Ādam possesses the names, which the angels do not have'.[18] For this reason, then, 'Ādam is the successor of God'.[19]

In likening the angels to the sensory powers or faculties of a human body in his sufi metaphysical metaphor of the universe as the Great Man, Ibn ʿArabī gives them too a role in the metaphysics of being. This is natural and necessary in Ibn ʿArabī's obvious fidelity to the Qur'ānic Ādam story. Here, then, in Ibn ʿArabī's metaphysical discourse, the angels are minor, subsidiary and limited forces, characterised in a mainly negative way by their non-possession of the divine comprehensiveness (*al-jamʿiyya al-ilāhiyya*), in contradistinction to Ādam.

17. *Ibid.*
18. *Fuṣūṣ*, p. 51.
19. *Fuṣūṣ*, p. 55.

CHAPTER

3

The Wisdom of Exaltedness in the Word of Mūsā

MOSES AND MŪSĀ: BIBLICAL AND QUR'ĀNIC

Moses is a focal figure in the Biblical tradition, in Judaism, in Christianity[1] and in Islam. The great lawgiver, communal guide and liberator of his people in his most prominent visage, Moses has a variegated body of stories attached to him, within each of the traditions as well as more universally across their borders.

Both Christianity and Islam also saw him as precursor and exemplar for their own founding figures and thereby use him in a way which draws an integrated web among the traditions. In the Qur'ān, Mūsā occupies a prime position among the body of prophets, with his life, personality and religion being related at great length and in much detail. Some of the main Qur'ānic stories are: Mūsā as the model for, and as prophesying the coming of, Muḥammad (7: 157); Mūsā's killing of the Egyptian, in defending a threatened Israelite (18:1–28); Mūsā's various encounters with the burning bush (20:9–48); Mūsā's tense relationship with Pharaoh in its many manifestations (7:109–126; 10:75–78; 28:4–13; 7:127; 18:60–82); Mūsā's meeting with al-Khiḍr whom he asks to be his guide (18:60–62); Mūsā's spending forty nights with God (7:142); and Mūsā and Hārūn's involvement in the incident of the golden calf (7:148;

1. For a good general survey, see *The Encyclopaedia of Religion*, entry 'Moses', Volume 10, pp. 115–121.

20:77–98).[2] All of the Mūsā stories in the Qur'ān are, of course, elaborated in the post-Qur'ānic Islamic literatures, with new (and sometimes somewhat different) stories being added. Because of Mūsā's status in Islam, the corpus of material on him is very extensive, as it was, for the same reasons, in Judaism, Christianity and associated popular Near Eastern traditions.

IBN ᶜARABĪ'S DISCUSSION

Ibn ᶜArabī's overall discussion of Mūsā in the *Fuṣūṣ* hangs on a series of Qur'ānic vignettes of encounters between Mūsā and Pharaoh and Mūsā and al-Khiḍr. These vignettes comprise most of the main Qur'ānic stories about Mūsā as these were mentioned above. As is his wont, Ibn ᶜArabī recounts these stories by way of effecting a Qur'ānic–metaphysical synthesis. I shall be concerned solely with Ibn ᶜArabī's rendering of the story of Pharaoh's edict, calling for the killing of all Israelite sons in order to be sure to eliminate the infant Mūsā, and its implementation.[3] This story distils Ibn ᶜArabī's main conception of Mūsā's identity as prophet and the particular spiritual wisdom—*ḥikma ᶜuluwiyya*, the wisdom of exaltedness—which Ibn ᶜArabī associates with him. My discussion of this story is organised in four parts, following what I believe to be Ibn ᶜArabī's own order and organisation.[4]

'THE WISDOM OF KILLING THE SONS'

In an obvious allusion to the title of the chapter and Mūsā's 'wisdom of exaltedness', Ibn ᶜArabī opens this chapter with the

2. These Qur'ānic references are examples and are not meant to be exhaustive.

3. Qur'ān, 28:4–13, 40:25, 7:127, 2:49, 14:6.

4. I realise that the division of any text into parts, as I have done here, is inevitably somewhat arbitrary and that other divisions might also be proposed. However, I believe careful and close reading of the text does support the division suggested here. The entire discussion of Mūsā is on pp. 197–213.

words, 'the *wisdom* of killing the sons'—*ḥikma qatl al-abnā'*.[5] Here 'wisdom', *ḥikma*, so laden in Ibn ᶜArabī's usage in the *Fuṣūṣ* with his own esoteric metaphysical associations as well as with other, earlier, philosophical connotations, now is identified with Pharaoh's notorious practice of killing all the Israelite sons. *Ḥikma* is in most other contexts something positive. How can it here be part of such an objectionable action? What sort of 'exaltedness' may be found here? Surely, in the Qur'ān Pharaoh's edict is not connected with anything so positive. Nor is the contrast here only between the positive sense of *ḥikma* and Pharaoh's negative edict; for it is, more deeply, again the essential contrast between outer and inner, *ẓāhir* and *bāṭin*. Thus in Ibn ᶜArabī's view, 'the *ḥikma* of killing the sons' is indeed the deeper, esoteric meaning of this execrable act; and this meaning relates to Mūsā in a most uncommon way. Ibn ᶜArabī continues in explication of this wisdom: 'The wisdom of the killing of the sons because of Mūsā was in order that the life of each one of those killed because of him should revert to Mūsā, as each [of the others] was killed on the supposition that he might be Mūsā.'[6]

The killing of the sons has, then, a deeper meaning than is indicated on the surface. But this meaning is not yet very clear. Ibn ᶜArabī elaborates further, first by saying that each of these sons' lives is 'pure, in its nature, which is not sullied by the desires of the [worldly] soul'.[7] This, he says, is 'according to the nature of "Yes, certainly"',[8] alluding, it appears, to Qur'ān 7:172, where God produces the human race—Ādam's descendants—from the loins of Ādam's children. In answer to God's question to them, 'Am I not your Lord', they respond, 'Yes, certainly, we do witness.' This Qur'ānic notion of the universal human covenant with God through the assent of the pure

5. *Fuṣūṣ*, p. 197; Qur'ān, 28:4–13, 40:25, 7:127, 2:49, 14:6.
6. *Fuṣūṣ*, p. 197.
7. *Ibid.*
8. *Ibid.*

human lives in their inception provides Ibn ʿArabī with a further link between Mūsā and the doomed Israelite sons. In their purity with unsullied souls, all the sons, then, affirm God in covenant as their only Lord on behalf of all humanity. And Mūsā, continues Ibn ʿArabī, is 'the collective life of those sons, who were killed because he was he'.[9] Mūsā was himself among these sons, but he represents them all in being the one who 'caused' them, as it were, to be killed. This extends to the particular essential identities and propensities (*istiʿdād rūḥihi lahu*) of those killed—for, says Ibn ʿArabī, all this 'was in Mūsā, peace be upon him'.[10] This is 'a special divine trait in Mūsā which nobody before him has possessed'[11] and its implications are great. It means that 'the wisdoms of Mūsā are manifold',[12] incorporating all the inner characteristics of all the other sons and that 'Mūsā was born only to be the collectivity of many spirits, who concentrates [within himself] active powers'.[13]

Ibn ʿArabī's full meaning here will emerge only later, through a series of additional transformations of Qur'ānic and traditional concepts. The foundation, however, is clear: Mūsā's relation to the other Israelite male infants is as a repository of all their essential qualities and their (philosophical/mystical) wisdom (*ḥikma*). This, for Mūsā, is the *ḥikma* of the killing of the sons which is unique to him. Thus all the sons will die in order that Mūsā might live, while the sons' lives 'revert' to Mūsā. In the further and broader context of Qur'ān 7:172, these particular sons are for Ibn ʿArabī part of the collectivity of Ādam's emerging descendants who universally make the covenant with God for humanity. The connection—or parallel—between Mūsā and Ādam will become clearer later, but it is mooted here: in all of the discussion of Mūsā thus far, in his role as repository of the

9. *Ibid.*
10. *Ibid.*
11. *Ibid.*
12. *Ibid.*
13. *Ibid.*

spirits and wisdom of the killed sons he already appears, much as the *insān kāmil* (in its various manifestations), as the mystical locus of all Godly attributes. Ādam for Ibn ᶜArabī is similarly described.[14]

The Qur'ān's stories of the infant Mūsā, and Pharaoh's edict and its image of Ādam's progeny accepting the covenant with God, have generated some special meanings through Ibn ᶜArabī's method here. That method has thus far been quite straightforward: Ibn ᶜArabī has simply viewed the Qur'ānic story of Mūsā and the killing of the sons—not cited by him literally, but in basic framework and conception—as having the meaning he ascribes to it. The Qur'ānic story is for Ibn ᶜArabī most definitely *not a metaphor* for his truth. On the contrary. For him, as always, it simply *is* the truth which he claims for it, as in all his Qur'ānic interpretations. Ibn ᶜArabī's *method* here (and elsewhere), then, is to proceed on the basis of a *certain knowledge* of the Qur'ān's meaning. There is a link here between method and knowledge, method being based on knowledge. Other types of Qur'ānic exegesis, as we know, found their sources of knowledge in historiographical accounts, *ḥadīth* or in other parts of the Qur'ān itself. This knowledge—'public' by its nature—presumably gave legitimation to the particular exegesis. As we know, Ibn ᶜArabī's particular knowledge is generally very different from these more 'conventional' and 'public' sources of knowledge. He tells us this again here, after saying that 'the wisdoms of Mūsā are manifold': 'I shall, God willing, expand on them in this chapter, to whatever extent the divine command takes hold of my thought.'[15] Ibn ᶜArabī's claimed epistemic source, here as elsewhere, is divine inspiration. The knowledge underpinning his method is dictated by God himself. This inspiration is his muse. The method using this knowledge presumably assures absolute certainty in interpretation and a

14. See Ibn ᶜArabī's chapter on Ādam in the *Fuṣūṣ* and our discussion of it in this book.

15. *Fuṣūṣ*, p. 197.

perfect correspondence between the Qur'ān and one's understanding of it.

MŪSĀ'S POWERS AND WATER

Ibn ʿArabī goes on to explain why Mūsā's role as repository of the spirits of the killed sons also makes him a centre of 'active forces':

> Because the younger controls the older. Do you not see the child controlling the adult in a special way, where the adult descends from his supervisory role towards the child, playing with him, clucking at him and approaching him with his reason? The adult here is dominated by the child without realising it. Then the child occupies the adult through the adult's raising him, protecting him, looking after his interests and making him comfortable, lest he suffer any unease. All this is by way of the younger controlling the older and is because of the power [residing] in the position [of the younger].[16]

Himself an infant, and incorporating the spirit of all the killed sons, Mūsā's possession of such active forces, *quwā faʿʿāla*, is now understandable: a certain extraordinary *active* power resides in the seemingly *passive* nature of the very young. Their very 'passivity' compels others who are 'more powerful' to serve and to care for them, thereby inverting the apparent power relationship between the two parties. The spirits of these young, innocent souls, unsullied by the worldly desires, are extraordinarily powerful. Mūsā is the repository of these souls, for reasons stated above, so he is, consequently, the seat of the 'active forces', *i.e.*, power. So strong is this power of the 'weak' against the strong that Pharaoh himself, head of a great empire, is overcome by it, his plans for Mūsā thwarted by the simple evasive measures of those who cared for the infant: putting Mūsā in the basket in

16. *Ibid.*

the water and all the associated ensuing events. Ibn ʿArabī further elaborates on this power of the very young, ascribing it to their closeness to their origins in divine creation:

> The young have most recently been with their lord, as this is the newness of creation, while the elders are more distant. And those who are closer to God may subjugate those who are farther, as the king's close associates exercise power over those who are more distant, because of their closeness to him.[17]

Of course, a king's closest associates may normally be considered to be powerful, as opposed to the very young. It is the principle of *closeness* to the source of power which is meaningful in Ibn ʿArabī's use of this analogy here. His main principle—the apparent weakness of those who are in fact most strong—seems for the moment to have receded in order to emphasise the principle of closeness. But Ibn ʿArabī then returns to this point with an illustrative story about the Prophet Muḥammad. The prophet, says Ibn ʿArabī:

> ...would expose himself to the falling rain and uncover his head to it so that the rain would strike it, saying that the rain was fresh from its Lord. Look at the knowledge of God possessed by this prophet—how brilliant, elevated and clear it is. But the rain overcame this most superior human being, because of its closeness to its Lord...[18]

And from the rain, says Ibn ʿArabī, the prophet gained '...what the rain brought from its Lord'.[19] There is a 'message' in all this: 'This is the message of water from which God made every living thing. So understand!'[20]

Let us look at Ibn ʿArabī's logic here: those who seem weak

17. *Fuṣūṣ*, pp. 197–198.
18. *Fuṣūṣ*, p. 198.
19. *Ibid.*
20. *Ibid.*

control and overcome those who seem strong. This, in the examples so far given by Ibn ʿArabī, is explained as being the result of these 'weak' parties—the young sons—being closer to their origins in God. In the story of the rain and the Prophet an additional factor seems to be involved: Water itself here represents *the basic element of life*, in addition to its having come fresh from its Lord and being 'weak' and 'passive'. This meaning of water becomes the transition through which Ibn ʿArabī passes over to the next theme.

MŪSĀ'S *TĀBŪT*

Ibn ʿArabī now returns to a particular aspect of the Mūsā narrative in the Qur'ān, referring to the placing of Mūsā in a box and throwing the box in the water:

> As for the wisdom associated with placing Mūsā in the box and throwing it in the water: The box is his humanity and the water the knowledge he obtains through the body and which is provided by the ratiocinative and sensual faculties. These and similar faculties of the human soul exist only through the existence of the physical body.[21]

The box (*tābūt*) that Mūsā is put in, then, is his humanity (*nāsūt*) and this would seem to be related to (or represent) the body (*jism*). The mental and sensual faculties mentioned are related to the soul and distinguished from the body though, it appears, they are also dependent on the body.[22] Knowledge which is derived from those faculties, though presumably transcending the body, is thus bound to it. Ibn ʿArabī explains this more precisely, relating it to Mūsā and the box:

> Thus when the soul is joined to the body and is commanded to act in it and to organise it, God makes these faculties for the soul as tools through which one may attain what God wishes in organ-

21. *Ibid.* and Qur'ān, 20:39.
22. Again, for Ibn ʿArabī the spiritual is manifest only through the physical.

> ising this box in which the Lord's presence resides. Thus was Mūsā cast into the river, in order to obtain—through these faculties—all sorts of knowledge.[23]

The exoteric (*ẓāhir*), the humanity, the physical represented by the box, is the locus of the esoteric (*bāṭin*) spiritual knowledge represented symbolically for Ibn ʿArabī by the water. The nexus between outer and inner, box and water, physical and spiritual, body and soul, is the Lord's presence which resides in the box.

This image of the pure esoteric truth and God Himself being made manifest in the phenomenal world and its various parts is, as we know, a basic principle for Ibn ʿArabī. He will shortly use the present example as an avenue for making the point in expanded contexts. The nexus between 'physical' and 'spiritual' posited here by Ibn ʿArabī as 'the Lord's presence' in the box is itself a Qur'ānic example, found in Qur'ān 2:248 where 'the presence of your Lord' (*sakīna min rabbikum*) is mentioned. This presence is within the ark or box (*tābūt*) which was promised to the Israelites. Also in the box would be 'things left by the families of Mūsā and Hārūn'.[24] This *tābūt* is not the one from the Qur'ānic story of the infant Mūsā, but because it is another story connected with Mūsā and another *tābūt*, Ibn ʿArabī uses the *sakīna* in this narrative, applying it to the *tābūt* in the other story. He thus, it seems, 'conflates' the two narratives, but for him here, as elsewhere, the Qur'ān is in any case one integral fabric. And the *sakīna* of the Lord in the new context provides Ibn ʿArabī with a divine presence that serves as the channel

23. *Fuṣūṣ*, p. 198.

24. Qur'ān, 2:248. What I have translated as 'the Lord's presence' from Ibn ʿArabī's *sakīnat al-rabb* is quite clearly 'presence' for him. I have also translated the Qur'ānic *sakīna min rabbikum* (2:248), to which Ibn ʿArabī seems to refer, as 'presence'. In a narrower Qur'ānic sense it might better be rendered as 'your Lord's tranquillity'. See ʿAfīfī, pp. 293–294, in his commentary on the *Fuṣūṣ*, for a discussion of *sakīna* with interesting comments on the Jewish mystical and philosophical *shekhina* as a possible model for Ibn ʿArabī here.

through which spiritual knowledge comes to Mūsā in his physical form. Thus: 'So Mūsā was thrown into the river in order to attain—through these [bodily] faculties—all kinds of knowledge.'[25] But Ibn ʿArabī is, again, keen not to relinquish the bodily side once the 'higher' knowledge has been attained. And from this we see an extrapolation of the idea culminating in a metaphysical point derived from this story of the infant Mūsā.

THE METAPHYSICS OF THE INFANT MŪSĀ

Ibn ʿArabī begins on this path by further clarifying the relationship between body and spirit in Mūsā's acquisition of knowledge. The issue is not simply the necessity of the body-based faculties in the acquisition of the higher spiritual knowledge, as we have thus far understood. For in this process one feature is most important: the seeming 'complementarity' of 'lower' and 'higher', body and knowledge, and so on, is actually much more; it is, in essence, an organising, controlling and directing force (*tadbīr*) which derives from the 'lower' party's control of the process. Again, there is an inversion of sorts, with a purpose we shall soon see. Continuing from his statement that Mūsā was put in the water in order to acquire knowledge, Ibn ʿArabī says:

> God thereby informs Mūsā that though the controlling spirit was sovereign over him [in his body], it could direct him only through himself. Indeed, God delegated to him those faculties which exist in this [his] humanity, which is understood as 'the box', by way of [esoteric Qur'ānic] allusion and philosophical insight.[26]

The very nature of the subject of a 'higher' force, then, actually directs the manner in which that force may work—much as, in a different context, the infant controls the adult (in

25. *Fuṣūṣ*, p. 198.
26. *Ibid.*

the example given above). In short, the nature of the box, as Mūsā's humanity and mental and sensual faculties, determines the nature and extent of the higher knowledge given to him. God's organisation of things is thus—even in His own relationship with the world He created. And here begins Ibn ʿArabī's extrapolation from Mūsā's situation to the 'larger universe'. He says:

> Likewise is God's organisation of the world. [For] God's organisation of the world is effected only through the world itself or through its form. This is like the dependence of the child on the generative power of the father, of effects on their causes, of the conditioned on their conditions... All of that is from the world and it is God's organisation in it. Consequently, He does not organise the world but through the world itself.[27]

Ibn ʿArabī's commitment to this principle is obviously thoroughgoing. He proceeds to develop it further, addressing in particular the seeming structural inversion in God's relationship with the world.

This he does by an explication of a phrase in his statement quoted above concerning God's direction of the world as being determined through the world itself, '*or through its form*':

> As for our saying, 'or through its form'—that is, the form of the world—I mean the beautiful names and the highest attributes by which God is named and described. Thus no name of God reaches us unless we have found the meaning of that name and its spirit in the world. God does not organise the world, then, except through the form of the world.[28]

This explanation, focusing on the phrase 'in its form', makes clear that it is not just the world in general that is meant here, but the whole variegation of phenomenal reality which consti-

27. *Fuṣūṣ*, pp. 198–199.
28. *Fuṣūṣ*, p. 199.

tutes God's names and attributes. The *form* of the world *is* God, in this sense: He is 'constrained' and 'directed' by this form, in creating and ordering the world and He is immanent in the world, its form being *His own*. And in microcosm, man in spiritual perfection represents it all:

> Thus did God say about the creation of Ādam, who is the exemplar comprising the characteristics of the divine presence which is [God's] essence, attributes and actions: 'God created Ādam in His form.'[29] And God's form is nothing other than the divine presence. God created in this noble microcosm, who is the Perfect Man, all of the divine names and the realities which emerge from this man into the external macrocosm. And God made him the spirit of the world, rendering the high and the low submissive to him, because of the perfection of form [in him].[30]

Now to bring everything together: Mūsā's form, his *tābūt*, his *nāsūt*, his body, determines his highest spiritual knowledge, through the 'presence of the Lord' within the *tābūt*. The *tābūt/nāsūt* are an expression and manifestation of this knowledge. God and the world are similarly related: the form of the world expresses and manifests God's characteristics; the form of the world is the divine presence (*al-ḥaḍra al-ilāhiyya*). The Perfect Man, as Ādam, is the world in microcosm, manifesting God's names and attributes and the Perfect Man is symbol for all humanity, to whom all of creation is made subservient. In all of these formulations the basic structure is the same: the transcendent and esoteric are made manifest and have a presence in the phenomenal and the exoteric. From this angle, God and His creation are as one, the multiplicity and diversity in creation expressing God's individual names. Mūsā, as the locus of the spirits of the sons killed by Pharaoh, exemplifying their freshly God-given virtues—the theme with which Ibn ʿArabī began—may now be seen also in this present framework as the tran-

29. al-Bukhārī, *Ṣaḥīḥ*, LXXXIX:I.
30. *Fuṣūṣ*, p. 199, Qur'ān: 31:20.

scendent manifest in the phenomenal. In this sense, Mūsā is on the model of Ādam.[31] For Ibn ʿArabī, the *esoteric knowledge* is the core of the divine presence manifested in these phenomenal realities. 'Therefore, *the form* of putting Mūsā in the box and casting it into the river is, on the face of it destruction, while *in essence* it is his salvation from being killed. Thus is he spared..., *by knowledge*, from the death of ignorance. As God, Most High, said: "Or one who was dead",[32] that is, by ignorance'.[33]

Not only was Mūsā spared from physical death by being cast upon the water in the box when to all outward appearances he was doomed, but he also attained a deeper salvation that from ignorance to spiritual knowledge. For death is ignorance and salvation knowledge in Ibn ʿArabī's terms. And Qur'ān 6:122—'Or one who was dead'—continues, saying that God gave life and a 'light' (*nūr*) to this person 'with which he can walk among men'. 'Light' for Ibn ʿArabī, as spiritual knowledge, was precisely what Mūsā received from God's presence in the box in the water.

It ought now to be clear, I think, that Ibn ʿArabī, in these passages from the chapter on Mūsā in the *Fuṣūṣ*, interweaves the Qur'ān and his own thought in a running commentary on the sacred text. Using aspects of the Mūsā narratives and other passages in the Qur'ān as well, Ibn ʿArabī here relates his particular view of Mūsā's prophetic nature and the spiritual wisdom ('the wisdom of exaltedness') associated with the Word of this eminent prophet.

31. As again are all the Prophets for Ibn ʿArabī, in their different ways.

32. Qur'ān, 6:122.

33. *Fuṣūṣ*, p. 199.

CHAPTER

4

The Wisdom of Leadership in the Word of Hārūn

THE STORY IN SCRIPTURAL HERITAGE

The Qur'ānic narrative about Hārūn is diverse and rich. Almost always connected with stories of Mūsā, the tales of Hārūn embody the complexities of that brotherly relationship which contribute to the delineation of the two personalities. The figure of Hārūn is largely defined against the foil of his brother's very substantial presence. Mūsā may be younger than Hārūn, but his position is for many—and obvious—reasons superior to that of his brother. Despite this situation, however, certain contexts reveal a maturity and wisdom in Hārūn which may, by way of contrast, indicate some limitations in Mūsā. These lineaments of the brotherly relationship and the finer details and nuances of their respective traits and characteristics in the Qur'ān are also documented in the Biblical and post-Biblical traditions concerning Aaron and Moses. In that context, of course, there are sometimes quite different emphases and concerns from those in the Qur'ān. Prominent in this long narrative tradition, as it continues through the Qur'ān, is the dramatic story of Hārūn, Mūsā and the golden calf. The momentous incidents of the making and worship of the calf, Hārūn's role in this evil and Mūsā's own awkwardness in dealing with it after his experience of the divine presence on Sinai, all combine most impressively to highlight the personalities of the protagonists. The ways in which the brothers' personalities are highlighted in the stories of this event, greatly significant for the three prophetic monotheisms, have also proved influential in the general perception of the two men. As we shall see, all of this provides a focus for Ibn ʿArabī in his treatment of the figure of Hārūn.

The scriptural framework stories may for our purposes be recounted briefly, with an eye towards similarities and differences between the stories in the two traditions of the Bible and the Qur'ān. The Biblical story is itself highly complex and even, according to some commentators, in parts contradictory. It is important for us mainly as relevant background. I shall, then, consider it primarily from the perspective of Aaron's role in the worship of the calf, the culpability (whose?) for this incident and the attitudes evinced towards this form of idolatry.[1] In discussion of the Qur'ānic accounts, I shall follow the same main points, in a somewhat more detailed and comprehensive way.[2]

THE BIBLICAL AND POST-BIBLICAL STORIES

The Biblical account of the incident of the golden calf appears in Exodus, 33:1–7. While Moses is with God receiving the Tablets of the Law, the people, in their impatience and lack of understanding, clamour for some discernible form of God which they might worship. Aaron requests from them their 'gold ear-rings'—from their 'women, sons and daughters'. He then puts it all in 'a mould' from which he produces 'the image of the calf'. They call the calf 'God' (Elohim)—the God who 'brought you out of Egypt'. Aaron builds an altar for worship of the calf, saying: 'Tomorrow, the feast of God.' The following day the people do indeed worship the calf and celebrate. God quickly warns Moses what is happening and threatens the

1. The story has occupied a central position in post-Biblical religious thought, Jewish and Christian, as well as in Islam. For a good survey, see: Pier Cesare Bori, *The Golden Calf.*

2. The detail here is obviously important for an understanding of Ibn ʿArabī's discussion of Hārūn.

people. Moses pleads forgiveness and God relents. Moses rushes back in anger, breaking the Tablets, upon seeing the sorry spectacle of idolatry. He reduces the calf to dust and powder, sprinkles it in water and forces the people to drink it. Moses again ascends Mt. Sinai with two new Tablets and again receives God's commandments.

Aaron's role in this Biblical account is clearly a central one. He accedes to the demands of the people for an image of God to worship, even taking charge of the whole process of producing the image. Aaron's culpability in this idolatry seems unquestionable, Moses's anger reasonable and the Bible's attitude towards this religious conception and practice wholly negative. Indeed, within the subsequent history of post-Biblical Jewish and Christian commentary on the story, this is the general picture, despite a Jewish exegetical tendency in some circles to offer an exculpatory explanation of sorts for Aaron's behaviour. For both the Jewish and Christian outlooks, the story of the golden calf provides a dramatic and instructive lesson in the fundamental principles of prophetic monotheism: whatever position one took on Aaron's culpability, the idolatrous religious practice—in particular the naming of the idol as 'God'—was universally and strongly condemned in Jewish and Christian circles. Indeed, this practice, coming as it did after the Israelites' covenant with God, was traditionally invoked as an exemplar of human duplicity and depravity. Treachery against God was the nature of the act—some have even seen here 'the nearest Jewish equivalent to the concept of original sin'.[3]

IN THE QUR'ĀN

The Qur'ānic narratives of the incident of the golden calf are found mainly (though not exclusively) in 7:148–155 and

3. M. Aberbach and L. Smolar, 'The Golden Calf Episode in post-Biblical Literature', p. 6. Also: Bori, *The Golden Calf*, pp. 9–27.

20:85–94. These stories serve as the basic sources from which Ibn ʿArabī constructs his sufi metaphysical tale of Hārūn, Mūsā and the golden calf. Though certain central elements of the Qur'ānic story are the same in these two *sūras*, some significant differences do exist. It will be important for our purposes here to see what is the same and what is different.

The story in *sūra* 7 appears in the midst of a 'cycle' of stories where Mūsā is the central figure, focusing on his encounters with Pharaoh, God's saving of the Israelites from Pharaoh's depredations and the religious lessons to be learned from all this. The story begins with the Israelites during Mūsā's absence suddenly taking 'a calf [constructed] from their bangles',[4] in the form of 'a body that lowed'.[5] They worshipped it, felt contrite and then worried about divine retribution. Mūsā, upon his return to his people, chastised them, cast aside the Tablets of the Law and in anger dragged Hārūn by the head towards him. Hārūn, in fear and in attempted self-exculpation, beseeched his brother, 'Oh, son of my mother, the people considered me weak and came close to killing me. Do not make [my] enemies gloat over me and do not make me one of the iniquitous'.[6] Mūsā then sought God's pardon and mercy for himself and Hārūn, saying at the same time that those who took the calf for their god would be visited by His wrath. When Mūsā's 'anger had abated',[7] he picked up the Tablets and found there 'mercy and guidance for those who venerate their Lord'.[8]

This story is quite a compact narrative of the idolatrous event. It presents it in brief scope, devoid of much elaboration. Mūsā's initial anger with Hārūn is soon mitigated, with Hārūn's own plea of his difficult situation among the people. Unlike the Biblical story, this tale portrays Hārūn in a somewhat more positive way.

4. Qur'ān, 7:148.
5. *Ibid.*
6. Qur'ān, 7:150.
7. Qur'ān, 7:154.
8. *Ibid.*

He does not actually take a hand in making the calf, nor does he encourage the people in their worship of it. If anything, the story conveys a sense of Hārūn's weakness and ineffectiveness which is consonant with, and in part derived from, his own attempt at self-exculpation before Mūsā. The sin of making, worshipping and considering the calf to be God is most prominent. Hārūn has *failed to prevent* this crime, rather than instigating and encouraging it.

The story in *sūra* 20 is rather more detailed than that in *sūra* 7 and is different from it in certain ways. The opening of the story has God asking Mūsā why he had left his people in such haste, with Mūsā answering that it was to please God by coming to Him. God replies that after Mūsā left '... the Samaritan has led them in error'.[9] Mūsā then returns to the people remorseful and very angry, accusing them of impatience in awaiting his return and of risking the divine wrath. The people reply that this was not their fault, as they were 'weighed down' with all of their collective bangles and thus threw them in the fire, as did the Samaritan.[10] The Samaritan then from this material produces the golden calf, here, as in *sūra* 7, 'a body that lowed'.[11] The people called the calf Mūsā's god and the Samaritan's god, in total ignorance of the true divinity and in seeming oblivion of the inability of this idol to respond to them or indeed either to help or to harm them.[12] Hārūn implores them to obey him and to recognise the true God and to follow Him. They resist, avowing their intention to worship the idol until Mūsā returns. Mūsā asks Hārūn why he did not act more forcefully to restrain the people, questioning Hārūn's very loyalty to him, 'Have you gone against my order?'[13] Hārūn pleads for mercy, calling Mūsā, as in *sūra* 7, 'son of my mother', asking Mūsā not to pull him

9. Qur'ān, 20:85.
10. Qur'ān, 20:87.
11. Qur'ān, 20:88.
12. Qur'ān, 20:89.
13. Qur'ān, 20:93.

by the beard or head (as in *sūra* 7), and expressing his fear that Mūsā may have accused him of dividing the Israelites and disobeying him.[14] Mūsā responds by turning to the Samaritan, 'What was your interest here, Oh, Samaritan?'[15] Somewhat cryptically, the Samaritan answers that he has seen 'what they [the people] did not see'.[16] This unseen was 'the messenger', *al-rasūl*, said in later commentaries to have been Jibrīl (Gabriel) approaching Mūsā.[17] The Samaritan says then that he took 'a handful of dust'[18] from the messenger's track and threw it on the calf presumably to bring it to life. Mūsā, unimpressed by this explanation, expels the Samaritan, asking him to look at this god to whom he is so devoted: 'We shall burn it and scatter it widely in the sea.'[19] Then, in a reaffirmation of strict monotheism, Mūsā instructs the Samaritan that '... Your god is God. There is no God but He.'[20] Those who reject this, says Mūsā, shall bear a weighty burden on the Day of Judgement.[21]

The differences between the two Qur'ānic accounts are obvious, while they incorporate the same basic framework story. The most striking point of similarity—and one which is crucial to Ibn ʿArabī's sufi metaphysical exposition—is *the implicit exculpation of Hārūn*. In *sūra* 20 this point is made even more forcefully than in *sūra* 7. The added force resides in the figure of the Samaritan (*al-Sāmirī*). Immediately upon Hārūn's plea for mercy from Mūsā in his attempt at self-exculpation, Mūsā turns towards this new and mysterious figure, whose culpability in the making and worshipping of the golden calf is then made absolutely clear. Hārūn appears, as in *sūra* 7, complicit

14. Qur'ān, 20:94.
15. Qur'ān, 20:95.
16. Qur'ān, 20:96.
17. *Ibid.* For a typical exegetical reference to Gabriel, see: al-Ṣuyūtī and al-Maḥallī, *Tafsīr al-Imāmayn al-Jalālayn.*
18. Qur'ān, 20:96.
19. Qur'ān, 20:97.
20. Qur'ān, 20:98.
21. Qur'ān, 20:100.

at most in his weakness, but not in any enthusiastic and active participation. And his awareness of the evil of such idolatry is patent. The Samaritan serves as a 'lightning rod' conductor of blame for the calf, by implication making it difficult to lodge any serious accusations against Hārūn.[22]

In *sūra* 20, as in *sūra* 7, no real person is identified as being responsible for the idolatry of the calf. In both *sūras*, Hārūn is suspect, but the case against him is weak. In *sūra* 20, the Samaritan is clearly responsible, but he is not a known person nor does he seem to represent a known group. His position is more as a dramatic device whose purpose, it seems, is to provide a 'culprit'. In both *sūras*, the clear focus is on the vileness of the idolatrous *idea* and *practice*. Ibn ᶜArabī adopts, adapts and transforms all this in his own story of Hārūn, Mūsā and the golden calf.

IBN ᶜARABĪ ON HĀRŪN AND MŪSĀ: LEADERSHIP AND MERCY

In the *Fuṣūṣ*, Ibn ᶜArabī's story of Hārūn is entitled 'The Bezel of the Wisdom of Leadership in the Word of Hārūn'.[23] That 'wisdom of leadership' (*ḥikma imāmiyya*) would construe the figure of Hārūn as 'leader', *imām*, presumably of the Israelites, in the absence of Mūsā. This 'quintessence' of Hārūn found in leadership is balanced for Ibn ᶜArabī with another virtue reflected in this prophet and his life: mercy. Indeed, for Ibn ᶜArabī, Hārūn's quality of mercy seems even more central to his character and spiritual nature than does his leadership. Whatever their balance of prominence here, leadership and mercy as virtues related to Hārūn, provide Ibn ᶜArabī with the basic stuff from which he develops the metaphysics of Hārūn's role. Thus after the title of the chapter expressing Hārūn's *ḥikma imāmiyya*, Ibn ᶜArabī

22. This, in fact, constitutes a near-total exculpation of Hārūn.
23. *Fuṣūṣ*, pp. 191–197.

then opens with a Qur'ānic reference to the Hārūnī mercy, 'Know that the existence of Hārūn, peace be upon him, is on the plane of mercy, by God's (Most High) saying: "We have given to him from our mercy", that is, to Mūsā "his brother, Hārūn, a prophet."'[24] Here in Qur'ān 19:53, God from His mercy gives to Mūsā his brother Hārūn as a partner in the task of confronting Pharaoh. This is in answer to Mūsā's plea to God for this helper. Mūsā felt in such need due to his speech impediment which caused him to fear being tongue-tied in his approach to the tyrannical Egyptian leader. Ibn ᶜArabī then continues: 'Thus is his [Hārūn's] prophecy on the plane of mercy; and while Hārūn is older than Mūsā, Mūsā is greater than Hārūn in prophecy.'[25] Despite the differences in their ages, Mūsā, the younger, is superior to Hārūn, the elder, in his prophetic qualities—as would be clear in general, given Mūsā's very particular superior status among all the prophets. But one must remember that this great prophet has been laid low by his fear and his speech infirmity. He pleads with God to make his older brother his support in the (for Mūsā) daunting presence of Pharaoh. Hārūn here is the very embodiment of God's mercy. At the same time, Hārūn is himself in a position of contrition, seeking mercy and pleading with Mūsā not to humiliate and punish him for his (suspected) role in the idolatry of the calf. Thus, Ibn ᶜArabī says that, 'Since the prophecy of Hārūn is on the plane of mercy, consequently he says to his brother Mūsā, "Oh, son of my mother". He calls him after his mother and not his father, as mercy belongs to the mother and not the father ... Were it not for that mercy, the mother would not have patience for the rearing up of the child.'[26] Ibn ᶜArabī, then, conflating passages from *sūras* 20 and 7, refers to Hārūn's plaintive pleas to Mūsā: 'Do not pull me by my beard or my head and do not cause [my] enemies to gloat over me.' 'All of this,' says Ibn

24. *Fuṣūṣ*, p. 191; Qur'ān, 19:53.
25. *Fuṣūṣ*, p. 191 and for the whole story see pp. 191–197.
26. *Ibid.*

ʿArabī, 'is a breath of [divine] mercy',[27] alluding thereby to the central sufi, and more general Islamic, notion of 'the breath of the merciful' (*nafas al-Raḥmān*).[28]

Mercy for Ibn ʿArabī becomes a central feature of the idolatrous event, as it serves to delineate the personalities of the two brothers in their own relationship and in their attitudes towards the calf and their stance towards God. It has thus far outweighed the Hārūnī virtue of leadership which characterises this prophet in the chapter's title. Indeed, in any straightforward way, Hārūn would hardly seem to embody this virtue of leadership, *as the story has thus far been told.* Mercy also becomes God's angle of involvement with the two brothers and with respect to the idolatry.

In finer detail, Hārūn represents and embodies God's mercy from two sides: he serves as the *instrument* of God's mercy towards Mūsā in confronting Pharaoh and he pleads for forgiveness and mercy for himself from Mūsā. The two brothers' personalities become clear in this. Mūsā, the great Lawgiver who had direct experience of God, suffers from a most ordinary human defect in his timidity engendered by his faulty speech, while Hārūn appears already as a rather weak figure, fearful of being blamed for something he did not do or did not agree to. The cohesive force in all this, Ibn ʿArabī says, is God's breath of mercy. Mercy is required to resolve the issue and to compensate for weaknesses in the prophetic personalities.

This emphasis on mercy—divine and human—is obviously central to the story and Ibn ʿArabī treats it as such. In Ibn ʿArabī's larger metaphysical scheme, however, mercy, *raḥma*, as we know, represents the unitary principle which defines the world as pure undifferentiated being. The resonances of mercy

27. *Ibid.*

28. Here for Ibn ʿArabī, the breath of the Merciful is specifically related to God's instilling of existence in His creation, as we shall see. For a general overview of the concept and also its specific meanings in Ibn ʿArabī's works, see Suʿād al-Ḥakīm, *al-Muʿjam al-Ṣūfī*, pp. 1023–1027.

register through all spheres of existence, from the personal, ethical notion (as expressed in the story thus far) to this most abstract, undifferentiated principle. Though the latter has not yet appeared in Hārūn's story as told by Ibn ʿArabī, we shall in retrospect find it certainly to have been adumbrated. The unlikely personality of Hārūn *as leader* may also later be better understood through the notion of mercy.

Ibn ʿArabī next moves on to discuss the nature and meaning of the worship of the calf. Implicitly, the question is: what are we to think of this practice, the people associated with it and the tense moments in its aftermath, upon the return of Mūsā? Taking the latter first, Ibn ʿArabī says 'the cause' of the ensuing fray was with Mūsā:

> For had he looked in them [the Tablets] discerningly, he would have found in them guidance and mercy. Guidance is the clarification of the occurrence which had angered [Mūsā, in Hārūn's presumed culpability for the idolatry] and which was really something Hārūn was innocent of. There was mercy here for [Mūsā's] brother, Hārūn, as [Mūsā] did not grab him by his beard for his people to see, because of [Hārūn's] being older than [Mūsā]. That was as well a kindness from Hārūn towards Mūsā, because Hārūn's prophecy is from God's mercy and thus nothing other than [mercy] could come from him.[29]

Finally, to cap his discussion of the immediate tense aftermath of the idolatrous act, Ibn ʿArabī cites Qur'ān 20:94, where Hārūn says to Mūsā, 'I was afraid you would say "You have divided the Children of Israel."'[30] Ibn ʿArabī says this means 'You [Mūsā] would make me [Hārūn] [appear to be] the cause of the division of the people.'[31] But, in a further twist in the exculpation of Hārūn, Ibn ʿArabī says of the other people that 'the worship of the calf divided them—some of them worshipping it, following after the Samaritan and in obedience to him and

29. *Fuṣūṣ*, p. 191.
30. *Fuṣūṣ*, pp. 191–192.
31. *Fuṣūṣ*, p. 192.

some of them desisting from worshipping it until Mūsā would return to them, so they could ask him about that. Thus did Hārūn fear that that division would be attributed to him.'[32]

This rather fraught period in the wake of the idol worship, with Mūsā's return, serves Ibn ʿArabī as an opportunity for further character delineation of the main figures and for glossing basic ideas and values derived from and reflected in the story. This, in turn, he will use in addressing the questions raised above concerning the meaning of the idol worship. Ibn ʿArabī thus makes quite explicit the exculpation of Hārūn which is mooted in the Qur'ānic stories. Mūsā's (unseemly) impatience with Hārūn is also underscored in Ibn ʿArabī's comment that if only Mūsā had been more discerning at first he would then have found 'guidance and mercy' in the Tablets (which, in any case, he did do after his outburst at Hārūn). This guidance made clear Hārūn's innocence, while the mercy was reciprocal between the two prophet-brothers: Mūsā bestowed it upon Hārūn by not humiliating him publicly, while the incident of Mūsā's suspicion and anger at Hārūn was a merciful benevolence from Hārūn to Mūsā. Indeed, anything connected with Hārūn is, *by definition and nature*, mercy. This requires clarification: Ibn ʿArabī's meaning here would seem to be that the whole complex of factors in the idolatry of the calf forced Mūsā, through the sequence of anger with Hārūn, to mercy for Hārūn and proper recourse to the Tablets, to 'wake up', as it were. Hārūn's great mercy to his brother, then, was just that: Hārūn's pleas and entreaties to Mūsā, in forcing him to realise Hārūn's innocence (through the Tablets, as well), were the kindness which in turn caused Mūsā's kindness to Hārūn and his return to the Tablets. Hārūn, exemplifying mercy in this way, though ostensibly weak in his collapse before idolatry and fearful of being blamed for that evil, in his own way 'led' Mūsā back to the truth God had revealed to him. Hārūn's 'leadership', in this sense, derived from his very

32. *Ibid.*

passivity and his pleas for mercy which themselves became an act of mercy to Mūsā. Leadership and mercy are linked here: each, again, seems in a sort of *inversion* to derive from its opposite.

Leadership occurs out of lack of leadership and fervent pleas for mercy become a great act of mercy toward the very one to whom the pleas were made. This linkage between leadership and mercy is based on their being paired in Hārūn in this particular 'inverted' way. And the *effect* of this inversion is most profound: Mūsā, having descended from the highest spiritual state in God's very presence, and then all too humanly diverted from his Tablets of truth by his anger, is led back to those Tablets and their truth by Hārūn's own reaction to Mūsā's anger. This in 'first interpretation' is the 'wisdom of leadership' attached to Hārūn by Ibn ᶜArabī in the title of this chapter and the 'mercy' connected with Hārūn in the first two lines. Of greatest importance here is the role of mercy which, in its Hārūnī passivity, and its Mūsāwī bestowal, drives Hārūn's leadership in bringing Mūsā back to his destiny. Mercy as yet has here the *personal quality* of its usual connotation in ordinary language and thought. It will subsequently retain its centrality in the discussion, while being transformed in Ibn ᶜArabī's metaphysical mill.

IDOLATRY, THE CALF AND THE METAPHYSICAL STORY

Having laid his foundation for Hārūn's tale in his 'Qur'ānic story-telling' and delineation of character, Ibn ᶜArabī moves into the central theme whose explication provides a focus for the remainder of the discussion: the worship of the calf and those questions concerning it. Thus, following on from the reiteration of Hārūn's voiced fear that the rift among the people over the calf would be linked to him, Ibn ᶜArabī says:

> But Mūsā was more knowledgeable about that matter than Hārūn, as he knew what the disciples of the calf were worshipping, because of his knowledge that God had decreed that only He

> be worshipped; and that God does not decree something but that it happens. Thus was Mūsā's rebuke of his brother Hārūn due to his [impetuous] rejection of the matter and his lack of vision.[33]

There is a double transition here, in subject and in level of discussion—from Ibn ᶜArabī's Qur'ānic narrative of character delineation, with description of the high, dramatic events, to his focused discussion of the nature of the idolatry, and secondly, from the level of 'ordinary language' narrative to that of metaphysical narrative. For the dialectic of the brotherly relationship, in the complex interweaving of character traits which posits both the conventional hierarchy of Mūsā's prophetic superiority to Hārūn *and* an implicitly *inverted* hierarchy of Hārūnī passive merciful leadership of Mūsā, has brought us from personality and character now to Ibn ᶜArabī's main metaphysical point. With Hārūn's 'instruction' and 'leadership' of Mūsā, Mūsā is awakened to the superior knowledge which is part of his superior prophethood. This knowledge is an 'inversion' of the more conventional wisdom concerning idolatry, parallel to the 'inversion' in the normally superior/inferior relationship between the brothers: for Mūsā '... *knew what the disciples of the calf were worshipping...*'. This knowledge emerged in the give-and-take between Mūsā and Hārūn, in particular with Hārūn's fear of being seen as the source of communal division and his consequent pleas for mercy from Mūsā. Mūsā was thus provoked into his merciful response and his awareness of God's decree that nothing be worshipped but Himself was rekindled. Thus Mūsā's knowledge of what the idolaters were really worshipping: God Himself. And here, then, is another inversion: a straightforward understanding of God's decree above might be that *only God may be worshipped* and that He would enforce that injunction. But for Ibn ᶜArabī it seems that here a different, inverted meaning may also be construed: some things—perhaps even all things—

33. *Ibid.*

worshipped *are* God. Hārūn's mercy to Mūsā was to return him to this truth. Neither Hārūn nor the sinful ones among the people would, by this standard, then, have been guilty of anything, even if they were unaware of this. Also, the communal division caused by the idol worship was likewise not of any true import. The deepest inversion then is that of mercy, which within its more manifest function in the brotherly relationship begins to evince its esoteric sufi metaphysical meaning, as in Ibn ᶜArabī's special vocabulary.

Ibn ᶜArabī continues in this metaphysical vein:

> For the gnostic is one who sees al-Ḥaqq in everything; indeed, he sees [al-Ḥaqq] as every thing. Thus would Mūsā inculcate knowledge in Hārūn, despite his being younger [than Hārūn]. Consequently, when Hārūn said to [Mūsā] what he said [*i.e.*, his pleas for mercy], Mūsā turned back to the Samaritan, saying to him: 'What is your concern here, Oh Samaritan' [in your turning toward the image of the calf], in particular, and your making of this figure from the jewellery of the people, even stealing their hearts, when obtaining their wealth?[34]

If Hārūn's mercy to Mūsā lay in jolting his brother back into his higher prophetic truth, then here the relationship reverts to Mūsā's being in the 'dominant' position in answering Hārūn's pleas and thereby attempting indirectly to inculcate in him the full esoteric knowledge. This confirms that Mūsā did indeed know what the people were worshipping and that in God's decreeing in the Qur'ān the worship only of Himself, the full esoteric truth was intended: *al-Ḥaqq* is immanent, *in* and *as* everything, including, here, most particularly, the golden calf. Thus did Mūsā turn away from Hārūn toward the Samaritan, in this way indicating the exculpation of Hārūn. But this exculpation, though in the story obviously on the personal, merciful plane, in esoteric metaphysical terms is derived from the fact that *there was no real sin committed—God was indeed being*

34. *Ibid.*

worshipped. Even where the blame seems clearly to lie with the Samaritan, Ibn ʿArabī reveals a deeper meaning which calls this too into question.[35] Thus, continuing on from his 'accusation' against the Samaritan for stealing the people's hearts 'in getting their wealth', Ibn ʿArabī, with much language play, says:

> So Jesus said to the Children of Israel, 'Oh Children of Israel, the heart of every man is where his wealth is. Make then your wealth in heaven and your hearts will be in heaven.'[36] He calls wealth 'wealth' only because of its being essentially the inclining of hearts toward it in worship. [Wealth] is the greatest desire in hearts, then, because of their inherent need for it.[37]

Whereas the Samaritan's central role in extracting their baubles from the people to create a glittering idol for them to worship is at first glance a manifest corruption, as is the people's seeming need for such worship, in Ibn ʿArabī's somewhat 'inverted' gloss a different meaning may be inferred and the culpability even of the Samaritan may now be reconsidered. For here, Ibn ʿArabī has actually transmuted that tarnished combination of human material concerns and idolatry into a golden worship of the true God. Human concern with—even worship of—wealth is natural and positive and may even be 'sublimated' in an elevated, heavenly form, as in Jesus's admonition to the Children of Israel. Indeed, in deeper inversion the 'base' material concerns of ordinary people may even 'paradoxically' be their main way into 'higher' spiritual realms. Materiality itself is nothing to be concerned about in Ibn ʿArabī's view, as material

35. Again, though in the Qur'ān the presence of the Samaritan does by strong implication exculpate Hārūn, the Samaritan's 'offence' is called into question if, as Ibn ʿArabī has been implying, there is no real offence.

36. *Fuṣūṣ*, p. 192. 'Wealth', *māl* here in Arabic, from the root *m-w-l*, is structurally identical to the verb *māla*, 'to incline towards', from the root, *m-y-l*. Hence Ibn ʿArabī's particular association of *meanings* with the structural identity of these words. Ibn ʿArabī seems here to be citing some variant version of Matthew 6:19 (The Sermon on the Mount).

37. *Fuṣūṣ*, p. 192.

objects are ephemeral in any case, while at the same time they may also be sites of divine manifestation. Thus:

> Material forms have no permanency, so the passing of the form of the calf was inevitable, had Mūsā not rushed to burn it. But fervour overcame him, he burnt it and scattered the ashes in the sea. Mūsā then said to the Samaritan, 'Look at your god.' Thus did Mūsā call the calf a god, by way of instruction, because of his knowing that it was a divine manifestation.[38]

The inversion is now complete: the calf was of no real consequence, as—like all material things—it was destined to fade away. But, in its status as a divine presence (*baᶜḍ al-majālī al-ilāhiyya*), it was not an improper object of worship for those who saw it as religiously attractive. Ibn ᶜArabī's recitation of Mūsā's comment to the Samaritan, 'Look at your God', obviously, then, plays on two possible interpretations (for Ibn ᶜArabī) of this statement: (1) The 'obvious' Qur'ānic meaning 'look at' what has become of the pathetic thing—in mocking, scolding tone, or (2) 'Look at your god', it really *is* 'God', *as a divine presence.* The word 'god', *ilah*, provides Ibn ᶜArabī with the focal point here for his gloss of inversion—'inversion', as the surface meaning of the passage in its Qur'ānic context remains the first one. Mūsā, then, though driven momentarily by thoughtless zeal in his anger at the idol worship and his burning of the idol, knows better and this is clear for Ibn ᶜArabī in Mūsā's call to the Samaritan to look at his 'god'. This call, says Ibn ᶜArabī, is really 'instruction' (*tanbīh, taᶜlīm*) concerning the true divine status of the calf. Implicit here, at the same time, is an exculpation of the Samaritan.

Ibn ᶜArabī's portrayal of the characters of Mūsā and Hārūn, interwoven in the themes of the drama of the Israelites' idol worship, has led inexorably to his full metaphysical inversion of the evil of this act. However, in his usual way Ibn ᶜArabī maintains a creative tension between the poles of *ẓāhir* and *bāṭin*,

38. *Ibid.*

thus *understanding*, but in no way *condoning* the calf-worship. Having made his basic point, Ibn ʿArabī expounds and elaborates on it from various perspectives, in the remainder of the chapter.

SUBJUGATION

One of these perspectives, following immediately on from the opening thrust above, is that of 'subjugation', *taskhīr*, involving an extremely long and abstruse argument attempting to carry the basic point further, in a quite different form. Thus, after saying that Mūsā knew the idol was 'a divine manifestation', Ibn ʿArabī cites, in slight paraphrase, Mūsā's pronouncement that he would burn the idol, as the point of departure for his 'argument from *taskhīr*'. Ibn ʿArabī's main concern in introducing *taskhīr* here is to provide another framework in which to consider the issue of multiplicity and unity as it is reflected in the story of Hārūn, Mūsā and the calf. To begin, then, Ibn ʿArabī says:

> The animality of man acts without limitation in the animality of animals, because of God's having subjugated [the animality of animals] to man. This is especially so, as man's essence is not animal. However, the calf is [here] the most subjugated because [something] inanimate has no will—rather, it is under the sway of one who directs it, without its objection. But the animal has will and aspiration and, consequently, sometimes objection when some [attempted] control is evinced from it. Thus if it has the power to manifest defiance of what man wants from it, then it will, or if it does not have this power, or if man happens to agree with the aspiration of the animal, then the animal may passively submit to what man wants from it, just as man, like the animal, submits to the command to do that through which God elevates him, on account of the riches which he hopes for from God. These riches are sometimes considered as recompense, as in God's saying, 'We have raised some of you above others in ranks, in order that some of you might take others in subjugation.'[39] However,

39. Qur'ān, 43:32.

no person has someone subjugated to him who is like him, but through the animality [of the subjected], not his humanity. Thus two like individuals may [in certain respects also] be different and conflicting [in status]—for example, the higher in position of wealth or status subjugating the lower through his humanity, while the other is subjugated by him from fear or ambition through his animality, not his humanity. In this sense, the subjugator has not really subjugated a like individual. See even how the beasts can be in conflict with one another, though they be 'alike'. 'Like beings', then, may indeed also be adversaries. Thus did [God] say He 'raised some of you above others in ranks'[40]—meaning the subjugated is not in the same rank as the subjugator. Subjugation, then, occurs for the sake of ranks. Subjugation is of two types: Subjugation through the wish of the subjector, the dominant 'active participle' in his subjecting of the subjected individual. [This is] like the master's subjection of his servant, though he be like him in [the quality of his] humanity and like the sultan's subjugation of his subjects, though they be like him [in their humanity]. Thus does he subjugate them by rank. The other type is the subjugation of circumstance, like the subjects' subjugation to the king who oversees their affairs in protecting them, watching over them, fighting their enemies and guarding them and their possessions. All of this is by subjugation through circumstance of subjects who [themselves may subjugate their ruler]; it is more precisely called 'the subjugation of position'. Thus [for example] position here dictates to the king in that matter. Among kings is the one who goes his own way [oblivious of this matter] and the one who knows the matter, knowing that through position he is thereby in subjection to his subjects. He thus knows their power and their right and God in consequence rewards him for that with the reward of those who know the matter as it really is. Such a reward is according to God, in His being [involved] in the affairs of His servants. Thus the whole of the world subjugates by circumstance the very One whom it is impossible to designate as 'subjugated'. He, Most High said, 'Every day, He is there, prominent'.[41]

40. Qur'ān, 43:32; *Fuṣūṣ*, pp. 193–194.
41. Qur'ān, 55:29; *Fuṣūṣ*, p. 194.

It is important to reduce this long digression/example to its main points and principles, while clarifying its relation to what came before and to what will follow. Understanding its *purpose* in the totality of Ibn ᶜArabī's discussion of Hārūn, Mūsā and the calf *through its basic arguments* is the goal.

Mūsā's rash and for Ibn ᶜArabī unnecessary and inconsequential burning of the calf-idol was the point of departure for his digression on subjugation. This link for him should now be clear in the context of subjugation in the four relationships, as mooted here: human/inanimate object; human/animal; human/human; and divine/creation. Mūsā's burning of the calf is subjugation of the first and most absolute type, between human beings and inanimate objects. An inanimate object, devoid of will, cannot resist or oppose in any way what a person may wish to do with it, even its destruction. This is what—needlessly in Ibn ᶜArabī's view—had occurred in Mūsā's action. How needless it was and the reasons for that will be reiterated and argued further later, with respect to Hārūn. The other types of subjugation illustrate, in subtle detail, other facets of this relationship of dominance, in a seeming 'evolutionary' scheme, to a 'high point' which then will serve as Ibn ᶜArabī's transition from subjugation to his return to, and further discussion of, Hārūn and leadership.

Thus, between human beings and animals subjugation may be different than with inanimate things, because animals have will. They therefore sometimes resist human direction and sometimes their will may be consonant with what their human master wants from them. But human beings will always remain dominant over them.

To emphasise, *within the human realm*, subjugation—the Qur'ānic hierarchical notion of the ordering of people in 'ranks' (*darajāt*)—is more complex and serves a necessary function of preserving social order. For unlike animals whose collective animal nature is singularly prone always to conflict and therefore requires human domination, humans are hierarchical in their virtues, abilities, powers and other propensities, with some thereby *naturally and rightly* subjugating others for the common good of an ordered society. Human beings, however, have a dual nature, part animal and part human; it is the animal nature which is operative in the subjugated person's subjugation, while his subjugator does this from his human nature. Why? It seems there is for Ibn ʿArabī a crude fact of animal life which is relevant also to humans: creatures of the same animal species will always be in conflict, thereby requiring a human master to subjugate them. Humans, also being of one species and *in part* sharing an animal nature, will by virtue of that also tend toward conflict with one another. But their *human nature,* which provides within their species a gradation and hierarchy of virtues, vices and power, engenders a self-regulating containment of conflict through subjugation. This is a positive human virtue derived from human nature in the subjugator and received by the subjugated *only* through his animal nature—*the human nature* of the subjugated, it seems, remains untouched, *and is as one with the human nature of his subjugator.* Thus do human beings regulate themselves—or at least the nasty, brutish aspects of their nature—unlike the animals who need man to do this for them and the inanimate beings which, in their state of most abject subjugation, have no volition and are therefore totally subject to man's subjugation of them.[42]

For humans, however, subjugation is of two types, that which is wholly derived from the will of the subjugator—a total domination of the kind discussed above, as with master and servants—and that which contains within it a certain reciprocity and, further, even a certain 'inversion' of power in which the subjugated may, from a particular angle, be seen to control his controller. The example of this which Ibn ʿArabī gives here is that of kings and their subjects, or at least of certain kings 'who know the matter as it really is'.[43] These 'rulers' understand in

42. Here Ibn ʿArabī seems to have in mind a sort of 'social contract' theory.

43. 'Knowing the matter as it really is' here is redolent of Ibn ʿArabī's main use of this expression: knowing the underlying oneness in things.

their relationship with their subjects their own 'subjugation' to the subjects *by virtue of their obligations to them*. This is called *subjugation by circumstance*—that is, the needs of the subjects *compel* the king to act in a certain way. This king for Ibn ʿArabī is the human analogue in this respect to God himself, in His relationship with the world He created. This is the ultimate *subjugation by circumstance*, the circumstance being God's omnipresence—immanence—in His created world and His being 'bound' there by the condition of His creation in which He appears and with which He is so identified. Thus the inconceivable becomes unavoidable: God 'subjugated' by His own creation, the ultimate inversion. Or is it? What does it mean? Here Ibn ʿArabī returns us again to Hārūn and the calf, using the new motif of subjugation *implicitly* as explanatory device, which at the same time thereby explains itself as well.

HĀRŪN'S REAL LEADERSHIP

Ibn ʿArabī picks up the thread in a return to the issue of Hārūn's behaviour in the presence of the calf and its worshippers, 'Thus was Hārūn's lack of restraining force on the worshippers of the calf by overcoming it, as Mūsā had overcome it, a wisdom from God, Most High, manifest in existence, in order that He be worshipped in every image.'[44] Mūsā's zealous burning of the calf was, then, an error in judgement and it was in fact contrary to Mūsā's own deeper gnostic knowledge, as Ibn ʿArabī has already stated. Here, however, the principle of subjugation by circumstance lends another dimension of understanding. For now Hārūn's weakness, in becoming a strength, is called a divine wisdom designed to enable God to 'be worshipped in every image'. God, like the most astute king, understands the 'two-way' nature of His subject realm: He subjugates it and through its

44. *Fuṣūṣ*, p. 194.

own structure of relationship with Him it subjugates Him, that is, it compels Him to respond to it in certain ways because of His own determination of its nature. The distinction between God and His creation is effaced here, functionally and substantively. And if part of God's creation is a deep human need to worship something, then such worship of all images is worship of God who is generally ever-present in His creation and, more particularly, is present in sites of worship (which are special sites of His presence, *majālin*). With respect to subjugation, the most thoroughgoing form of it, that between man and inanimate things (the special case being the calf here), is displaced by the least strong form of subjugation (between humans and the type which is 'by circumstance'). Indeed, this is hardly subjugation in any true sense—for it is really a sort of 'counterfeit subjugation', the ultimate inversion of subjugation through a total intermingling of subjugator and subjugated in a unity. Ibn ʿArabī then addresses the ephemeral nature of inanimate material bodies in this connection, obliquely referring back to his earlier assertion about the calf's being destined to disappear in any case, whether Mūsā had destroyed it or not. The implicit question raised and answered here, then, is: if God Eternal is worshipped in a mundane physical image, how could this God be manifest in something so ephemeral? Ibn ʿArabī's answer:

> Even if that image (*ṣūra*) disappeared after [being worshipped], then it would have disappeared only after being cloaked in godliness for its worshipper. Thus nothing remains which has not been worshipped, either through the worship of godliness or through the worship of subjugation. For any person of reason this would be necessary. And nothing in this world is worshipped except after being cloaked in sublimity for the worshipper and being manifest through a degree in his heart. Therefore, al-Ḥaqq is called 'Sublime in rank',[45] but He did not say 'in ranks'. Ranks, then, are numerous in one essence. God thus decreed that nothing should be worshipped but He, in numerous different

45. Qur'ān, 40:15.

> ranks, each of which provides a seat of [divine] manifestation in which He is worshipped.[46]

The eternal God is thus worshipped in the form of ephemeral things (an image here), without this in any way diminishing His eternal nature. Any *imagined* contradiction must be superficial and misleading; for the numerous different ranks, like the ranks in the subjugation by circumstance, really revert back to the mutuality in the relationship of the One to the many in which, ultimately, all are part of the One. Thus when the calf idol was destroyed (or if it would have been allowed naturally to decay), this did not show the falsity of idol-worship and 'prove' the practice of monotheistic worship, as is implied in the initial understanding of Mūsā's admonition to the Samaritan, 'Look at your god.' For as we saw earlier, from Ibn ʿArabī's perspective, Mūsā's words were by way of *instruction* concerning the calf's status as manifestation of the true God, Himself—no matter how fleeting the idol's existence in the physical realm: everything is the manifestation of the one essence, for however limited the life-spans of phenomenal beings, they are at the same time eternal in the One.

DESIRE, IDOLATRY AND UNITY

Though Ibn ʿArabī discussion has here attained a 'metaphysical peak', it has, again, occurred through a number of transformations in the narrative story of prophet-brothers and idol worship. Returning once more to the 'earthy substrate' of his sufi metaphysics, Ibn ʿArabī continues his explication of the divine manifestations, *majālin ilāhiyya*. This explication plumbs a psychological motif mooted earlier:

> The greatest and most sublime divine Self-Manifestation is desire (*al-hawā*), just as He said, 'Do you not see the one who takes his

46. *Fuṣūṣ*, p. 194.

> desire as his God.'[47] [Desire] is the greatest object of worship; nothing is worshipped but through it. Nor can desire be worshipped except through God Himself. So concerning this, I say: The truth of desire is that desire gives rise to [further] desire. Were it not for desire in the heart, desire would not be worshipped. And do you not see how perfect is God's knowledge of things, how instrumental it is in [the motivation] of one who takes his desire as his God? Consequently, God said, 'And God led him into error knowingly.' [48] 'Error' here is confusion. Thus when God sees this worshipper worshipping only his own desire, rigorously obeying desire's command in worshipping the one he worships, then even his worship of God Himself is also from desire. This is because if desire had not occurred to the worshipper in that most sanctified state, he would not have worshipped God or preferred Him to anything else.[49]

Ibn ʿArabī's psychological profile of desire and worship integrates a commonsensical observation with his unitive metaphysics. Desire in general, and the particular desire elevated as a god for worship, is for Ibn ʿArabī *empirically* 'the greatest object of worship', through which all other worship occurs. Human beings are fundamentally motivated by their desire; it is the driving force without which people would persist in torpor, unmoved and unmoving. The desire taken by some as their god for worship is for Ibn ʿArabī a *positive inclination*, as God Himself is thereby worshipped. The Qur'ān's negative tone and teaching with respect to those who practice this false worship is here inverted, with desire becoming a most positive human quality, leading to God Himself. The obsessive quality of desire—whatever its object—begets more desire. In human life all is desire. And though the Qur'ān seemingly speaks in derisory fashion about those who succumb to such motivation in the extreme act of actually worshipping their desire, it also says, in the same place, and in this connection, that 'God led him into

47. Qur'ān, 45:23.
48. *Ibid.*
49. *Fuṣūṣ*, pp. 194–195.

error knowingly'. How is this possible? Certainly the Qur'ān's oft-stated principle of God's omniscience and omnipotence, resulting in the determination of all human acts (good or bad), may on one level be invoked here. Ibn ʿArabī's gloss, however, would seem to lead in quite a different direction, toward the notion that God's directing of the one who worships his own desire as a god may, in fact, be something positive. For in referring to the phrase 'knowingly' ('in knowledge', *ʿalā ʿilm*) in this passage, Ibn ʿArabī speaks of the perfection of God's knowledge and its completion with respect to the worshipper of his own desire. Thus God, it would seem, does not lead into error such a one simply out of His own perfect power or out of some perverse motive in forcing His creature into sin. No. For God's perfect knowledge—completed in this act—informs Him there is a good to be found here. This good is that being led astray (*ḍalāla*) is 'confusion' (*ḥayra*). 'Confusion' in Ibn ʿArabī's general meaning is often a necessary prerequisite to esoteric knowledge of the metaphysics.[50] Desire as *ḍalāla*, in becoming *ḥayra*, has moved semantically from having a pejorative (Qur'ānic) connotation to a more neutral, sympathetic and even positive sense. Thus when God sees such an 'outrageous' act, He is pleased, as He knows that here is the foundation also of 'proper' worship, worship of Himself. Thus did He actually engineer the 'misdeed' through His comprehensive knowledge. Here the psychology of desire and worship begins again to merge with the absolute being and the immanent God.

Ibn ʿArabī pursues this line in two stages. First, he says, referring back to his statement above, that 'if desire had not occurred to the worshipper in that most sanctified state, he would not have worshipped God or preferred Him to anyone else'. Thus, as mooted earlier, the psychology of desire is such that desire feeds upon and begets itself, increasing inexorably as a concomitant of human existence. In this process, many things may be

50. See Suʿād al-Ḥakīm, *al-Muʿjam al-Ṣūfī*, pp. 353–357.

worshipped, in the building of a worshipful fervour which culminates compellingly in the worship of God. Thus does God lead man 'astray' into a 'confusion' of worshipful objects engendered by insistent desire, that man might find his way to God. But secondly, and by extension, man is in any case worshipping God in all of those 'lesser' objects of worshipful desire. 'Confusion' of worship here is in fact the recognition of *God immanent* in all things. This unity has its human counterpart, then, in a unity of belief, despite the wide variation of its worshipped objects which may for their worshippers be exclusive of the favourite objects of others. In a further gloss on the passage 'And God led him into error' (45:23), Ibn ʿArabī says:

> [God] confused him 'knowingly' [for God knows] that every worshipper worships only his desire and only his desire subjugates him, whether [his desire] is contrary to *Sharīʿa* law or not. However, the accomplished gnostic is one who sees every object of worship as a manifestation of al-Ḥaqq in which He is worshipped. Thus do they [the worshippers] name all of them [the worshipped things] 'a god', despite their [also] being called specifically a stone, tree, animal, man, heavenly body or angel ... Godliness is a quality which causes the worshipper of something to imagine that it is a quality of the object of his worship. But [godliness] is in reality a manifestation of al-Ḥaqq before the eyes of the worshipper who is devoted to this object of worship in this particular divine manifestation.[51]

The variety of forms of human worship, whatever their object and whether or not the worshippers themselves understand the true nature of their practice, are in fact then worship of God, *al-Ḥaqq*. The godliness imagined by the worshippers to be in their objects of worship is in fact there, because these things are foci of divine presence. In calling the worshipped animal, rock or tree 'a god', the worshippers *are* correct, not only because *for*

51. *Fuṣūṣ*, p. 195.

them the object appears divine, but because it is a seat of *true* divine presence. The pagan practice may be 'wrong' according to Sharīʿa, but it is 'right' in its underlying nature, which *as worship of God Himself* is actually the goal of true religion. Though human desire swings in all directions toward worship of all manner of things—whether 'licit' or 'illicit' in Sharīʿa terms—the 'illicit' becomes 'licit' in the way here described.

The calf-worship in Hārūn's story has led Ibn ʿArabī through various paths of Qur'ānic narrative and sufi metaphysics to the conclusion that such a practice is not as it may seem on first superficial glance. On deeper contemplation, it may well appear a pious act of true worship, in sharp contrast with its usual designation as idolatry.[52] This reconsideration was in fact given exemplar status with Mūsā himself, as Ibn ʿArabī tells that story in relation to Hārūn. Ibn ʿArabī concludes his intricate discussion of Hārūn and the calf with a summary statement of the main issues, here emphasizing a hierarchy of knowledge. He also brings fresh Qur'ānic evidence to bear on the case.

Thus in referring to the pagan idol-worshippers mentioned in Qur'ān 39:3 and 38:5, Ibn ʿArabī says that even 'some of those who speak in ignorance would say, "We worship them [the idols] only that they might bring us closer to God." [39:3] Indeed, they [also] had already called the idols gods, when they said, "Has he made the gods one God? How wondrous that would be." [38:5]'[53] For Ibn ʿArabī, then, the Qur'ān itself affirms that even some benighted pagans in their very idolatry evince a modicum of recognition that God is somehow associated with their idols. This obviously runs contrary to a more literal reading of these passages in their original Qur'ānic contexts. The passage from 39:3, for example, seems to indicate a disingenuousness on the part of the pagans, in their attempt to evade the divine challenge, while the passage from 38:5 obviously indicates a

52. But, again, for Ibn ʿArabī it can be—and is—*both*.

53. *Fuṣūṣ*, p. 195.

sarcastic response from the pagans to the notion of one God. However, with his subtle irony Ibn ʿArabī never 'loses faith' in the pagans, saying, by way of deepening the exegesis:

> So they did not, then, reject God. Rather, they expressed wonder [at the possibility that there might be one God transcending all the others]. Nevertheless, though, still they continued adhering to the numerous forms which they considered to be divine. Thus did the apostle come to them and call them to one God, whom they had acknowledged, but whom they could not see, making them unable to affirm him. However, again they did believe in Him, in their saying, 'We worship them [the idols] only that they might bring us closer to God'. This was because they knew that those forms were [really only] stones—and thus was the argument turned against them, with God's saying, 'Say: So name them.' But they could name them only because they knew that those names have a reality.[54]

For Ibn ʿArabī, the pagans, then, did believe in God *through their idols* which they knew 'were really only stones', the idols presumably serving as a tangible aid in moving closer to the intangible true God. Ibn ʿArabī thus takes the pagans' 'declaration of faith' in Qur'ān 39:3 at face value, in contradistinction to the Qur'ān's seeming emphasis on its lack of substance. Indeed, for Ibn ʿArabī, the pagans' realisation that the idols were only stones and that something greater must exist beyond them served God's purpose well in His further challenge to them *to name their gods*. For in the Qur'ān, this challenge would reveal the depth of the pagans' error, with any such naming of their gods being a mere display of empty words, informing God of nothing new and thereby devoid of reality. Thus in Qur'ānic terms was the argument decisively 'turned against them', as Ibn ʿArabī says. And the Qur'ānic implication here is that the pagans, should they wish to see the light, would have nowhere to go but to God Himself, indicating a crushing defeat of their

54. *Fuṣūṣ*, pp. 195–196.

claim to some sort of reality for their idols. For Ibn ʿArabī, God's argument against the pagans here *is* decisively turned against them, as he says. And he certainly is in agreement with the basic Qur'ānic idea that God and His Prophet are trying to move recalcitrant pagans away from their worship of idols. For Ibn ʿArabī, though, the emphasis and perspective have been, and continue to be, different. Thus as his response to Qur'ān 39:3 and 38:5 involved a dedicated attempt to see there a positive monotheistic impulse and tendency for the pagans, in some contrast with the Qur'ān's apparent meaning, so here, in his understanding of 13:33, he sees the pagans' anticipated reply to God's command to name their gods as a turning-point which underscores and confirms their monotheistic proclivities which, for Ibn ʿArabī, were mooted in 39:3 and 38:5. While the Qur'ān sees the command to name as a turning-point in exposing the emptiness of those names and, in consequence, the absence of a reality for those idols, Ibn ʿArabī declares that the pagans could name them 'only because they knew that those names have a reality (*ḥaqīqa*)'. That reality for Ibn ʿArabī is obviously God. The command to name is in Ibn ʿArabī's view, then, also a turning-point for the pagans, but toward the reality of God behind the empty stone idols.

THE HIERARCHY OF KNOWLEDGE

Why is Ibn ʿArabī's understanding of idolatry, then, 'different' in conception from that in the Qur'ān? Any answer to this would, of necessity, concentrate on metaphysics and his notion of an immanent God, which have been our focus thus far. Also highly relevant and related to this, is his notion of the appropriate types of knowledge and understanding for different classes of people, in general and in particular. Ibn ʿArabī concludes with this issue. It will return us to another important perspective of his, as well as providing a final revisit to the brothers Hārūn and Mūsā in their special relationship. Ibn ʿArabī says:

> The gnostics are those who know the matter as it really is. They publicly manifest a form of rejection of the [pagan] images that are worshipped. This is because their level of knowledge renders them subject to the normative standard of the Prophet's era and, thereby, to the dominion of the apostle in whom they believe and through whom their being called believers is determined for them. For [the gnostics] are worshippers [of God, bound by] their knowing that the pagans did not worship those images as such, but rather that they worshipped God in them, consonant with the power of the divine manifestation which the gnostics recognised [in the idols]. But one who rejects [the idols] without knowing of the divine manifestation [in them] is ignorant of this. And the accomplished gnostic hides [this truth] from any prophet, any apostle and any of their heirs.[55]

The hierarchy of knowledge and the roles which derive from it are clear: the gnostics *know the full truth* concerning idolatry, but they are honour-bound not to disclose this truth, even to the prophets, the apostles and their heirs, for these all have their divinely-appointed roles in curbing idolatry and promoting the worship of God *in their time and in their situation.* The gnostics, *as believers*, in deference to God and the apostles, are obliged not to disclose and even deliberately to hide their deeper truth, thereby remaining under the authority of the apostle's situation (time and context/*al-waqt*).[56] The God to whom the apostles and the prophets call the people, says Ibn ʿArabī, is known only in the most general way. He cannot be seen, as the Qur'ān says, because 'Eyes do not see Him', but 'He sees the eyes' (6:103). This, as Ibn ʿArabī has said, is 'because of His opaqueness and His diffusion in the essences of things…'. Human eyes cannot see Him, as this would be like seeing their own 'external shapes', for He is immanent in the eyes, as He is in all things. [57] Thus,

55. *Fuṣūṣ*, p. 196.

56. Ibn ʿArabī seems here to mean by *al-waqt* the original temporal situations and contexts of the Prophet which all his later followers would be obligated to acknowledge and show fidelity to.

57. *Fuṣūṣ*, p. 196.

again citing Qur'ān 6:103, 'He is opaque and knows all', God's 'knowing' in Qur'ānic language (*khibra*), says Ibn ʿArabī, in a gloss on this passage, 'is taste and taste is [God's self-] manifestation and [His self-] manifestation is in images. Thus are the images and God both necessary, as it is axiomatic that one who sees [God] in his desire thereby worships Him—if you will understand. And the path leads to God'.[58] Here God's own attribute of 'knowing' is one with that of the gnostic (taste/ *dhawq*) and this in turn is God's appearance (self-manifestation/ *tajallī*) in all things. God and the forms, then, are both necessary, as they are the two sides of the same coin. And the calf here is one of the forms.

58. *Ibid.*

CHAPTER

5

The Wisdom of Ecstatic Love in the Word of Ibrāhīm

THE FIGURE OF IBRĀHĪM/ABRAHAM

The Qur'ānic figure of Ibrāhīm makes available to Ibn ʿArabī a wide range of themes for expressing certain essential features of his sufi metaphysics. Appearing numerous times in the Qur'ān,[1] Ibrāhīm exemplifies various religious principles and conditions. Prominent among these are pure monotheism or Ibrāhīm as *ḥanīf*,[2] Ibrāhīm's willingness to fulfil God's command to sacrifice his son,[3] Ibrāhīm's establishing of the Kaʿba,[4] Ibrāhīm's offering of hospitality and food to strangers[5] and Ibrāhīm's status as 'friend of God', *khalīl Allāh*.[6] Some of these motifs are of course Biblical as well, at least in general theme if not in fine detail and identical stories.[7] In the chapter on Ibrāhīm in the *Fuṣūṣ*, Ibn

1. Ibrāhīm appears in 25 *sūras*, second only to Mūsā in this frequency. For an overview of Ibrāhīm in the Qur'ān and Islam, see the article 'Ibrāhīm' by Rudi Paret in *The Encyclopaedia of Islam*, new edition, pp. 980–1. Also, for a good post-Qur'ānic and extra-Qur'ānic account of Ibrāhīm in Islam, see Reuven Firestone, *Journeys in Holy Lands*.

2. Qur'ān, 4:125. (The following Qur'ānic references in notes 3 to 6 are suggestive and not always exhaustive.)

3. Qur'ān, 37:100–11.

4. Qur'ān, 2:224–225.

5. Qur'ān, 11:69; 51:24–30.

6. Qur'ān, 4:125.

7. Here, as in other such instances in the *Fuṣūṣ*, it is again important to recognise the *continuity* of religious culture in the transmission of popular story themes from a reservoir of ancient tradition (oral and written) and their absorption and expression in different contexts.

ᶜArabī makes use mainly of two of these Qur'ānic/Biblical ideas: Ibrāhīm as friend of God and Ibrāhīm as offering hospitality and food to others.[8] Some other Qur'ānic themes concerning Ibrāhīm may be implicit—particularly that of the pure monotheism associated with him—but it is these two which are here most prominent. Of the two, Ibrāhīm as friend of God is the most central, though both are understood by Ibn ᶜArabī as exemplifying the metaphysical unity which is so central to his sufi metaphysics. Here through the Qur'ānic figure of Ibrāhīm, Ibn ᶜArabī expresses, in a somewhat more explicit way than in many other discussions, the full structure of his metaphysics.

Ibn ᶜArabī also employs other Qur'ānic motifs which have no explicit connection with Ibrāhīm, but are rather associated with other prophets and other Qur'ānic ideas. Like the ideas explicitly associated with Ibrāhīm, these others for Ibn ᶜArabī reveal and allude to the metaphysical truth of the universe. These Qur'ānic motifs work in concert with the two main Ibrāhīmī ideas, to create for Ibn ᶜArabī a full explication of this truth. There are five such Qur'ānic references in the chapter on Ibrāhīm: 'Praise be to God' (*e.g.*, 1:2, 6:1, 6:45, 7:43, and so on); 'God has the decisive argument' (6:149); 'He made things difficult for them' (68:42); 'If He wills' (4:133); 'There is none of us but has a known rank' (38:164).

In exploring how this whole Qur'ānic collection is understood by Ibn ᶜArabī as the core of his more general metaphysics, three subjects will serve as the framework for discussion of his exposition of Ibrāhīm's story: Ibrāhīm's wisdom in the title of the chapter; the *takhallul* of God and man; the ethical dimension and God's freedom and efficacy with respect to that. These three constitute the main themes in Ibn ᶜArabī's discussion of Ibrāhīm, though he often interweaves them in such a way that they may not always appear as separate ideas.

8. *Fuṣūṣ*, pp. 80, 84. The relevant Biblical references are: Isaiah, 41:8, for friend of God; Genesis, 18:1–16, for hospitality.

IBRĀHĪM'S WISDOM

Ibn ʿArabī titles the chapter on Ibrāhīm 'The Wisdom of Ecstatic Love in the Ibrāhīmī Word': *ḥikma muhayyamiyya fī kalima Ibrāhīmiyya.*[9] The adjective *muhayyamiyya* attached to *ḥikma* conveys a basic idea here round which Ibn ʿArabī builds his metaphysical explication of Ibrāhīm's essential truth: a rapturous, ecstatic, even reckless love through which one loses oneself in another. This loss of self (or transcendence of self) may also imply the effacing of the self's boundaries: loss of self in rapturous love of the other may then mean a final blending which renders the self inextricable from and part of the other. The connotations here remain emotional and personal. Indeed, rapturous love may even be associated with being 'out of one's senses', 'beside oneself' or, 'confused, puzzled, baffled'. But why, one might ask, does Ibn ʿArabī associate Ibrāhīm with this sort of personal experience and how does this idea serve as the foundation of the sufi metaphysics which Ibn ʿArabī explicates generally in the *Fuṣūṣ* and with such sharp clarity in this chapter?

Ibn ʿArabī's wisdom of rapturous, mad love in the word of Ibrāhīm is for him associated with Ibrāhīm's status in the Qur'ān (4:125) as 'God's friend': 'And God took Ibrāhīm as a friend' (*khalīl*). Thus does Ibn ʿArabī begin with a comment on Qur'ān 4:125: '*Al-khalīl* is called *al-khalīl* because of his penetrating (*takhallul*) and encompassing everything by which the divine essence is characterised.'[10] Seeing in the Qur'ānic *khalīl*, friend, other associations with that linguistic root (*kh-l-l*), Ibn ʿArabī has, then, in particular designated the verbal noun *takhallul*, 'penetrating', 'encompassing', 'pervading', as the root meaning which for him most aptly reflects the deeper Qur'ānic sense of Ibrāhīm's status as 'friend of God'. This 'language game' for Ibn ʿArabī goes far beyond a simple exercise in word and root

9. *Fuṣūṣ*, p. 80.
10. *Ibid.*

association. While there is indeed a playful poetry of language here, emanating from Ibn ʿArabī's deep knowledge of the Arabic language and the Qur'ānic text, the meaning of *takhallul*, as the core of *khalīl* for Ibn ʿArabī, signifies the 'impersonal' and abstract realm of the oneness of being or absolute being. Just as Ibn ʿArabī develops this notion elsewhere in the *Fuṣūṣ*, his development of it in relation to Ibrāhīm begins here. Let us look more carefully at what he has thus far done.

TAKHALLUL

From mad, self-dissolving love, to the more sober notion of 'friend of God', to one who pervades and is himself characterised and pervaded by all the attributes which define the divine essence, this is the bare framework of Ibn ʿArabī's initial interpretative thrust. It incorporates the first two parts of the basic tripartite structure of his discussion, Ibrāhīm's *ḥikma* and the *takhallul* of God and man. The *takhallul*, as the philosophical extension of the *ḥikma muhayyamiyya*, begins to unlock the metaphysical world by providing some terminology of abstraction rather removed from emotional and personalised love and friendship.

This terminology posits a divine essence (*dhāt ilāhiyya*) and divine attributes (*ṣifāt*), the basic formulation and description of God's nature found in various trends of Islamic thought. There it conceptually 'divides' God into these 'two spheres': His essence, which usually may not be known to us (the theological perspective), and His attributes, which are the 'face' He presents to His creatures through which they will certainly be capable of knowing and understanding Him in some way. The attributes in this formulation are generally derived from God's names in the Qur'ān.[11] As is well-known, many versions of this two-fold

11. See, *e.g.*, Abū Ḥāmid al-Ghazālī, *al-Maqṣad al-Asnā fī Sharḥ Maʿānī Asmā' Allāh al-Ḥusnā*, ed., Fadlou A. Shehadi, translated into English by D. Burrell and N. Daher, *Al-Ghazālī on the Ninety-nine Beautiful Names of God.*

conception of understanding God were expressed in Islamic thought, sometimes resulting in fierce intellectual polemics. Particularly contentious was the issue of the *relationship* between the divine essence and attributes: were the attributes, for example, 'added' to the essence, in which case, according to some, God's oneness might be compromised? Or might some other explanation of this relationship, according to others, obviate the doctrinal danger?[12] Ibn ʿArabī does not here address this aspect of the question.[13] He simply employs the formulation of essence and attributes, in his own way and for his own ends. This is, again, in order further to extend the main issue of the divine-human encounter from the personal to the more abstract, as a basis for his own subsequent, metaphysical explication of the relationship between God and man.

The main difference in Ibn ʿArabī's use of the essence-attributes model applied to God from its more 'conventional' use by other thinkers is in the notion that a particular human being (*al-khalīl*, Ibrāhīm) can enter into and fully possess those attributes which characterise the divine essence. Here man would appear fully to take on the traits of God—an absurd (indeed, dangerous) notion from ordinary theological standpoints.[14] Ibn ʿArabī reinforces and further explicates this idea, first with a brief line from an unnamed poet and then with examples drawn from a discussion of the way ordinary things possess attributes. The line of poetry, 'I have entered the way of the [divine] spirit within me; thus was *al-khalīl* named *khalīl*'.[15] This asserts that man becomes clothed in this divine garb by joining the divine spirit (*rūḥ*) *within himself* (*bihi*). God (or His

12. See F.A. Shehadi's 'Introduction' to al-Ghazālī's *al-Maqṣad al-Asnā*, pp. XV–LI, for a good general discussion of these ideas.

13. But he does, obviously, formulate his ideas against this background in *ʿilm al-kalām*, Islamic discursive theology. See note 23 below.

14. This is obviously different, in its metaphysical implications, from the Islamic idea of man striving to *emulate* God in some of His main attributes.

15. *Fuṣūṣ*, p. 80.

spirit) being *within man*—using Ibrāhīm as human paradigm—is thus made central here. The notion of the interior of man as the venue of the human adoption of divine attributes exemplifies Ibn ʿArabī's central idea of the true God as dwelling within His creation.

In explicating the 'mechanics' of this human adoption of divine attributes, Ibn ʿArabī gives a further example, again referring to this same line of poetry. Here he likens the human entrance into the divine essence, and the human appropriation thereby of the divine attributes, to the colour which enters into and pervades something which is coloured. Comparing this process with that of the attribute (*ʿaraḍ*) in its relationship to the substance in which it inheres (*jawhar*), Ibn ʿArabī warns against thinking this is like an entity filling an empty space. For while in the former there is presumably a true pervasion of one side by the other (Ibn ʿArabī's meaning with respect to *al-khalīl*), in the latter there is not. Further, as we have seen, there is a reciprocity in this relationship in which the pervader *receives* something from the pervaded. Ibrāhīm thus partakes of the divine attributes, absorbing them within himself. The model of divine essence and attributes or—more mundanely—the substance (*jawhar*) and accident (*ʿaraḍ*) which Ibn ʿArabī uses as his framework here, while possessing some general suggestive intellectual value for him, falls very far short of carrying his own most important meanings.[16] Ibn ʿArabī's next move in the discussion takes this divine–human intertwining (*takhallul*) even further, with the suggestion of a thoroughgoing reciprocity between the divine and the human which envisages an 'exchange' of attributes from one side to the other. This was earlier strongly implied, but it is here made explicit.

Ibn ʿArabī says there is either the perspective already

16. This is mainly because, for Ibn ʿArabī, the construct of attribute and thing (or being) characterised by that attribute—whether God or some part of His creation—is essentially a 'paradoxical' pointer towards a unity of being where such attributive functions are rendered irrelevant.

discussed—the human within and partaking of the divine—'or [the situation is thus] because of God's pervasion and incorporation of the existence of the form of Ibrāhīm, peace be upon him'.[17] Either attribution (*ḥukm*)—*i.e.,* the divine–human connection from either side—'is valid' says Ibn ʿArabī, 'Do you not see God manifested in the attributes of created beings and thereby revealing Himself, even taking on [human] attributes of deficiency and blame?'[18] And, in stating the full mutuality of God and Ibrāhīm, 'Do you not see the created thing manifested in the attributes of God… all of these divine attributes being right for it, just as the attributes of created beings are right for God?'[19]

The discussion thus far is a highly particular formulation of Ibn ʿArabī's sufi metaphysics, focused in this divine-human mutuality of attributes, all of it from the perspective opened by Ibrāhīm's status as *khalīl* and the derived notion of *takhallul.* The conventional notions of divine essence and attributes and 'substance' and 'accident' are again, for Ibn ʿArabī, suggestive but not determinative in this particular formulation of his metaphysics. Especially noteworthy here is the idea of God's full adoption of human characteristics, even those of '*deficiency and blame*'. This is the basis of what will later become the Ibrāhīmī version of Ibn ʿArabī's general ethical angle in his metaphysics of the divine-human encounter. For as the metaphysical nature of this encounter in Ibn ʿArabī's thought makes the two parties in this meeting as one, it thereby renders their ethical relationship different from its more conventional interpretation in scriptural and theological formulations. Further metaphysical elaboration here through the figure of Ibrāhīm will now often be intertwined with the ethical side.

17. *Fuṣūṣ*, p. 80.
18. *Ibid.*
19. *Ibid.*, pp. 80–81.

QUR'ĀNIC AND GRAMMATICAL POINTERS IN ETHICS AND METAPHYSICS

Two Qur'ānic citations—these not directly related to Ibrāhīm—serve Ibn ʿArabī as a basis for this elaboration. The first, from 1:2, like numerous other verses, is the classic Qur'ānic formula expressing wondrous praise for God, 'Praise be to God' (*al-ḥamd lillāh*). For Ibn ʿArabī, this utterance expresses the truth that, 'Therefore the referents of praise, whether the praiser or the praised, originate in God.'[20] This follows logically from, and deepens, Ibn ʿArabī's idea above that the attributes of created beings are right for God just as God's attributes are right for His creation. The praiser (*ḥāmid*), then, and the praised (*maḥmūd*) both refer to God. Conventionally, it might seem somewhat unusual. For though God is always praised, the one who praises him is man. But it is also true, however, that as the Qur'ān itself provides the notion of praising God, this is in any case God's word. And God for Ibn ʿArabī, therefore, *is* praising Himself. Thus continues Ibn ʿArabī, citing Qur'ān 11:123, 'To him the whole matter returns with God.' This identification of God and His creation in Ibn ʿArabī's Qur'ānic gloss then points towards the ethical side in his further and conclusive remarks on 11:123, 'Consequently, God comprises what is blameworthy and what is praiseworthy—indeed, there is nothing but the blameworthy and the praiseworthy.'[21] God here is explicitly dressed in the shabby garb of human imperfection, as well as in the glorious robes of divine praise.

Ibn ʿArabī then continues further in this vein, now using the ethical statement above as a 're-entry' into the issue of *takhallul*, here employing some language of Arabic grammar as his way of understanding:

> Know that nothing pervades something else unless it already resides within it. The pervader—the active participle—is, then,

20. *Ibid.*, p.81.
21. *Ibid.*

> hidden within that which it pervades, the passive participle. The passive participle is thus the external side, while the active participle is the hidden passive side. [This passive party] is nourishment for the active, like the water which permeates wool causing it to swell and to expand. If, however, God is the external side, man is consequently hidden within Him and man assumes all the names of God, His hearing, His sight and all His characteristics and ways of understanding. If, however, man is the external side, God is hidden within Him, and God assumes man's hearing, vision, hand, foot and all of his faculties.[22]

Using the grammatical analogy of active and passive participles to clarify further the *takhallul* of Ibrāhīm and God, Ibn ʿArabī thus gives additional insight into the process: the passive participle—the praised (*maḥmūd*), for example—corresponds with the external (*ẓāhir*), while the active participle—the praiser (*al-ḥāmid*), for example—corresponds with the internal (*bāṭin*). Grammatically, the passive participle is that which receives the verbal action—in this case, pervasion or penetration—and the active participle is the agent of the action, here the penetrator. The grammatical analogy of active and passive for Ibn ʿArabī signifies in particular the giving of characteristics or attributes (the active) and the receiving of them (the passive). But such an 'interactive' language for this particular relationship still implies *two parties*, when Ibn ʿArabī's ultimate meaning, of course, is the very unity and ontological 'indivisibility' of these two parties. If, however, one bears in mind that in Ibn ʿArabī's formulation and understanding the attributes 'exchanged' in this interaction are *already present* in their *receivers*, then the larger unitive dimension will be apparent: God and His creation are as one. The language of discussion of this oneness, though, still implies a *pair, two things*, because of the very structure of the language and the religious worldview it reflects. This is to be expected in a monotheistic theology founded on the notion of a gulf

22. *Ibid.*

(physical, ontological and ethical) between the creator and creature. Ibn ʿArabī's technique of integrating *the two* here has been to view the relationship through the exchange of attributes, this based on the concept of God Himself—as a somehow integrated pair of essence and attributes—as various schools of Islamic theology and philosophy postulated His nature.

THE DIVINE ESSENCE AND ATTRIBUTES IN *TAKHALLUL*

Ibn ʿArabī's difference, even uniqueness, in this respect lies in his notion of the divine–human *exchange of attributes* as a new conception of the relationship, very different from the various established formulations. This is also apparent in Ibn ʿArabī's treatment of Zakariyyā, in the chapter devoted to that prophet. Another side of the issue still remains to be brought out and explicated in this general discussion of *takhallul*: *God's nature* within His relationship to His creation. This has lurked in the discussion without having been made explicit in the exposition. In itself and in its essential connection with the issues thus far discussed, the subject is crucial to a full picture of Ibn ʿArabī's metaphysics.

Ibn ʿArabī plunges into the issue of God's essence and attributes now within a more narrowly conventional and theological type of discourse. He then takes the resulting formulations back to the sufi metaphysical discourse on *takhallul* and combines the two. Thus:

> The [divine] essence, then, if it were stripped of these connections [*i.e.*, the attributes], would not be a god. But our own fixed essences (*aʿyān thābita*) create these connections, and we, therefore, make God a god, through our own divinity. He, consequently, is not known until we are known. The Prophet, peace be upon him, said, 'He who knows himself knows his lord.' And the Prophet is the most knowledgeable of us concerning God. But some philosophers and Abū Ḥāmid al-Ghazālī claimed that

God may be known without our looking at the world and this is an error.[23]

Ibn ᶜArabī's conception of God as essence *and* attributes here again takes on a decidedly different colouring than the conception held by the theologians and philosophers. For whatever their particular angle on the issue, the divine essence for these thinkers had a significance *in itself*, stripped of its attributes. Indeed, the divine essence was in a sense the 'true' God, the attributes being there for God's own reasons with respect to His creation. For Ibn ᶜArabī, though he does talk about the divine essence, it is meaningless without the attributes. Ibn ᶜArabī's God *is* His attributes. As we have also seen, however, *we are His attributes*. And here precisely lies the radical difference which Ibn ᶜArabī introduces: the created world—and humanity as its essential manifestation—for Ibn ᶜArabī *is* God. Ibn ᶜArabī's understanding of the divine attributes here (*ṣifāt Allāh*) and the connections (*nisab*) between God and the world is that they *are* the created world, for each attribute or divine name represents another aspect of creation. 'Creation' here is the *appearance of God* in a 'created form', the form itself being God. Created being, therefore, is not 'created' in the usual sense of a thing produced from nothing by a creative agent. 'Created' here is a metaphor for the manifestation of God (as *tajallin*) *through* His creation. In contradistinction, then, to Ghazālī, and other 'conventional' thinkers, the formula of divine essence and attributes is here used very differently: It is now the vehicle for *erasing* the distinction between a creator God and His creation, whereas previously it presupposed and investigated various aspects of that

23. *Ibid.* This is, in a sense, the crux of Ibn ᶜArabī's disagreement with the 'conventional' thought which posits the divine Essence–Attribute distinction where there may be an 'essential God' who is somehow (indirectly) knowable to us apart from His attributes. For Ibn ᶜArabī, the attributes *are* God in the form of the phenomenal world (His names) where His divinity itself is manifested. For a 'conventional' view see al-Ghazālī's *al-Maqṣad al-asnā*, Chapter Four of Part One.

distinction. God's attributes are also for Ibn ʿArabī, as he terms it in various places, 'the God created [conceived] in the religious doctrines'.[24] *We* conceive that God through our understanding of these religions. God, as formulated in these systems *is* the attributes—*i.e.*, He can be known in no other way than through these descriptions of Him. This is our 'creation of God'. Though Ibn ʿArabī *in principle* does hold that the 'true God' is ineffable but yet a reality and that the 'created God' is, somehow, but a pale version of the 'true God', this seems also for him to be formulaic and devoid of any significance. For the 'true God' is at best an *intuited* 'first cause' behind everything. But this has no intellectual value for Ibn ʿArabī and does not figure significantly in his thought. Ibn ʿArabī makes this point clearly and forcefully in what he calls two 'revelations' (*kashfayn*), introduced here as further support for what he has already argued.

THE *KASHFAYN*, METAPHYSICS AND ETHICS

The first *kashf* 'reveals':

> That God Himself is the very proof of Himself and his divinity, that the world is nothing other than His appearance in the forms of their [created beings'] fixed essences whose existence is impossible without Him and that He is manifold in appearance as forms, according to the natures of these essences and their modes.[25]

This *kashf*, says Ibn ʿArabī, comes after knowledge derived from us 'that God is a God for us' (*annahu ilāhun lanā*).[26]

Here, in greater detail, is what Ibn ʿArabī meant when he said that God is not known 'until we are known'. God appears according to the fixed essences (*al-aʿyān al-thābita*) of His creation (we, in particular), in which He appears (in a *tajallin*) *as* that

24. See note 8 in chapter one for discussions of and references to this term.
25. *Fuṣūṣ*, p. 81.
26. *Fuṣūṣ*, pp. 81–82.

creation. The fixed essences—paradigms of later 'created' beings—God's names and God's attributes are virtually all the 'same', constituting the created or phenomenal world. In this sense, God *as the world* is 'proof of Himself and His divinity', for proof must in this case be empirical. We—and Ibrāhīm as a perfect specimen of us—*as the world* also have, as Ibn ʿArabī said earlier, our own divinity (*uluhiyyatunā*), for God appears in us and in the whole world.

Ibn ʿArabī's 'second revelation' (*al-kashf al-ākhar*) emphasises this latter point, serving thereby to complete the metaphysical explanation of the *takhallul* of Ibrāhīm and God:

> Thus do our forms appear to you in God. Consequently, some of us appear to others in God and some of us know others and are distinguished from one another [in God]. Some of us know that in God this knowledge occurs to us and some are ignorant of the plane in which this knowledge occurs in us. May God keep me from being among these ignorant ones.[27]

If God appears *in* the world and *as* the world, as has been established, then we exist in our mutual relations, and indeed in everything related to our lives, *in God* or *in the world*. This whole structure and process are inexorable, according to the patterns of fixed essences through which God is made manifest in the forms which constitute the phenomenal world. And we, as His main creation, *are* these forms in fulfilment of our own fixed essences. God's names and attributes reflect and express this. 'We', as reality and microcosm of the whole 'created' universe, 'determine' our own lives and destiny, and, by extension, the destiny of the universe: 'With the two revelations together, [it may be known that] we are not determined except through ourselves. No, indeed, we determine ourselves, through ourselves, but in God.'[28]

It is important to understand what Ibn ʿArabī means here by

27. *Fuṣūṣ*, p. 82.
28. *Ibid.*

his various uses of 'determine', from the Arabic root *ḥ-k-m* This is a good example of Ibn ʿArabī's common method of infusing key terms in his thought with metaphysical meaning, while continuing also to intend the ordinary meaning. In this case, derivatives of the root *ḥ-k-m* may ordinarily signify determination or control of something and this certainly is one sense in the passage above, as will later become even clearer. Thus, we determine—have power over—our own lives *in God*, in this phenomenal 'creation' which is God's empirical reflection. This formulation is redolent of 'free-will' doctrines—*i.e.*, we determine our lives and thus *bear responsibility* for our actions. But the notion of *ḥukm* for Ibn ʿArabī also is a key metaphysical concept, connoting the nexus of metaphysical efficacy and order between various planes of being. A clear example of this usage, as we know, may be found in the chapter on Zakariyyā in the *Fuṣūṣ* where Ibn ʿArabī says that God's mercy touches everything, *wujūdan wa ḥukman*—in 'its existence-giving nature' and 'in its ontological governance'.[29] The ensuing metaphysical *order* is a result of the decisive effect of *ḥukm*. Thus, for example, the fixed essences 'descend' into the phenomenal realm which their earthly manifestations inhabit through the *ḥukm* which connects each essence with this realm. Here 'we determine' ourselves in an abstract metaphysical sense, with the process of 'our' fixed essences taking their phenomenal forms *inexorably*, according to the nature of things. Ethical responsibility and metaphysical necessity, then, serve Ibn ʿArabī as a dual approach to the 'same' issue. The continuing discussion exemplifies this, further deepening the mutuality of ethics and metaphysics for Ibn ʿArabī and, by extension, raising another aspect of God's nature and His relationship to His 'creation'.

As proof-text for these preceding statements on our determining (*ḥukm*) of ourselves, Ibn ʿArabī cites Qur'ān, 6:149, 'To God belongs the decisive argument'. The direct Qur'ānic

29. *Ibid.*, p. 117.

context for 6:149, to be found in 6:148, is the argument of 'those who associate partners with God' (polytheists), that if God had not wanted them to worship other gods, He somehow would have prevented them doing that; as He has not done so, then the practice must be permissible. God disagrees, instructing the Prophet to tell these heathens that they have no solid evidence for this and that they do nothing but lie. At that point comes 6:149, 'Say: "To God belongs the decisive argument", continuing, "If He had wished, He certainly could have guided you all."' But He did not, as by implication He obviously expected ethical responsibility from His creatures who would have free choice in ethical matters. God's 'decisive argument', then, refutes these claims of the polytheists. Ibn ʿArabī, however, says it is a decisive argument 'against those who are veiled (*al-maḥjūbūn*), since they say to God, "Why did you do this and that to us?", which did not correspond with their desires'.[30] The fate of these veiled ones, says Ibn ʿArabī, is revealed in Qur'ān 68:42, 'The shin shall be exposed for them', *i.e.*, the Day of Judgement shall hit them hard.

Apart from his reference to 'those who are veiled', Ibn ʿArabī has been speaking here mainly on the level of ordinary ethical responsibility in a quite usual way: we determine ourselves by choosing freely to do or not to do what God has enjoined; and we will receive our recompense accordingly. The personal, ethical discussion is constructed as Qur'ānic interpretation and seems intended to serve as support for the preceding, mainly metaphysical, explication on our determining of ourselves. This 'shift' is an instance of Ibn ʿArabī's method of interweaving and alternating between the personal and the metaphysical, using Qur'ānic verses as the 'interface' between the two. And this process here constitutes his 'exegesis'.[31] He is now ready to 'return' to the metaphysical.

30. *Ibid.*, p. 82.

31. In this sense, as I have said previously in other contexts, the *Fuṣūṣ* may be considered an exegetical work.

In his 'shift' above, Ibn ʿArabī did not completely leave the metaphysical for the personal (he never works solely on one or the other level). For he dropped a 'metaphysical marker' in the midst of his Qur'ānic gloss on ethical responsibility, in his designation of those in Qur'ān 6:149 against whom God's 'decisive argument' is deployed, as 'the veiled ones' (*al-maḥjūbūn*). In the Qur'ān itself, this verse does not contain that term, nor could this sense easily be construed. Again, in the previous verse (6:148), where the present narrative (in 6:149) really begins, these people are identified as 'those who associate partners with God' (*alladhīna ashrakū*), a common Qur'ānic way of referring to polytheists, idol worshippers and others of their ilk. 'The veiled ones' would not normally be a Qur'ānic designation for such persons. But of course in sufism 'the veiled ones' is a central term and concept referring in general to any person or group who have not attained the higher mystical truths, whether their veiling is manifested in idol-worship, low spiritual insight, intellectual weakness or whatever. Being veiled is contrasted with 'true knowledge' (*maʿrifa*, gnosis) or mystical 'taste' (*dhawq*). For Ibn ʿArabī, the intellectual component of that knowledge, or taste, is central and paramount. *Maʿrifa* for him, though perhaps in broader sufi context does incorporate an experiential aspect, is in conception and practical application largely intellectual. It means an understanding of Ibn ʿArabī's metaphysical system in all its intellectual subtlety and in its association with Islamic intellectual traditions and history.[32]

We must, then, look with interest at how Ibn ʿArabī defines and understands the veiling or ignorance which impedes the understanding of the veiled ones (polytheists in the Qur'ān) who complain to God that He has ordered their lives in ways not consonant with their wishes:

> It is the issue which the gnostics (*al-ʿārifūn*) have discovered here. Thus they understand that God does not do to the polytheists

32. In my view, Ibn ʿArabī 'inverted' traditional sufism, with his intellectualisation, thereby rendering 'gnosis' more objectively accessible.

> what they claim He has done and that this is most certainly from themselves. God can indeed know them only as they are. Their argument is consequently thwarted and God's decisive argument remains.[33]

In saying 'God can know them only as they are', Ibn ʿArabī interweaves the ethical and the metaphysical, preparing a full return to a metaphysical gloss on the ethical. For in Ibn ʿArabī's special language 'as they are' (*ʿalā mā hum ʿalayhi*), here, and in other similar formulations elsewhere, means 'as this derives from the fixed essences'. In other words, the polytheists *ethically* do what they do *themselves*—God neither impelling nor impeding them—but *metaphysically* their selves are derived from their fixed essences which are unalterable. God really can do nothing to change this. In this perspective, personal ethical responsibility—'they did such-and-such and must reap the fruits of it'—becomes 'they are what they are and do what they do because their *aʿyān thābita* determine it, *impersonally*'. In both instances, and from both sides, God is uninvolved and unable to alter things as they are. He is 'bound' by the order—at once moral and metaphysical, deriving from, reflecting and manifesting His own being. Ibn ʿArabī goes on to discuss the ramifications of this truth for the very nature of God.

In a hypothetical dialectical form reminiscent of Islamic discursive theology, Ibn ʿArabī next asks the question:

> If you say, what is the use, then, of God's (Most High) words, 'If He had wished, He certainly could have guided you all?' We say, 'If He had wished' [employs] the particle 'if' (*law*) which is a hypothetical grammatical particle that denies an impossibility [implying that God could do whatever He wished, but in the issue at hand He chose not to do something]. However, in fact God does not wish [to do anything] except that which is as it is (*mā huwa al-amr ʿalayhi*).[34]

33. *Fuṣūṣ*, p. 82.
34. *Ibid.*

To clarify further: the hypothetical disputant, presumably supporting the assertions of the polytheists in the Qur'ānic passage in question, is asking why did God Himself say He could have guided you all if He had wished? What was the use of His saying that, if it was not true? And, if it was true, this then supports our claims that if He had wanted to guide us away from worshipping our gods, He would have; as He did not, we can only conclude that He did not wish to, and thereby He sanctioned our practices. This expanded, hypothetical form of the polytheists' argument presupposes an omnipotent God: what He chose not to do He could have done, had He wished. This God determines everything. In the polytheists' worldview, the conception of a sole, all—powerful divinity was normal, even if they did not believe in Him. And in the above Qur'ānic passage, such a God is also presupposed. The difference, however, is that in the Qur'ānic view He did not choose to guide all, because He wished to allow free choice for ethical responsibility, while for the polytheists and their enhanced and expanded hypothetical argument, as Ibn ʿArabī formulated it, God chose not to guide them toward monotheism, because He did not object to their polytheistic practices. In both views, God had the ability to do what He had chosen not to do. He simply chose not to.

GOD DETERMINED

To return now to Ibn ʿArabī's own position, as stated above, that God only chooses to act *in accordance with the way things are*, there seems here to be a sort of 'determinism' for God Himself: He seems to be constrained in some way by the nature of His own 'creation'. This, if truly Ibn ʿArabī's view, would run contrary to the positions discussed above, that of the Qur'ānic God in 6:149, that of His pagan adversaries in that same verse and that of Ibn ʿArabī's hypothetical disputant, all these positions presupposing an omnipotent God. Ibn ʿArabī goes on to explicate his position further, using language and concepts derived from Islamic discursive theology and philosophy.

Thus, says Ibn ᶜArabī, 'The essentially contingent may either become something or not, in logical terms. Whichever of these logically possible events occurs has to do with the nature of the particular contingent in its state of latency.'[35] This means the *contingents*, in Arabic philosophical terms, *mumkināt*, may or may not be actualised, but *logically* it is possible for all contingents to be actualised. However, this will happen or not, as the case may be, according to the state of fixed latency of each contingent (its *thubūt*). The nature of the contingent's latency *determines* whether or not it will be actualised. The *mumkināt,* as Ibn ᶜArabī refers to them here in a more philosophical/theological manner, are interchangeable with his own term *al-aᶜyān al-thābita*, as is made clear with this application of the term *thubūt*, fixed latency, to the *mumkināt*.

The upshot of all this, then, is that God's behaviour for Ibn ᶜArabī is truly 'constrained' by the nature of the world He has 'created'. God would thereby be 'bound', from the perspective of conventional terms which presuppose a creator God 'out there' and separate from His 'creation'. In this conventional context, Ibn ᶜArabī's God would indeed be different from the main God of the Qur'ān and of much of the later religious thought in Islam. For that God apparently may not be so constrained. Ibn ᶜArabī, however, sees the conventional outlook as pointing towards its own inner, deeper truth. As we know, for Ibn ᶜArabī this deeper truth is most often a seeming *inversion* of the surface truth. The deeper truth here tells us that God is not 'determined' by His own 'creation' in a paradoxical formulation, impossible conventionally, as would appear, but rather that this is a matter of God *as creation*, 'determined' by His own nature. Again, the gulf between 'creator' and 'created' is here collapsed. Ibn ᶜArabī gives an example which not only

35. *Ibid.*

explains, but also strikes at opponents of his idea by making the opponents themselves a part of the example: 'The meaning [in 6:149] of "He would have guided you" is, He would have made clear to you [the deeper truth]; but not every contingent being in this world has its inner eye opened by God to the thing in itself, according to what it is. Some people know and some are ignorant.'[36]

Human beings, then, may or may not be divinely-guided or enlightened concerning the nature of things. This happens according to their makeup in their fixed latency and 'guidance' thus becomes a metaphor for 'the way they are'. God 'guides' some and not others, *not as a personal God* in a personal way, but rather only in the sense that the fixed essence of everything that is actualised is itself an expression and manifestation of God. The knowledgeable and the ignorant are as they are for this reason and both in this sense are divine manifestations. The knower of truth knows this. And this very truth explains to him why he knows, just as it would explain to the ignorant why he does not know. The inherent ignorance of the ignorant person, however, precludes this knowledge. Ibn ʿArabī's opponents on this issue would be in this category.

KNOWING AND BEING

In sum, Ibn ʿArabī has here, then, made the very issue under discussion and the human understanding of it an example of itself, as it were, and in the process he has explained the nature of the 'ignorant', the reasons for their ignorance and the 'inability' of God to have guided them to knowledge (whether one sees the ignorant in conventional Qur'ānic terms—as deniers of monotheism—or in 'mystical' terms—as the 'veiled ones'). Thus, says Ibn ʿArabī, 'God did not so wish, so He did not guide them all; and He does not so guide; and He will not. It is likewise

36. *Ibid.*

[for the similar Qur'ānic expression] "If He wished". For how can God wish to do something which is not to be?'[37] This now makes the issue absolutely clear: some things *are not to be*, for all the reasons given thus far. So why would God wish to do them? Indeed, He *could not* do them *because they are not to be*. This has to do with the nature of God's will and its relation to the world and to His power:

> God's will is, consequently, uniquely related to the world, in a connection dependent on [His] knowledge. [His] knowledge, however, is itself a connection dependent on that which is known. And that which is known is you, what is as it is and your states. Knowledge, then, has no influence on that which is known. Rather, that which is known influences knowledge. Indeed, that which is known itself bestows knowledge of what is as it is in its fixed essence.[38]

The things known (*al-maᶜlumāt*, intelligibles) which are 'us', *i.e.*, 'creation', *as they are in their fixed essences,* determine the nature of knowledge of them and, by extension, the ability (or lack thereof) of their 'Creator' to influence them by way of change or alteration. 'We/humanity', as microcosm of 'creation', may actually 'determine' our own natures and that of our 'Creator'. This will be discussed further below, but again it is clear here, as before, that the language of 'Creator', 'created', 'knower', and 'known', to cite some of Ibn ᶜArabī's choice contrasting terminological pairs, are but the conventional talk of a worldview of monotheistic bifurcation: Creator/creation. Taking a deeper view, however, this formulation would then be seen as a pointer towards its own 'contradiction'. The external language, though not 'untrue', must be interpreted in a way which is consonant with and revealing of the meaning of that language; as in most instances with Ibn ᶜArabī, the *meaning* of religious formulations based on a worldview of *multiplicity* is the

37. *Ibid.*, pp. 82–83.
38. *Ibid.*

opposite, i.e., a worldview of *unity, oneness*. The link between the 'external' and 'internal' meanings of religious language for Ibn ʿArabī, as for much of sufism, is some sort of special 'knowledge' (*maʿrifa, ʿilm, kashf*) held only by a small 'elite'. As we have also seen, for Ibn ʿArabī this special knowledge is largely *intellectual* rather than primarily 'spiritual' or 'experiential' (if indeed this distinction can be made here in that way). But he usually does not describe and define the processes constituting this knowledge *in a direct and complete way*. Nor does he ever completely reveal the 'how' and 'what'—*i.e., how* one knows in this way and exactly *what* one knows. This does not, however, mean such things are not present and that we must invoke 'ineffable experiences'. For again, Ibn ʿArabī wants—indeed demands—that his reader understand him through the intellect. But this understanding is not through the conventional intellect of conventional reason.

A special channel of 'revelation' is required here to achieve the sought understanding. In explicating this point, Ibn ʿArabī discusses the language in which God presents His truths and the human exegesis of this language:

> The divine discourse is revealed only according to what is appropriate for those who are addressed by it, according to what intellectual reasoning provides; [divine] discourse is not revealed according to what mystical revelation (*al-kashf*) provides. Consequently, believers are numerous while the gnostics, possessors of mystical revelation, are few.[39]

In Ibn ʿArabī's view, then, God sends his revelations in the language of the many. This is the language of 'intellectual [discursive] reasoning', *al-naẓar al-ʿaqlī*. Though perhaps not the 'highest order' of conventional, ordinary reason with respect, say, to philosophical discourse, it is part of *the genre of expression* found in conventional reason. It is this sort of reason which

39. *Ibid.*, p. 83.

typifies those who are 'mere' believers as opposed to the small 'elite' group of gnostics. But the gnostics in the context of Ibn ᶜArabī's discussion are not simply emotional recipients of some divine inspiration which forms the basis of their mystical understanding. For Ibn ᶜArabī they are, rather, people who 'know' through a 'different' intellectual process: a type of reasoning that connects 'contradictory' elements in the synthesis which transcends the 'contradiction'. Thus, if the Qur'ān says explicitly that God can do anything He wishes, but that He wishes and chooses not to do certain things, as in the present case, the 'mystical understanding' of this (at least in Ibn ᶜArabī's 'mysticism') is not that God is absolutely 'omnipotent', as a more straightforward text-reading might indicate, but, rather, that His 'omnipotence' is *qualified* by the very nature of the world He has 'created'. This 'restriction' on God's power means that He is 'bound' by His own rules which are in fact an expression of His own nature and being. The fixed essences, which are one stage in an 'emanating process' of divine self-expression, *determine* God's choices, wishes and abilities. The 'gnostic' will 'know' this truth, which may seem to 'contradict' the literal meaning of the text, not through an 'experiential' or 'emotional' realisation, but rather through a knowledge and understanding of the sufi metaphysical theories associated with Ibn ᶜArabī. One tenet of these theories themselves is that such knowledge is for an 'elite' class of 'gnostics' (*ᶜārifūn*) as opposed to 'ordinary' believers (*mu'minūn*) and there are few of the former and many of the latter. And the many are the ones for whom God's word is formulated, along with their 'exegesis' of reason (*ᶜaql*), in reason's conventional and straightforward sense. This division of humanity is natural for Ibn ᶜArabī and derives (like everything) from the nature of a universe which is itself an expression of God. The knower and the known are, then, intertwined in the most profound way.

According to this view—and supporting it—for Ibn ᶜArabī is God's corroborative statement in Qur'ān, 37:164, 'There is not among us anyone who does not have a known station.' That is, one's Qur'ānic 'known station' (*maqām maʿlūm*) is in Ibn ʿArabī's understanding one's fixed essence, 'And it [*i.e.*, the 'known station'] is what you were in your fixedness [*thubūt*] through which you became manifest in your existence—this is, of course, [only] if existence were fixed for you.'[40] Whether one is a 'gnostic' or not is, like everything else, decided by virtue of one's characteristics determined through one's fixed essence in the realm of *thubūt* (in Qur'ānic terms, for Ibn ʿArabī, one's *maqām maʿlūm*). This much is clear. But with his statement about this being true 'if existence were determined for you', *i.e.*, if your fixed essence contained a potential *wujūd*, Ibn ʿArabī begins a line of thought which explores the intertwining of all the components involved thus far in the discussion.

In order to proceed in this line, it is first necessary to know exactly what Ibn ʿArabī means here by 'existence' or 'being' (*wujūd*). As a cornerstone of his sufi metaphysics, this term and concept have figured prominently in Ibn ʿArabī's thought. Often, it has been considered to be the central idea in Ibn ʿArabī's intellectual system, particularly in the form of *waḥdat al-wujūd*, 'unity of being' (or existence), which some have attributed to Ibn ʿArabī and his 'school'. More to the point here, I believe, and as I have mentioned elsewhere, is Ibn ʿArabī's common division of *wujūd* into *wujūd muṭlaq* and *wujūd muqayyad*, absolute being and conditional being. Absolute being is close to what later writers termed unity of being: the dimension wherein, or perspective wherefrom, multiplicity is seen as the 'epiphenomenal overlay' reflecting various facets of the oneness of being which is the true condition of things. Absolute being is 'God' conceived non-theistically, as first principle or ultimate fount of all. Conditional or phenomenal being—theistic 'multiplicity' as opposed to 'unity' —expresses and reflects 'God's' nature in all its facets; but for those who 'know', theistic 'multiplicity' refers back to the unitive

40. *Ibid.*

principle, 'God' in non-theistic terms. The tension between these 'two Gods' is the relationship between absolute and conditional being, between 'monism' (oneness) and monotheism (multiplicity).

ANOTHER PERSPECTIVE

The issue above has to do with the nature of potential, conditional being before it 'descends' into its phenomenal manifestation. This is in the larger context of the relationship between God and His 'creation', with respect to who 'determines' whom and whether or not God may in fact do anything He wishes. Thus, it seems in one's latency (*thubūt*) one may or may not have potential *wujūd* (here, *wujūd muqayyad*). If one does, then this is one's *maqām maᶜlūm* 'through which you appear in your existence'. This is one possibility, then, concerning the issue of one's nature—and very presence—in this phenomenal world and God's ability to alter that in any way. In this perspective, your nature, *ᶜayn thābita*, includes existence, so you exist in the phenomenal realm. But, Ibn ᶜArabī goes on to say, 'if it is the case that existence belongs to God and not to you, then in any event the determinative force *is* no doubt yours without God's existence'.[41] This is *not* for Ibn ᶜArabī an *alternative* to the first possibility above; it is a different perspective on the *same* truth, as the phenomenal world (*wujūd muqayyad*) is what it is because of the 'preordained' nature of things in their *aᶜyān thābita* and this 'natural order' is the very manifestation of God Himself. God is, then, again 'bound' by His 'creation' because that 'creation' is God. Thus, the two perspectives both mean that whether one sees existence as being ('belonging to') for man or God, the reality is the same: you—and all phenomenal being—are what you are as a result of your nature, thus *you* have the determinative power, *ḥukm*. Finally, Ibn ᶜArabī presents one other possible perspective on this issue:

41. *Ibid.*

> Or it may be affirmed that you are the existent [in which case] determinative power is yours without any doubt. And even if the determiner would [in this case] be God, anyway the only role He would have is the pouring of existence on you; but the determinative power would [still] be yours over yourself. So do not praise or blame anyone other than yourself. For God, nothing remains except praise [of Him] for the pouring of existence, because that is His, not yours. You, then, are nourishment for Him through [your] determinative power while He is nourishment for you, through [your] existence.[42]

Here again, the meaning remains the same, albeit from yet another angle and with further implications in the metaphysical and ethical spheres. Thus, if one conceives the matter as the creature ('you') being an 'existent' (*mawjūd*) intrinsically, again the determinative power is yours, while God is the 'determiner', as He pours existence on you (and all else). But here too, as in the other perspectives, *you* 'determine' what you are by virtue of your fixed essence, itself a manifestation of God. So do not bother praising or blaming anyone but yourself—you are what you are *because of you*, not because God plays a part in the matter. Praise only yourself for what you have and blame only yourself for what you are. Let us now, however briefly, focus very precisely here on Ibn ʿArabī's method and language, as a clear example of his way of intertwining exegesis, metaphysics and ethics toward a full expression of the worldview so commonly found in his works.

This is exegesis because, as we have seen, the framework of Qur'ānic citations constitutes a focus for discussion through which central issues of metaphysics and ethics are expressed and formulated. But—again, always to be borne in mind—for Ibn ʿArabī 'his' ideas *are* the meaning of the Qur'ān and for him this is the first and foremost significance of his thought in the *Fuṣūṣ*. Metaphysics constitutes the mirror of meaning in which the Qur'ān's purpose is known. Ethics, in the broadest sense, and

42. *Ibid.*

itself also through the mirror of metaphysics, is the pattern of relationship between God and His creation. Here God's very nature is discernible in this relationship, as well as that of His creation. Thus, as was said above in various contexts, God and His creation are in reality as one, but, seen as separate and multiple for creation they may, and do, appear in a different light. God is here bound by the nature of creation. Your ethical status and your fate in this world—whatever they may be—are, consequently, determined by you (your *ḥukm*) and this, from another viewpoint, also determines God Himself, as we have seen. Using a metaphor resonating with the earthy motif of Ibrāhīm's hospitable offering of food to his angelic guests, Ibn ʿArabī puts the issue in a most succinct and straightforward way:

> So you nourish Him with determinative power and He nourishes you with being. And what is incumbent upon Him is incumbent upon you. The matter, then, is from Him to you and from you to Him, though you are called the 'commanded'. But in fact, He commands you only with respect to what you request, according to your own condition and your own nature. Nevertheless, God is not referred to as 'commanded', [grammatically] a nominal direct object.[43]

The generous 'nourishment' in the relationship between God and man is reciprocal: God feeds you with your very being while you feed Him with the order and structure—your nature—which determine the manner and specific content of this 'feeding'. The metaphysics of the matter is here reiterated as above, while the intertwined ethical aspect becomes more focused with Ibn ʿArabī's use of the term 'commanded' in referring to man, as he is called in his relationship with God. The word Ibn ʿArabī employs here, *mukallaf*, is the standard Islamic technical legal and theological usage for the human being as the object of God's revelatory commands of belief and action (the

43. *Ibid.*

taklīf). A Muslim, who 'submits' to God in the literal meaning of the term, becomes by virtue of that a *mukallaf*, the submission now being within the realm of specific legal obligations. This is what it means to be a Muslim in the full Islamic legal and overlapping ethical sense. Here one will be judged according to the standard of one's performance as *mukallaf*. This criterion is obviously at the heart of mainstream Islamic tradition. But for Ibn ʿArabī there is a profound difference. This difference is that the conventional use of *mukallaf* in reference to man is simply that—*convention*. Thus, but for that convention 'the matter is from Him to you and from you to Him'. That is, there is a full reciprocity and ontological intertwining between God and man, as variously explained above and as already mooted in Ibn ʿArabī's introductory remarks on the *takhallul* of Ibrāhīm and God. Even the complementary roles of seemingly 'uneven' influence possessed by God and man, in God's outpouring of existence on man, are in Ibn ʿArabī's broader view not uneven at all. For, as we have seen, this 'outpouring' is controlled, contained and directed by man's very form and nature and it would be otiose without man. This terminology of God as existence-giver and man as existence-receiver, implying an 'unequal' relationship of divine 'superiority' to human 'inferiority' is not, I believe, meant that way by Ibn ʿArabī in an absolute sense—certainly not in that broader context of his thought discussed above with respect to Ibrāhīm (and elsewhere). Why, then, these two 'different' meanings? Let us look at the issue from a slightly different angle, in order to answer this question.

THE TWO PLANES OF INTERPRETATION

As we know, Ibn ʿArabī works on two planes and in the space connecting them: the Qur'ānic and the metaphysical. Each plane has its own language and style and in the intermediate space these languages subtly merge, combining in various ways, as well as detaching from one another. What happens in this space is Ibn ʿArabī's thought. Here he employs, most prominently, the language and logic of the Qur'ān and 'conventional' religious thought where God and man, no matter how close in some ways, are separated by a chasm of difference: God as Master, man as servant; God as omnipotent, man as impotent; God as moral arbiter, man as morally obligated; God as true reality, man as ontologically void; and so on. More schematically, we might here see it thus: *Allāh/khāliq* and *al-insān/makhlūq*, *ʿabd*.

The second plane of Ibn ʿArabī's discourse, the metaphysical, would then comprise *al-Mūjid* and *al-mawjūd*, God and man from the metaphysical perspective. On the first plane, the core relationship between the two sides is through God's *creation*—*khalq*—of man, while on the second, it is through *ījād*, the infusing of being through all things. Terminologically, there are 'two planes' here, which one might call the *moral* (monotheistic) and the *metaphysical*, in further refinement of what was otherwise discussed earlier. They may be seen as *reflections* of one another for Ibn ʿArabī, expressed in the two vocabularies from which they are derived.

A DARING SUMMATION

For his summation of the wisdom of Ibrāhīm and of the particular metaphysical ideas associated with him, Ibn ʿArabī presents two poems. The first poem is:

> He praises me [in my existence] and I praise Him
> He worships me and I worship Him
> In a state [of being] I indeed confirm Him
> In [the realm of] fixed essences, I deny Him
> He knows me and I know Him not
> But yet I know Him and witness Him
> So where is [His presumed] independence [from us]
> when I do help Him and make Him happy?
> Thus does God cause me to be, while I inform Him

and cause Him to be
in this way does the [divine] word come to us and
God realises its objective in me.[44]

Expressed in Ibn ᶜArabī's characteristically daring sort of formulation, particularly evocative and metaphysically redolent of his general doctrine, this piece is a summation of Ibrāhīm's *takhallul.* The reciprocal nature of praise and worship between God and man in the first two lines utilises the 'ethical' scriptural idiom to signify the deeper metaphysical situation. 'Praise' and 'worship' in this sort of posited mutuality obviously create an 'ethical paradox': how can we speak of God praising and worshipping man when only God may be praised and worshipped and man's task is to do just that? But again, for Ibn ᶜArabī the metaphysical import, *in its own abiding conceptual and terminological context*, means exactly that sort of mutuality. The 'paradox' remains between the 'ethical' and 'metaphysical' outlooks, while Ibn ᶜArabī's 'true intent' continues to be towards the metaphysical. This is indicated in lines three and four in the contrast drawn there between the human–divine mutuality expressed in the first two lines and another aspect of that relationship which is devoid of their mutuality. In the latter case, the human side in its 'fixed essence' must 'deny Him', as in that state 'He knows me and I know Him not'. The 'fixed essences' are the indicator of Ibn ᶜArabī's metaphysical intent, as in his larger thought the realm of the *aᶜyān thābita*—as potential conditional being—is indeed 'one-sided', with God the only truly existing thing, His 'creation' a mere pattern of what will be.

These lines for Ibn ᶜArabī, however, serve to place the poem squarely in the metaphysical realm, first by introducing the terminology of potential existence (*fī'l-aᶜyān*) and then by using this as a point of sharp contrast with his main intent, the metaphysical thesis of divine–human mutuality and intertwining. The metaphysical takes pride of place in the poem expressed in

44. *Ibid.*

its 'personal' poetic style. The rest of the poem then emphasises, in suggestive poetic 'metaphor', a divine–human mutuality and intertwining (Ibrāhīm's *takhallul*) which for Ibn ᶜArabī are the 'true' meanings inspired by Ibrāhīm. Thus, 'I know Him and witness Him'; 'I do help Him and make Him happy'; He 'does cause me to be', 'while I inform Him and cause Him to be'; thus do we receive God's word while 'God realises its objective in me'. All of this is 'metaphor' for Ibn ᶜArabī's sufi metaphysics in which in our phenomenal, conditional existence (*wujūd muqayyad*), we (and all creation) are the locus (*maẓhar*) in which God, absolute, unconditional being, (*wujūd muṭlaq*) is manifest, expressing His names and attributes. Thus do we 'help' Him; thus do we make Him 'happy'; thus do we make Him 'be'; and thus does His word need us to achieve its goal. Our being, though 'qualified' in contrast with His 'absolute' being, *is* His being, expressed necessarily as His creation. 'His [presumed] independence from us', as Ibn ᶜArabī rhetorically asks about it, is in metaphysical terms only with respect to our potential existence which is theoretical and here unimportant. It is also, presumably, the same independence of God and the gulf between Him and His creation posited in the external, superficial formulation of His word—the only aspect of His word understood by those who lack a deeper understanding.

Ibn ᶜArabī's own commentary on this most abstruse metaphysical poem reverts to the earthy 'metaphor' of food and the feeding of guests associated with Ibrāhīm's scriptural story:

> As *al-Khalīl* possessed this degree [of being] because of which he was named *khalīl*, thus did hospitality become established custom... Through nourishment, the feeding of those nourished occurs. The nourishment, then, permeates the very one being nourished. This proceeds in such a way that nothing remains of the nourishment except its dispersion. Thus the food pervades all parts of the one being fed—indeed, here there are no parts. And

thus does God pervade all the divine stations which are designated as [His] names, and His essence—He most high and sublime appears in them.[45]

The two Ibrāhīmī scriptural themes which provide the 'story-telling' side of Ibn ʿArabī's discussion of Ibrāhīm's special wisdom are here combined with the metaphysics of absolute being. Ibrāhīm as God's friend (*khalīl Allāh*) and Ibrāhīm as bestower of hospitality, particularly food, indicate the intermingled being of God and His creation (*takhallul*) and the thoroughgoing nature of this intermingling in the analogy of the digested food which can no longer be distinguished from the body which assimilates it. If God is the nourishment, then the body in which He is absorbed is this phenomenal world of His 'creation', designated as the divine stations which are His names. His being in the world is His self-expression through the names which *are* the world and which possess His essence.

The final poem:

We belong to Him, as our proofs establish, and we
belong to ourselves
He has no reality other than mine, so we are to Him as we
are in ourselves
I have two faces, He and I, but He has no I through my I
But His place of manifestation is in me, so for Him we
are as a vessel.
God says the truth and He guides [one to] the path.[46]

This poetic ending for Ibn ʿArabī is obviously a restatement, in slightly different formulation, of everything he said earlier. One point of emphasis in the poem is, however, necessary to consider: God has no 'I' through the human 'I'. Man, though, has 'two faces, He and I'. This may resolve the earlier question concerning Ibn ʿArabī's seemingly total identification of God

45. *Fuṣūṣ*, p. 84.
46. *Ibid.*

and man through the mutual assimilation of each other's personal attributes. It is now clear that this happens in such a way that man as *vessel* and *site* of God's manifestation retains his own 'face' wherein is reflected God's 'face', while man is as well God's 'face' in that he manifests God's appearance. God has no 'I' (*anā*) in creation as He is solely represented by man's 'I' which, in the poem's play on words, is God's 'vessel' (*inā'*). Such, again, is the necessary ambiguity in this issue of the One and the many which here, through Ibrāhīm, Ibn ʿArabī treats so creatively in the 'two languages' of monotheism and metaphysics.

CHAPTER

6

The Wisdom of Divine Unity in the Word of Hūd

HŪD IN THE QUR'ĀN

Hūd was one of the Arabian prophets in the Qur'ān, who served to warn his people, the ʿĀd, of the importance of belief in and worship of the one God, Allāh, rather than their established religion of belief in false gods and other pernicious and improper practices. Thus in one Qur'ānic account, Hūd said to the ʿĀd, 'Worship God [alone]. You have no other god. You are only slandering liars [in your false beliefs].'[1] But, as another Qur'ānic account tells us, the ʿĀd remained stubbornly resistant in their idolatry, claiming Hūd had not brought them any conclusive proof (*bayyina*) of his one God and that they could not, therefore, leave their own gods simply because of Hūd's claims. Nor could the ʿĀd believe in Hūd himself.[2] Hūd, however, continued to proclaim his belief in God, dissociating himself from the idolatry of the ʿĀd. Then the moment of truth arrived for the ʿĀd. As punishment for remaining adamant in their rejection of God's signs and in their disobedience, God then totally destroyed the ʿĀd except for Hūd and 'those who believed with him'.[3] As the Qur'ān says, in its powerfully pithy way, 'Then away with the ʿĀd, Hūd's people (*alā buʿdan li ʿĀdin qawmi Hūdin*).'[4]

1. Qur'ān, 11:50.
2. Qur'ān, 11:53.
3. Qur'ān, 11:58.
4. Qur'ān, 11:60.

This destruction of the ʿĀd, in the one verse where such detail is given, was effected by 'a wind in which there is a terrible punishment. It will destroy everything by the command of its Lord.'[5] And so it did. For, 'by morning there was nothing left to be seen, except for their houses.'[6] It was, in fact, these very houses which in the Qur'ān symbolised the prideful decadence of the ʿĀd and their consequent inability to acknowledge true belief in the one God. Finally, God says, 'Thus do we recompense those who do evil.'[7]

The Qur'ānic story of Hūd and the ʿĀd is, then, a tale of a people who dared reject God and his prophet, continuing instead to wax proud, to worship their false gods and to do evil on the earth. Thus did they lose the possibility of God's favour in this world and the next. At a higher level of abstraction, the tale of Hūd and the ʿĀd is a parable conveying, in the Qur'ān's unique and persistent fashion, the principle of the one God and His particular relationship with His creatures, of reward and punishment, in this world and the next. In various tales of prophets and in other contexts as well, the Qur'ān preaches this message continually as one of its essential and basic themes.[8] The story of Hūd and the ʿĀd is one of the most powerful renditions of this kind in the Qur'ān. It is noteworthy for its evocative strength and compactness of formulation. Unimpeded by any salient ambiguity, its message of divine might, human weakness and total human dependency on the creator comes forcefully through—as does the theme of human depravity and arrogance.

The Qur'ān and later exegesis also put the story of Hūd into certain broader prophetic contexts, of prophecy to people who were powerful, wealthy and arrogant in their unbelief. Not just ordinary idol-worshippers and arrant wrongdoers, but the worst

5. Qur'ān, 46:25.

6. *Ibid.*

7. *Ibid.*

8. See T. Izutsu, *God and Man in the Koran*, and Da'ūd Rahbar, *God of Justice: A Study of the Ethical Doctrine of the Qur'ān*, pp. 105–106 and 158–171.

of these, the high and mighty, were those who formed the natural fellowship of Hūd's people, the ʿĀd.[9] *Sūrat* Hūd contains the fullest account of the group of prophets who had been sent to such peoples, emphasizing non-biblical Arabian prophets, with Hūd prominent among them.[10] In the exegetical *tafsīr* and quasi-exegetical texts (for example, the *Qiṣaṣ al-Anbiyā'*) Hūd's lineage is often traced to Nūḥ in a way reminiscent of certain of Noah's Biblical lineages (where Hūd is, of course, not present). This implies an Islamic lineal 'Biblical connection' for Hūd, in addition to the Qur'ān's broad typological affinity indicated above.[11]

For Ibn ʿArabī, this Qur'ānic prophetic tale was the inspiration and source of his own thinking on what he calls in the *Fuṣūṣ* the 'wisdom of divine unity' (*ḥikma aḥadiyya*) in the word of Hūd (*kalima Hūdiyya*). As is his wont, Ibn ʿArabī here too takes a particular Qur'ānic story and message, those of Hūd, and makes them his main point of reference and the foundation of his ideas. I shall concentrate my efforts in particular on the first four pages of this brief chapter in the *Fuṣūṣ*. It is in these pages, I believe, that Ibn ʿArabi gives his understanding of the Hūd story and its essential teachings. In the remainder of the chapter, he elaborates on and presents from other angles the ideas formulated in this first part.[12] Following Ibn ʿArabī's order here, I shall organise my discussion according to four basic themes.

THE QUR'ĀNIC 'STRAIGHT PATH' IN METAPHYSICAL FORM

Ibn ʿArabī opens with a brief poem which is the quintessence of his later full interpretation of Hūd's story: 'God has a straight

9. Qur'ān, 48:27–30.

10. Nūḥ, Hūd, Sāliḥ, Lūṭ, Shuʿayb and, with a far smaller presence, Ibrāhīm and Mūsā.

11. See T. P. Hughes, *A Dictionary of Islam*, pp. 181–182. Questions abound here concerning a possible Ancient Near Eastern provenance which may have been present in the background of the Qur'ānic Hūd. These are questions which at present are unanswerable, in the absence of relevant sources.

12. *Fuṣūṣ*, pp. 106–114 for the entire story.

path, manifest universally and not hidden. He is omnipresent, in the small and in the great, in those ignorant of truth and in those knowledgeable. Consequently, His mercy encompasses everything, the lowly and the mighty.'[13]

Let us look closely at Ibn ʿArabī's ideas, terms and methods here, beginning with his main notion of God's 'straight path.' This, in Ibn ʿArabī's intention, is the *ṣirāṭ mustaqīm* of the Qur'ān, found, most notably, in the first *sūra*, *al-Fātiḥa*. There, in the chapter which Muslim scholars have so often referred to as *umm al-Qurān*, 'mother of the Qur'ān', the 'straight path' is the way in which God's servants request to be guided; for it is 'the path of those upon whom You have cast Your favour, not those who have been recipients of Your wrath, nor those who have gone astray.'[14] Here in the *Fātiḥa*, then, 'the straight path' provides, among other things, a conceptual division between 'those upon whom You have cast Your favour', on the one hand, and 'those who have received Your wrath' and 'those who have gone astray', on the other. As a dividing marker, the 'straight path' belongs completely to the first group, whose possession of it identifies them, while the other two groups do not possess it, either because God has poured his wrath upon them or because they have gone astray.[15] The Qur'ān here does not tell us the criteria involved in any of these categories, that is, what people must do or believe, or avoid doing, and avoid believing in order to be included in or excluded from any of these groups. But the main, general, point—and this is our concern—is that the *Fātiḥa* makes 'the straight path' *exclusive*, not inclusive. *Some* are on it, receiving God's favour, and *some* are not—presumably in all cases because of their good or bad behaviour.

13. *Fuṣūṣ*, p. 106.

14. Qur'ān, 1:6–7.

15. The two latter 'negative' categories might in fact be reduced to one, as those who were punished had obviously gone astray and the ones who had gone astray would be punished.

But for Ibn ʿArabī, God's straight path, as described in his opening poem, seems to be *inclusive*, rather than exclusive. It is '*manifest universally*', while God, to whom it belongs, is present in all things. And His omnipresence necessitates His Mercy's encompassing all things, 'lowly *and* mighty'; for, it may be assumed, God's mercy could not be absent from something in which He Himself is present. Most importantly, if one understands Ibn ʿArabī's conception of God's mercy (as he defines and discusses it in various places in the *Fuṣūṣ*) as ontological, that is, the receiving of divine Mercy means coming into being, then, by definition, everything has been included by God's mercy.[16] The very idea of God's mercy's encompassing everything is, of course, itself derived from the Qur'ān,[17] where it is seen prominently, for example, in *sūra* 7:156, in God's words, 'My mercy encompasses everything.' But this *general notion*, relating to God as essentially merciful (*Raḥmān*), in no way obviates his judgmental role and the ethical burden upon his creatures; these remain fundamental.[18]

To sum up, it would seem that Ibn ʿArabī has caused an implicit inversion of the key Qur'ānic ethical notion of *al-ṣirāt al-mustaqīm*. From being an exclusive path in the *Fātiḥa*, it has now become an inclusive path. Three main ideas have helped

16. See in particular the chapters in the *Fuṣūṣ* on Zakariyyā, Hārūn and Shuʿayb.

17. But where found it is usually linked to *general* divine beneficences to His creatures, such as creation of food in the earth (30:99), rain and water to drink (25:50–1), wind (30:45), cattle (16:5–7) and guidance provided by the apostles (21:107; 16:66; 45:19). These do not refer to individuals or smaller collectivities (tribes), but rather to humanity as a whole; and in general the gifts cited are those which make possible the maintenance of human life on earth and their moral law. With respect to individuals, the Qur'ān almost always requires compliance with proper belief and practice as prerequisite for the giving of mercy (for example, 16:47–9; 18:56–7; 50:31–3; 4:33–4, to cite just some references). Also, see Rahbar, *God of Justice*, p. 166.

18. Indeed, in 7:156, God also says, 'I will prescribe mercy for those who fear God, who pay alms and who believe in Our signs.' Thus here the principle enunciated above (note 17) is also illustrated.

Ibn ʿArabī to effect this change: (1) 'The straight path' itself, (2) his idea of God's being present in everything and (3) the notion of God's mercy encompassing everything (itself both Qur'ānic and, for Ibn ʿArabī, transformed from the Qur'ānic to the ontological conception).

THE QUR'ĀNIC INVERSION COMPLETE

If the straight path of God in the *Fātiḥa* is now inclusive, this would seem, by extension, to invert also the main message of Hūd's story in the Qur'ān. For that message, as we have seen, is one of divine retribution for evildoers. In its way, the literal message of the Hūd story is obviously at one with the 'ethical exclusivism' of the *Fātiḥa*'s straight path. Thus, immediately after the opening poem Ibn ʿArabī cites a verse from the Qur'ānic Hūd story as validation and foundation for what will shortly become a fully-blown inversion of the exclusive straight path. The verse, from *sūra* Hūd, 11:56, goes as follows, 'There is no creature that moves but that God holds it by its forelock.' Lodged in a Qur'ānic context where Hūd is disputing with the ʿĀd over their resistance to true religion, the statement in this verse is Hūd's rejoinder to the ʿĀd, expressing his confidence in God's ultimate protection for him, however fierce the opprobrium heaped on him. And indeed, Hūd is subsequently saved, along with a few other righteous souls, while the ʿĀd are destroyed.[19]

For Ibn ʿArabī, this verse is proof that indeed all will be saved, though contextually, in *sūra* Hūd, the verse seems to be surrounded and overwhelmed by the opposite meaning. But Ibn ʿArabī concludes from this verse that 'every being that walks is [by virtue of that] walking on the straight path of the Lord.'[20] And this means, invoking the language of the *Fātiḥa*, that every

19. Qur'ān, 11:58.
20. *Fuṣūṣ*, p. 107.

being is, from this perspective, neither the recipient of God's wrath [*maghḍūb ʿalayhim*] nor among those who have gone astray [*al-ḍālīn*]'.[21] Further, he asserts that both humans going astray (*ḍalāl*) and divine wrath (*ghaḍab Ilāhī*) are 'accidental' (*ʿāriḍ*).[22] Thus, 'All paths lead back to the mercy of God which encompasses everything.'[23] And, says Ibn ʿArabī, as verse 56 of *sūra* Hūd tells us, no creature moves along on its own; it is, rather, led by another—'through the force of following [that other] who is on the straight path.'[24] The other whom one follows and who leads one here is, of course, God.

The Qur'ānic inversion adumbrated in Ibn ʿArabī's opening poem has now been made complete and explicit through invoking the Hūd story. It is an inversion of the exclusive straight path of the *Fātiḥa* and of the framework story of Hūd. For the very idea of people who have incurred God's wrath and those who have gone astray—that is, those who are not on the straight path according to Hūd and the *Fātiḥa*—has now, seemingly, been nullified. In Ibn ʿArabī's view, *all* are on the straight path. God's anger and human error have been rendered 'ontologically void'. Ibn ʿArabī's method in achieving the inversion thus far has been to juxtapose various Qur'ānic concepts in 'corrective fashion'. Thus he takes the Qur'ānic straight path and its related ideas and confronts them with the notion of God's mercy encompassing everything, as well as the verse, 'There is no creature that moves but that God holds it by its forelock'. The metaphysical underpinning and meaning of the inversion, however, have not yet been made clear, though by mentioning God as being in all things and God's mercy encompassing everything, in his opening poem, Ibn ʿArabī did hint at this. In the two additional reflections, he makes it all explicit.

21. *Ibid.*
22. *Ibid.*
23. *Ibid.*
24. *Ibid.*

HELL, METAPHYSICAL

Ibn ʿArabī continues, discussing the various kinds of 'divine esoteric knowledge' and perceptions possessed by the 'People of God'.[25] These forms of knowledge vary according to those in whom they reside, but they all return to one source, God. Indeed, God *is* these forms of knowledge and these perceptions. In support of this, Ibn ʿArabī cites the well-known *ḥadīth qudsī*: 'God, most High, said, "I am his hearing through which he hears, his sight, through which he sees, his hand, through which he grasps and his foot on which he walks."'[26] Thus, 'God's very being, then, is the very limbs of the servant', says Ibn ʿArabī, 'and every limb has its own special esoteric knowledge'.[27] Though these are the élite of spiritual people, with their particular understanding, who are mentioned, they are for Ibn ʿArabī, as always, a metaphor for Everyman who may, if properly activated, possess the same intrinsic characteristics.[28] Indeed, all this, says Ibn ʿArabī, is 'the wisdom of the feet'.[29] For in the 'lowest' is the 'highest'. It is through the knowledge in the organs and limbs that one knows the truth (of Qur'ān 11:56, *viz.*, that God directs all creatures). And that truth again concerns God's leading everyone to their proper end, in the image of creatures moving, or being moved, *on foot*. Ibn ʿArabī turns then to a verse from *sūrat* Maryam, paraphrasing it as, 'He [God] will drive the evildoers to Hell.'[30] Then, in this connection, referring again to the ʿĀd, he says that these evildoers earned the place to which God drives them by the West wind and thus does He purge their souls with this wind. And, in a most interesting resolution of the fate of the evildoers of ʿĀd as they are driven to Hell,

25. *Ibid.*
26. al-Bukhārī, *Saḥīḥ*, LXXX 1:38.
27. *Fuṣūṣ*, p. 107.
28. For Ibn ʿArabī, the perfect human being (*al-insān al-kāmil*), the accomplished spiritual adept, is still *human* and represents the *potential* of all humanity.
29. *Fuṣūṣ*, p. 107.
30. Qur'ān, 19:86: 'We shall drive the wrongdoers to hell in a herd.'

'The straight path is for walking and that is done only with feet.'[31]

Here the larger aspects of Ibn ʿArabī's inversion begin to come into view. Thus, it seems, *by virtue of their (evil) actions*, the wrongdoers get close to God, with hell disappearing:

> For they were in their actions on God's straight path, because their forelocks were in the hands of the One who has this attribute [that is, being on the path]...Thus God takes them by their forelock and the wind drives them... to hell and hell is the distance which they had imagined [to be between themselves and God]. But when God leads them to that place they arrive at the very greatest closeness [to God], that [imagined] distance having disappeared. And for them the thing called hell vanishes.[32]

Furthermore, these wrongdoers 'gain the pleasant closeness [to God]', says Ibn ʿArabī, because '... they deserve it in their being wrongdoers'.[33] God does not lead them to this exalted state as a 'gift' to them; rather, 'they attain it because their very being deserves it by virtue of their [sinful] actions. And in these actions, they were walking on the straight path (*ṣirāṭ mustaqīm*) of the Lord.'[34] How is this possible? Does it not contradict the 'conventional' notions of hell and its denizens?

It is possible, says Ibn ʿArabī, because they walked to that divine presence through the divine 'determinative force'[35] (*ḥukm al-jabr*) and not under their own power. Again, the earthy images of creatures being pulled by their forelocks (from Qur'ān 11:56) and walking on their feet on a path are prominent. The feet, the path, the forelocks, the divinely directed movement, indicate that all are on the 'straight path', now made fully inclusive. Sinful or wrong actions, insofar as they exist, qualify their

31. *Fuṣūṣ*, p. 107.
32. *Fuṣūṣ*, pp. 107–108.
33. *Fuṣūṣ*, p. 108.
34. *Ibid.*
35. *Ibid.*

perpetrators—as existing beings—for the *qurb*, closeness to God, which is the ultimate end (and beginning) for all. This 'closeness' is indeed the metaphysical reality of all being on that true plane of existence where the true God and His creation are as one. 'Closeness' (*qurb*) here means unity and total identification on that plane. All 'achieve' this by virtue of their status as creation (*mawjūd*, existing), which is, for Ibn ʿArabī, God's projection of Himself outward.[36] The language and reality of moral differentiation in the 'conventional' exclusive straight path are 'true' in their qualified way. But it is this very way, the exoteric, which points towards its own inner truth. Ibn ʿArabī thus sees, in the exclusivist Qur'ānic notion of the straight path and in the moral framework story of Hūd, pointers toward an 'inverted' notion of the straight path, that is, the inclusivist idea. The paradox or contradiction which might be seen to arise from this 'inversion' was for Ibn ʿArabī only a seeming 'problem', if a problem at all. For in his view, the metaphysical unity which is the true nature of things absorbs such 'contradictions' within it. The 'contradictory' and the 'inversion' indeed serve to point up this 'higher' unitive truth. The exoteric meanings are not nullified but rather transcended, remaining, again, 'true' on their own level, in their own way. And, again, it is this level which provides the starting point and important spiritual hints toward its own 'inversion'. From the human spiritual and epistemological perspective, as well as from that of his own cosmology and metaphysics, Ibn ʿArabī next explains how this works and what it means.

THE IGNORANT AND THE GNOSTIC

Ibn ʿArabī says humanity is of two types: 'those who walk on a path knowing it and its appointed end; for these people the path

36. Ultimately, that is, there is no *real* difference between God and His creation; such difference as appears is accidental and insubstantial. But for Ibn ʿArabī, this accidental and insubstantial difference is real and true in its own, very important, realm.

is a straight path. The other type of people walk on a path while ignorant of it and its appointed end. This is in fact the same path which the first kind of people know.'[37]

The 'straight path' referred to here is, of course, Ibn ʿArabī's inclusivist definition of this path, the reality of all creation, beginning and ending in (the metaphysical) God. Thus, says Ibn ʿArabī, though 'the spiritual adept (*al-ʿārif*) appeals to God with spiritual insight (*bi'l-baṣīra*), while the non-adept (*ghayr al-ʿārif*) appeals to Him in blind faith and ignorance (*ʿalā al-taqlīd wa'l-jahāla*)',[38] the way in which both walk is the same. There is a 'special knowledge' here, derived from 'that which is lowest', because 'the feet are the lowest part of the person, anything lower than they being only the path [on which the feet tread]'.[39] Epistemological and spiritual capacity, then, ultimately make no difference metaphysically. For the path or way—the 'lowest' of things—is the lowest common denominator representing the all-inclusive metaphysical reality which is the 'highest' of all things. But those who know—*ʿārifūn*—*do* live with a greater awareness of the truth and an understanding of who they are: 'For those who know that *al-Ḥaqq* is that path know the matter fully (*ʿalā mā huwa ʿalayhi*). In Him do you [really] walk and travel, since He is the only thing known and He is existence, the walker and the traveller. Thus He is [also] the only knower. Who are you? Know your own reality and your own way'.[40]

The unity, oneness and essential sameness of God and His creation are here made absolutely clear. Thus, differences of moral status, 'highness', 'lowness', and 'proper' or 'improper' behaviour, if correctly understood, may then give way to meanings that posit the *absence* of all such differentiation. This 'inversion' of revealed exoteric conceptions was for Ibn ʿArabī

37. *Fuṣūṣ*, p. 108.
38. *Fuṣūṣ*, pp. 108–109.
39. *Fuṣūṣ*, p. 109.
40. *Ibid.*

not a rejection of these conceptions, but rather their fulfilment and complete truth. The *apparent* message of the *Fātiḥa* and the Hūd story is, then, employed by Ibn ʿArabī in its own esoteric transformation. This is Ibn ʿArabī's method of 'Qur'ānic exegesis', as we know, here and in much of the *Fuṣūṣ,* the method of continuous interplay between the Qur'ānic text and his sufi metaphysics.

CHAPTER

7

The Wisdom of the Heart in the Word of Shuʿayb

SHUʿAYB IN THE QUR'ĀN

Shuʿayb, as we know, is one of three Arabian prophets in the Qur'ān, along with Hūd and Ṣāliḥ. These are among the Qur'ānic prophets who were rejected by their people and whose people were consequently destroyed by God. In the Qur'ān, the basic story of Shuʿayb is relatively simple and straightforward: Shuʿayb is sent to his own people of Madyan to warn them of the folly of their ways and of the dangers accruing to them if they do not repent. Apart from their idolatry, the Madyanites are in particular charged with dishonesty and fraud in their business and commercial practices. They do not accede to Shuʿayb's revelatory call, God then dispatches them with 'a massive quake' and thus do they 'lie prostrate in their houses, by morning'.[1] Divine retribution is enacted dramatically and conclusively, as recompense for the people's rejection of monotheism and their other evil deeds. Shuʿayb's personality, however, does not reflect the seeming harshness of that retribution. He is characterised by his modesty and gentle, patient and conciliatory approach to the people. No 'fire-and-brimstone' preacher he, Shuʿayb carefully calibrates his demands and responses, sometimes even backing off to avert fierce clashes. His entreaties are informed by an apparent sensitivity to the beliefs and practices of his people

1. As told in Qur'ān 7:91 and 29:37.

(though these be wrong and evil) which is remarkable for the situation.[2] There was, in addition, clearly a serious division among the Madyanites in religious matters, some of them being amenable to prophetic truth. Thus were Shuʿayb and this group saved, when the cataclysm came.[3]

Shuʿayb's story is told in four places in the Qur'ān, in varying complexity, length and detail, but essentially as described above: *sūra* 7:85–93; *sūra* 11:84–94; *sūra* 26:177–190; *sūra* 29:36–37. As we shall see, the story's content from these Qur'ānic accounts is not *directly* cited by Ibn ʿArabī in his discussion of Shuʿayb's wisdom. He rather cites passages from *other sūras* which have no explicit connection with this prophet, but which for him obviously do have relevance for Shuʿayb's 'wisdom of the heart.' The Qur'ānic story of Shuʿayb in its four occurrences does, however, inform Ibn ʿArabī's treatment of Shuʿayb. For though he makes no direct use of specific elements in the Qur'ānic tales of this prophet, Ibn ʿArabī does say explicitly what the connection is for him between Shuʿayb and Shuʿayb's 'wisdom of the heart.' Though highly succinct, this reference will help us to identify a more implicit aspect of the relation between Ibn ʿArabī's Shuʿayb and the Shuʿayb of the Qur'ān.

THE HEART, MERCY AND METAPHYSICAL MERCY

Ibn ʿArabī opens with remarks about 'the heart':

> Know that the heart—I mean the heart of the gnostic—derives from God's mercy and is more comprehensive than it. For the heart encompasses al-Ḥaqq, most exalted, while His mercy does not encompass [the heart]. This is the language of the most general formulation of this point. Thus is al-Ḥaqq merciful but not the recipient of mercy. Indeed, mercy has no dominion in Him.[4]

2. Qur'ān 7: 89 and 11: 86–90.
3. Qur'ān 7: 92 and 11: 94.
4. *Fuṣūṣ*, p. 119 and pp. 119–126 for the full discussion of Shuʿayb.

The heart and mercy, as Ibn ʿArabī's main ideas here, will be the focus of our attention. 'The heart of the gnostic' (*qalb al-ʿārif*) is the seat of the deeper mystical understanding in Ibn ʿArabī's sufi psychology. The heart in this passage derives 'from the mercy of God.' This is consonant with Ibn ʿArabī's general emphasis on God's mercy having a deeper, transformed metaphysical meaning as well as its conventional personal sense. What, however, does he mean in saying the heart is 'more comprehensive' than God's mercy and that it 'encompasses al-Ḥaqq' while 'His mercy does *not* encompass the heart?'—and even that 'mercy has no dominion in Him?' Is not God's mercy (*raḥmat Allāh*) in Ibn ʿArabī's system the most universal of concepts, encompassing everything, in its metaphysical sense of engendering being (*ījād*)? Does mercy not even encompass itself and God Himself, thereby rendering Him 'recipient' of mercy (*marḥūm*) as well as merciful (*rāḥim*), as Ibn ʿArabī says in his discussion of Zakariyyā, though in seeming contradistinction to what he has said here?[5]

Ibn ʿArabī does himself provide implicit answers to these questions, while also more explicitly clarifying concepts and resolving the apparent contradiction regarding the nature and dominion of divine mercy. The following 'exegetical comments' on some issues in these opening lines will, I hope, provide a basis for an understanding of what Ibn ʿArabī says.

As we know, 'God' in Ibn ʿArabī's outlook, whether designated as *al-Ḥaqq* or *Allāh*, possesses 'two faces', 'the remote' and 'the manifest'. Though ultimately reducible to one 'combined' visage only, God does, from the perspective of His creation, evince this 'dual nature', at least for man's purpose, the better to understand Him. For the remote God is in Himself unknowable to man, His existence being a conceptual necessity and a mystically-intuited presence. The manifest God, however, is for man the remote God's 'appearance' or 'self-manifestation' *in*

5. See the chapter on Zakariyyā in this book.

and *as* the multiplicity and flux of the phenomenal world. The *absolute* must, then, be reduced to the *conditional*, in order for it to be knowable to the conditional world. 'Existence' or 'being' (*wujūd*) for Ibn ʿArabī, in its two aspects of absolute (*wujūd muṭlaq*) and conditional (*wujūd muqayyad*) thus corresponds with the *remote* and the *manifest* God. And the second part, in both formulations, is, again, 'different' and 'separate' from the former only in a qualified way. This qualified separation, however, is for Ibn ʿArabī essential in its function of maintaining the tension between the One and the many, between God ('in the religious beliefs') as Creator from nothing and God as unitive principle. The tension ultimately provides that creative ambiguity which, as we know, is one important foundation of Ibn ʿArabī's thought.

Seen from this angle, Ibn ʿArabī's opening claim that the gnostic's heart is more comprehensive than God's mercy may then be understood as referring to the *remote God* and to the *qualified mercy*. For the gnostic's heart is the seat *where the true God is intuited*, while God's mercy here may be understood in its metaphysical sense of *conditional being* and its active aspect of engendering existence, *ījād*. Mercy transformed from the personal still applies to the world of the many, reflecting, but not representing the One. God's mercy in this sense cannot encompass the gnostic's heart, as, again, that heart is on the plane of the absolute, while the mercy in question is that which corresponds with the conditional (*wujūd muqayyad*) and the phenomenal. *Al-Ḥaqq*, then, cannot here be the recipient of this category of mercy, but only its bestower (which is also consonant with the more 'conventional' exoteric understanding). Indeed, as Ibn ʿArabī remarks, this mercy 'has no dominion in Him' (*ḥukm*)—it cannot have, as it is His 'other side', manifest as the phenomenal world. Having said the above, Ibn ʿArabī, in his typical dialectical manner, continues with a view on the other side of the issue, pointing here toward the world of creation. Thus, now 'in the language of the most particular formulation of the point', Ibn ʿArabī says '...God characterises Himself as breath, which is breathing'.[6]

Let us pause for a moment to see what this statement means in preparation for the unfolding argument. 'Breath' (*nafas*) and 'breathing' (*tanfīs*) are, of course, terms from Ibn ʿArabī's special lexicon which denote the Qur'ānic Divine Merciful Breath of creation, in his particular sufi metaphysical gloss.[7] Here His breath not only puts life into God's creation, as the force in creation's inception (in the general Qur'ānic 'exoteric' sense), but in Ibn ʿArabī's special sense it represents God's own immanence in, and oneness with, His creation. A staple in Ibn ʿArabī's thought, as we know, this idea evinces a number of formulations. Thus Ibn ʿArabī continues:

> [And know that] the divine names are the same as the one named, who is no other than He; and that [the names] seek what they receive from the realities and these realities which the names seek are nothing other than the world. Thus 'divineness' seeks that which has been made a god and 'lordship' seeks that which has been made a lord, while the names have no essence—existentially or in being defined—but through the world. And God (al-Ḥaqq) from the side of His essence is independent of the world. But 'lordship' does not have this connection, and the matter, consequently, remains between what 'lordship' seeks and what the divine essence necessitates, in [its] independence of the world. Lordship, in reality and [in its] relation, is nothing other than this [divine] essence.[8]

God now becomes manifest in and as the world in 'stages', through His names—exemplified and represented here as His

6. *Fuṣūṣ*, p. 119.

7. The divine breath for Ibn ʿArabī is associated with God's mercy; he most often calls it 'the breath of the Merciful' or 'the merciful breath' (*nafas al-Raḥmān, al-nafas al-raḥmānī*). This association with God's mercy obviously has an ontological connotation in Ibn ʿArabī's ontological *raḥma*. See *Fuṣūṣ* pages 112, 119, 219, for other examples.

8. *Fuṣūṣ*, p. 119.

'divineness' and 'lordship'—while the 'realities' (*al-ḥaqā'iq*) which the names seek *are* 'the world' (*al-ᶜālam*). 'Divineness', then, seeks its correlative 'reality' (*ḥaqīqa*) in 'that which has been made a god' (*al-ma'lūh*), while 'lordship' seeks it in 'that which has been made a lord' (*al-marbūb*). These 'realities', which are the world, give life to the divine characteristics (His 'names', *al-asmā' al-ilāhiyya*).[9] He then becomes 'God' and 'Lord' concretely in this way; and all His names/attributes constitute the world in which He is immanent. The names indeed have no true existence nor can they be adequately defined *except as the world.* This is divine immanence in the most thoroughgoing way. However, divine transcendence and remoteness remain, as they must for Ibn ᶜArabī, in order to maintain the creative tension between these two poles which is so necessary for his outlook. Though 'the names are the very thing named who is no other than He' and this implicitly reduces all to a unitary principle, at the same time it is not so simple, as the issue remains 'between what "lordship" seeks and what the divine essence necessitates in its independence of the world.' 'What "lordship" seeks' here is, of course, its worldly manifestation, while at the same time the divine essence ('lordship' in its remote form) is of necessity cut off from the world. But coming full circle, '"lordship", in reality and in its relation is nothing other than this [divine] essence'. 'Lordship', as Godly attribute in His name and immanence, is *at the same time* His unmanifested essence—unmanifested, that is, except to the 'heart of the gnostic'. And this for Ibn ᶜArabī is true of *all* of God's names and attributes, not just 'lordship'. The phenomenal world as manifest, immanent God, living in creative tension with the remote, unknowable God, serves Ibn ᶜArabī well here and, as we have also seen, elsewhere, in expressing his theme of the unity/diversity perspective.[10] Ibn ᶜArabī clarifies some details of

9. In a sense, then, the realities and the names *are* the world, a notion typical for Ibn ᶜArabī, as we have seen.

10. Again, ultimately there is no true unity/diversity perspective, in the higher synthesis of non-duality.

the unity/diversity relationship, illuminating its *process*, while also clarifying his terse opening remarks on the 'heart of the gnostic' as 'more comprehensive than God's mercy'—remarks which I provisionally sought to explain above and which Ibn ʿArabī now helps us further to understand. Thus:

> When the situation becomes [internally diverse and] contradictory by virtue of the [variety of] relations, there occurs in predication [of God] that which God attributes to Himself as compassion to His servants. Therefore, the first [breath] God breathes from Lordship is his breath related to [His name] The Merciful (*al-Raḥmān*), by way of His bringing the world into being, the world which 'Lordship' in the reality sought and [likewise] all the divine names. From this perspective [then], His mercy encompasses everything—thus does it encompass God (*al-Ḥaqq*). The mercy is thus more comprehensive than the heart [of the gnostic] or [at least] equal to it in comprehensiveness.[11]

The situation which has become 'diverse and contradictory' in its 'variety of relations' is the nascent, phenomenal world. Here, viewing the realm of incipient multiplicity with its attendant clashes and contradictions, God breathes His breath of creation, 'desired' by His Lordship and 'breathing' in compassion His mercy (*nafas al-Raḥmān*) in His servants. This 'breath of the Merciful' effects God's bringing the world into being; it is what His 'Lordship' and all His other divine names seek, for in this process (*ījād*)[12] they are fully brought into being to become the phenomenal world. In this sense, *al-Rubūbiyya* and *al-Raḥmān* are 'archetypal' divine names, with *al-Raḥmān*'s correlative quality of *raḥma* being the 'motive force' in the process of coming into phenomenal being (*ījād*). Now is God's mercy all-encompassing, covering all the divine names *and God Himself* (al-Ḥaqq). Here, in contradistinction to Ibn ʿArabī's opening remarks, divine

11. *Fuṣūṣ*, p. 119.

12. For the most penetrating discussion in the *Fuṣūṣ* on this issue, see the chapter on Zakariyyā.

mercy is 'more comprehensive than the heart of the gnostic or, at least, equal to it in comprehensiveness'. How has this become possible? The 'change' results from *undefined terminology*—in both cases—expressing two perspectives, that of 'the remote God' and that of 'the manifest God' and the implications for the phenomenal world in both instances.[13] In his opening remarks, Ibn ʿArabī seemed to be referring to the remote God who could be apprehended and encompassed only by the heart of the gnostic. The divine mercy, all-encompassing with respect to the phenomenal world, its sovereign domain, was no match for the gnostic's direct apprehension of God in His essence. Al-Ḥaqq, God, was here understood to be this remote God precisely because of its particular relation with the gnostic's heart, while Ibn ʿArabī does not *explicitly define* al-Ḥaqq. Now, in the latter formulation, in the context of explication of the divine names as the phenomenal world in which the manifest God is immanent, the mercy suddenly *does* encompass al-Ḥaqq and now *does* hold sway with, even exceed, the heart of the gnostic. But al-Ḥaqq here is clearly what Ibn ʿArabī usually refers to as 'the created God', *al-Ḥaqq al-Makhlūq*, the only God ordinarily 'known', apart from the remote God in the quite extraordinary case of the gnostic's type of knowing.[14] Divine mercy, then, in Ibn ʿArabī's ontological transformation as agent of phenomenal being (*mūjid*, through *ījād*) does indeed encompass *al-Ḥaqq al-Makhlūq*, as God in this meaning (as 'created') has like all else been brought into being by the divine mercy. The heart of the gnostic cannot surpass that.[15]

Ibn ʿArabī's discussion here is the sort of 'conceptual knot' which, as we know, he places at certain junctures in the *Fuṣūṣ*,[16]

13. Such lack of terminological definition was, of course, a major method which Ibn ʿArabī used in effecting his 'creative ambiguity'

14. See the chapter on Zakariyyā.

15. Here the 'creative ambiguity' becomes transparent in its workings.

16. These 'knots' should not be seen as 'problems' in Ibn ʿArabī's thought; they are, on the contrary, to be used as means to understanding.

in order to reiterate, in different ways, certain of his basic truths. 'Untying the knot', through successful analysis, lays bare its various strands, each becoming visible independent of the others. The present 'knot', now analytically 'untied', in its dissolution clearly shows Ibn ʿArabī's pattern of thought in the issues of unity/multiplicity and the remote God and immanent God, as formulated here through the polarity of the gnostic's heart and God's mercy in Shuʿayb's 'wisdom of the heart'. One further aspect of this matter, however, remains for discussion. I think it appropriate to call this Ibn ʿArabī's 'creation myth'.

THE 'CREATION MYTH'

In all of Ibn ʿArabī's various discussions of the One and the many—whatever the formulation and particular perspective—there is implicit his conception of the 'origins of all being'. In our Shuʿaybī version here, this conception is particularly transparent and worthy of explication, as a simple model of Ibn ʿArabī's 'creation myth'.[17] The focal point is to be found in God's 'dual nature', as *remote* and *immanent* deity, and the relation between 'the two'. For it is the remote God who is in fact somehow made manifest in creation, as immanent God; and, ultimately, all *is* the remote God in His essence. Though characterised by His 'independence from the created worlds', in Ibn ʿArabī's poetry of being He also 'desired' the creation of these worlds *as His very self-manifestation.* He thus 'commissioned' His ontological mercy to effect this creation as the ultimate and necessary expression of His names. 'Creation', then, is simply the eternal and independent (*wujūd muṭlaq*) appearing as the temporal and dependent (*wujūd muqayyad*). God's 'dual nature' is in fact the opposite to duality—*it is unity conceived and encountered in two ways*, oneness and multiplicity. If there is a contradiction here,

17. I use this term to refer to Ibn ʿArabī's characteristic account of the 'origin of all being', an account which *fuses* the personal and 'mythopoeic' creation notion with the metaphysical dimension.

it is merely on the surface; both deeper intellectual apprehension of, and intuitive (gnostic) encounter with, the phenomenal manifestations of the eternal will transcend it. Indeed, as Ibn ᶜArabī continues in an evocative account of the gnostic's particular perspective and consciousness and with further intellectual explication:

> You must, then, know that God (*al-Ḥaqq*), Most High, as it is firmly established, is transformed in the [various] forms [of His appearance] in self-revelation; and that when the heart embraces God (al-Ḥaqq), it does not [at the same time] embrace any created thing—for it is as though God fills the heart [to the exclusion of all else]. This means that when the heart contemplates God (al-Ḥaqq) with His self-revelation to it, it is not possible that the heart should contemplate any other than God. The heart of the gnostic, with respect to [its capacity for] expansiveness, then, is, as Abū Yazīd al-Bisṭāmī said: "If the Throne and what encompasses it were one hundred million times in a corner of the heart of the gnostic, he [still] would not feel it." And Junayd said in this vein: "When the temporal joins with the eternal, there remains no trace of [the temporal]."[18]

The gnostic's heart, then, makes contact with a particular divine self-manifestation which completely fills it. There is no room for any created thing in it, as the reported remarks of Bisṭāmī and Junayd make clear. But that very same divine self-manifestation which so fills and is so embraced by the gnostic's heart to the exclusion of anything temporal *is itself a temporal form*. Indeed, as Ibn ᶜArabī says, the gnostic's heart gravitates toward the phenomenal form in its understanding of God's presence there. Again, there is no contradiction here, as the 'eternal' and the 'temporal' are but two perspectives on the One, 'experientially' for the heart of the gnostic and 'intellectually' in Ibn ᶜArabī's theoretical framework. Thus for the heart, 'when it embraces the eternal how can it recognise the temporal as

18. *Fuṣūṣ*, pp. 119–120.

something [truly] existent?'[19] But again, the temporal forms *as the self-revelation of the true God*, actually determine 'the spiritual dimensions' of the heart in its encounter with God: 'Since God's self-manifestation occurs in the [temporal] forms, then the heart will of necessity expand and contract according to the [temporal] form in which the particular divine self-manifestation occurs; nothing, then, will exceed whatever form in which the self-manifestation appears'.[20] Here the 'temporal'—as God's appearance—is actually *the determining force* in the experiential realisation of the 'eternal'. The heart's very spiritual dimensions are fixed in each of its encounters with a particular divine manifestation (temporal form). Ibn ʿArabī elegantly portrays this process in an anological image:

> The heart of the gnostic or the Perfect Man is situated exactly as is the setting of the stone of a ring, no more [than that in relation to the stone]; rather, the setting is in keeping with the dimension and shape of the stone, round if the stone is round, or square, hexagonal or octagonal or any other shape... Thus the stone's setting in the ring is in the likeness of the stone, not any other.[21]

The human heart, then, in this engaging analogy, again conforms totally to the divine self-manifestation, as the ring setting must, for obvious reasons, conform to the shape of the stone. In further clarification, and making a polemical point, Ibn ʿArabī says this notion is 'opposite to what the Folk refer to [in saying] that God, Most High, is manifested in conformity with the preparedness of the servant'.[22]

But it is 'not like that',[23] says Ibn ʿArabī. This preparedness of the servant—the *istiʿdād* which is so prominent in Ibn ʿArabī's

19. *Fuṣūṣ*, p. 120.
20. *Ibid.*
21. *Ibid.*
22. *Ibid.* Ibn ʿArabī uses the term *al-ṭā'ifa*, 'the Folk'; this usually refers to the sufis.
23. *Ibid.*

thought—is rather the servant's preparedness to conform to a particular form of God's phenomenal appearance. Indeed, this *istiʿdād is given by God to His servant.* Thus, in further explication:

> The servant, then, appears before God commensurate with the form in which God appears to him. The solution of this question is that God has two [kinds] of self-revelation, the self-revelation of the hidden and the self-revelation of the seen. From the self-revelation of the hidden is given the preparedness which the heart possesses; it is the self-revelation of the divine essence whose reality is the hidden and it is the Heness which He demands by calling Himself He. In Himself, He remains He, eternally. Then when this preparedness comes to the heart, so too does the self-revelation of the seen in [the very act of] seeing. And the heart sees Him in the form in which He is revealed to it. Thus He, Most High, gives to the heart that preparedness, [as evidenced] in His words, "He gave to each thing its nature."[24]

This passage is one of the most succinct and refined statements of the relationship between God eternal and 'God created', between unity and multiplicity, the one and the many, to be found anywhere in Ibn ʿArabī's works. It shows very clearly, among other things, the nature of this 'polarity' and, for Ibn ʿArabī, its resolution in the larger unity. Thus it is in the very realm of the gnostic's apprehension of the hidden God, the realm of eternal unity, that God gives to His servant the appropriate preparation (*istiʿdād*) which will equip him to receive the self-revelation of the seen God present in phenomenal forms. The servant, then, does 'see' God in this way, according to the servant's nature. The Qur'ān for Ibn ʿArabī—in his first reference to it here—indicates this truth. Where, then, is the boundary between the 'two poles' in this 'polarity'? The proper figure, perhaps, is Ibn ʿArabī's much-invoked 'circularity', in the eternal 'return' to a source which was never left, rather than

24. *Fuṣūṣ*, pp. 120–121; Qur'ān, 20:50.

linear-orientated boundary lines and polarities. Ibn ʿArabī continues with further explication of the immanent, revealed God, leading to the issue of the variety of religious beliefs in this world (his 'religious pluralism').[25]

As a concomitant of the process described above, says Ibn ʿArabī:

> God thus raises the veil between Himself and His servant. The servant then sees Him in the form of his own belief—indeed God constitutes the servant's very belief. Further, neither the [servant's] heart nor [his] eyes ever sees anything in God other than the form of his own belief. The God who is in the belief is, therefore, the one whose form the heart encompasses and he is the one who is manifest to the heart; in this way does the servant know Him. The eye [of the servant], then, sees nothing but the God of belief.[26]

THE 'GOD OF BELIEF'

The veil between God and man is lifted here by God, not in the experiential encounter between the two, with God as unseen essence, but rather in man's 'seeing' God in the phenomenal forms in which He is manifest. The heart is not the gnostic's heart encompassing the unseen God of divine essence—as in the opening lines of the chapter—but it is rather the gnostic's 'seeing' God in the created world. This is here described as 'the God of belief' (*al-Ḥaqq al-iʿtiqādī*) or, as Ibn ʿArabī describes it elsewhere, 'the created God in the beliefs' (*al-Ḥaqq al-makhlūq fī'l-iʿtiqādāt*).[27] This particular perspective on God immanent leads Ibn ʿArabī to expand on his notion of the multiplicity

25. *Fuṣūṣ*. p. 120. For a good discussion of this issue, see William Chittick, *Imaginal Worlds: Ibn al-ʿArabī and the Problem of Religious Diversity*, especially pp. 137–160.

26. *Ibid.*

27. Other synonymous terms used by Ibn ʿArabī are: *ilāh al-muʿtaqadāt, al-ilāh al-majʿūl*, and *al-ḥaqq al-muʿtaqad fī'l-qalb*. See Suʿād al-Ḥakīm, *al-Muʿjam al-Ṣūfī*, pp. 87–92.

of religious beliefs, their mutual competitiveness and their 'pluralistic', open relationship, from the angle of the gnostic's awareness.

'One who posits God in an exclusivist belief', says Ibn ʿArabī, 'will reject Him in anything other than his own fixed conception [of God], as God is made manifest [to him in this way]'.[28] What is implied here is a description of the 'typical' exoteric, exclusivist belief; truth in this view can only be present in one sort of belief, to the exclusion of all others. However, for Ibn ʿArabī there is another side to the issue:

> But one who frees God from [this sort] of fixed conception will not reject Him—he will, rather, affirm Him in every form in which He is pervasive and he will take Him from himself in the form in which He appears to him, infinitely. For the forms of divine self-manifestation have no limit at which they cease, just as knowledge of God has no ultimate specific goal with the gnostic at which he stops; rather, he remains a gnostic, in all times seeking enhancement in knowledge of Him, "My Lord increase me in knowledge;"[29] 'My Lord, increase me in knowledge'; "My Lord increase me in knowledge." Thus the matter is infinite from both sides. This, you may say, is God and creation.[30]

Religion from this angle—the deeper gnostic conception—transcends its exoteric exclusivist form, due to its particular understanding of the infinite forms of God's self-manifestation. On the exoteric side, then, one who sees only his own belief as true is missing that deeper reality of this 'pluralism' of beliefs and their objects, a 'pluralism' which bespeaks the *validity* of all beliefs, if not their *equality*. Indeed, by strong implication even equality *is* understood, because the beliefs—like all 'creation'—*are* God's self-revelation; and how could any aspect of God not be equal in value to any other? Here, it must be noted, there is

28. *Fuṣūṣ*, p. 121.
29. Qur'ān, 20:114.
30. *Fuṣūṣ*, p. 121.

an underlying assumption of the necessary unity and identity of beliefs and their objects. And for Ibn ʿArabī, as he has already indicated above, this is the main point. The gnostic, in his understanding, here exemplifies Ibn ʿArabī's general principle of the identity of knower, knowledge and known, in all spheres. 'Subject' and 'object', as separate categories, *at this level* do not exist. The issue of religious beliefs and their diversity here really constitutes a subsidiary of Ibn ʿArabī's 'foundation principle' of metaphysical unity. The 'religious pluralism' of Ibn ʿArabī's outlook, as some have seen this notion, is not so much derived from any principle analogous to modern religious pluralism with its 'liberal' ideological and social foundation, but, rather, from the non-dualist ontology underlying Ibn ʿArabī's thought. The real issue here is the ultimate intertwining identity of God and His creation; the unity of religions—like the unity of all else—comes within this remit. The gnostic knows this—so typically for Ibn ʿArabī—through a higher intellectual understanding rather than *via* an emotional, 'spiritual' understanding. The 'mystical experience' here is very much *an intellectual attainment* surrounded by an aura of 'mystical insight'.[31] Ibn ʿArabī formulates this intellectual and 'mystical' understanding in an astonishingly frank account. With regard to 'the two sides ... God and creation', Ibn ʿArabī says:

> If you consider His words, 'I am his foot with which he walks, his hand with which he hits and his tongue with which he speaks',[32] including also other faculties which are located in the limits of the body, then why do you differentiate [between God and man], saying the matter [may be reduced to] either all God or all creation? For in reality it is creation in one connection and it is God in [another] connection; but the essence is one. Thus a particular form is in fact manifested from within its own

31. This 'intellectualisation' of sufism—without loss of the 'experiential'—has been seen as the watershed achievement of Ibn ʿArabī, as was discussed in the first chapter of this book.

32. Bukhārī, LXXXI:38.

manifestation. God is then [both] that which is revealed and that which it is revealed to. Consider in this regard how wondrous is God in His Heness and in His connection to the phenomenal world in the realities of His beautiful names.[33]

And in a poem expressing the same idea:

Who is here and what is there?
The very here is its there
The one who has universalised it, has also particularised it

And the one who has particularised it, has also universalised it
There is only oneness
Whose very light is its darkness
One who neglects this will find his distress in himself
Nobody knows what we have said except the servant who possesses spiritual resolution.[34]

This truth for Ibn ʿArabī issues in a critique of conventional reason (*ʿaql*) and its proponents, those who profess the various doctrinal beliefs *(asḥāb al-iʿtiqādāt),* in favour of the gnostic's (*ʿārif*) way of the heart (*qalb*) and esoteric knowledge (*maʿrifa*). But this is not a simple 'sufi distinction' between 'deficient reason' and 'sublime religious experience'. We have already seen Ibn ʿArabī's nuances in that matter, with 'mystical understanding' constituting in fact a more productive sort of 'reason' than *ʿaql* in a conventional sense. Ibn ʿArabī will discuss this distinction (in its types) as part of a patchy general treatment of epistemological matters in the pursuit of truth. Here the heart, so prominent earlier on, again serves as a focus of discussion. Various examples of relevant approaches through discursive theology, dogmatic tradition, pure reason and others are presented towards clarification (in polemic) of Ibn ʿArabī's own views. Some important points in Ibn ʿArabī's epistemology are made. Shuʿayb's figure

33. *Fuṣūṣ*, p. 121.
34. *Fuṣūṣ*, p. 122.

in all of this finally emerges clearly as inspiration for this chapter in the *Fuṣūṣ*.

THE HEART

Ibn ʿArabī says the poem above is 'a reminder for the one who has a heart', citing directly from Qur'ān, 50:37, 'because of His transformation in the various forms and attributes'. God's transformation and appearance in these ways, then, seems for Ibn ʿArabī to be a matter of the heart, as opposed to reason, for 'God did not say "for the one who has reason"'.[35]

Ibn ʿArabī has created a seeming opposition here between the heart and reason, with respect to understanding the divine manifestation in forms and attributes; and it is for him the Qur'ān in 50:37 that provides the foundation for this formulation. The Qur'ān's 'reminder' for those who have a heart refers literally *in the Qur'ānic context* to an understanding of God's mercy and wrath *for their respective recipients*, while Ibn ʿArabī's reminder and heart have to do with God's manifestation *in forms and attributes*. Thus for Ibn ʿArabī *the referents are obviously the same*, enabling him to invoke this verse at this time. The Qur'ānic God who assigns some of His servants to paradise and others to the fire is indeed 'the created God in the beliefs', here manifested in His mercy and wrath. Reason, conventionally applied to this God, with respect to these or other of His attributes, cannot see the full truth, as Ibn ʿArabī argues *contra* the conventional thinkers:

> For [conventional] reason is restrictive, limiting the matter to one feature. But reality essentially denies [such] limitation. The 'reminder' is thus not for those who have only conventional reason, for they are the possessors of [exclusivist] religious beliefs who excommunicate and execrate one another, 'And they have no helpers'.[36]

35. *Ibid.*
36. *Ibid.* Qur'ān, 3:91.

The remainder of Ibn ʿArabī's discussion here is 'patchy' in texture, as mentioned above, and dialectical in its method, with the general framework of 'heart' and 'reason' remaining as the focus of attention.

To begin, the Qur'ānic phrase 'And they will have no helpers', (3:91) which Ibn ʿArabī adduces here as a supporting 'proof-text' for his critique of the *aṣhāb al-iʿtiqādāt*, is in the Qur'ān the dramatic culmination of a fierce attack on unbelievers (*kuffār*) who die in their unbelief ('*wa mātū wa hum kuffār*'); they will receive their just desserts—'a grievous punishment' (*ʿadhāb alīm*)—with no recourse to mercy: 'And they will have no helpers'. In the present context, the target of this dire pronouncement for Ibn ʿArabī is those people who hold the formulated exclusivist beliefs which set them against one another. The product of conventional reason, these beliefs are traps of mutual exclusivity for those who profess them. Each believer's god (*ilāh*) is devoid of authority and validity with respect to the god of another believer. Each believer defends his god and tries to help him in the competition with other gods. But his god cannot help the believer ('And they will have no helpers'): 'For God excludes any help from the gods of the beliefs, as each one of them is isolated within itself'[37]—and thus such a god cannot help anyone outside itself.

But while the Qur'ān here and Ibn ʿArabī's use and interpretation of it have a similar *structure*, where in both cases people who evince no true belief are doomed to being forsaken, in the Qur'ān the sin at issue is absence of belief in the one God and, as corollary, the presence of belief in false gods, while for Ibn ʿArabī the 'sin' is the belief in the divinities created by man *with his reason*, where each god becomes separate and exclusive, leading its adherents in the path of harmful exclusivity. Thus for Ibn ʿArabī, in contradistinction to the Qur'ān, no succour can be had from these gods, because they are the creations of a narrowly-applied

37. *Fuṣūṣ*, p. 122.

human reason, rendering each a solipsistic construction encapsulated by reason's internal regulations—*not because they are 'false'*. For the Qur'ān, however, they cannot aid their worshippers *because* they are false.[38]

Ibn ʿArabī's answer goes further than all this and is posited in the linguistic terms of Qur'ān 3:91, playing on the Arabic root *n-ṣ-r* from which the Qur'ānic *nāṣirīn* ('helpers') is derived: 'The one who is helped (*al-manṣūr*) is the totality, and the helper (*al-nāṣir*) is the totality. Thus God (*al-Ḥaqq*) for the gnostic is something known which cannot be unknown'.[39] This is the meaning of 'heart' (*qalb*) in Qur'ān 50:37, for:

> The gnostic knows the variability (*taqallub*) of God in physical forms, through his own transformation in form. Thus from himself, the gnostic knows [God as] himself. The gnostic's self, then, is none other than God's very identity; indeed, nothing that exists in creation is anything but the identity of God. In fact it is that identity'.[40]

If the *manṣūr* and the *nāṣir* are the totality (*majmūʿ*) and there is no distinction between them, then this is Ibn ʿArabī's basic metaphysical unity in another formulation. Here it gives deeper meaning to Qur'ān 3:91, saying, in essence, that these false gods cannot help their believers because their very separation and objectification (in their believers' construction of them) imply a negation of the truth of metaphysical divine immanence. From the Qur'ānic perspective, this negation renders the belief and its godly object *false* as well as *intellectually misplaced*.[41] For in the absence of a realisation of divine immanence the reigning false belief and its distinct godly forms is incapable of helping anyone in any way. Only if one sees in these godly forms a

38. For Ibn ʿArabī, the *logical status* of these gods has its exact *ontological correlation*.

39. *Fuṣūṣ*, p. 122.

40. *Ibid.*

41. That is, in the sense that its implications are not realised.

pointer toward their own effacement in the larger unity will any 'help' be forthcoming. This is the condition of the gnostic in his realisation of God's and his own *taqallub* in physical forms, his own forms changing and adapting as necessary in order to accommodate God's presence within. Thus, from within his own self does the gnostic find and know God. And:

> Thus is God the gnostic, the knower and that which is known in this form, while at the same time He is not the gnostic, not the knower and not known, in the other form. This is the destiny of one who knows God in His self-revelation and in seeing Him in that very totality. And hence God's words, "for the one who has a heart", that is, the one who becomes multiform in his transformations [in response to God's variegated self-manifestation].[42]

Ibn ʿArabī has with all this provided a model for the gnostic and his knowledge of the highest truth: One who has 'heart' (in Ibn ʿArabī's understanding of Qur'ān, 50:37), as opposed to mere reason in attaining religious truth. The possessor of heart realises the omnipresence and immanence of God within all phenomenal forms, including and, in particular, himself; indeed, the gnostic himself is continually transformed as God's appearances change. Thus does the gnostic know God within himself, as his own form adapts to conform to God's various self-revelations. The heart (*qalb*) of Qur'ān 50:37 in its pulsations is the organ-source of the continual transformations of both God and gnostic (*taqallub*), as God's changing self-manifestation (*tajallin*) directs the gnostic's own accommodative self-transformation (*taqlīb*). *Qalb, taqallub* and *taqlīb,* then, rooted for Ibn ʿArabī in the *qalb* of Qur'ān 50:37, constitute a 'node' of linguistic and semantic association which conveys the truth of God's immanence within all phenomenal forms, particularly in the heart of the gnostic. Here all barriers and boundaries between God and man are effaced, in the metaphysical unity which is

42. *Fuṣūṣ*, pp. 122–123.

presupposed in the foundations of Ibn ʿArabī's outlook. The subject/object distinction is removed, as God is both *knower* and *known*, as well as *not-knower* and *not-known*. Those who believe in 'the gods in the beliefs' will, therefore, have no helpers as Qur'ān 3:191 tells us, but here perhaps for reasons peculiar to Ibn ʿArabī's understanding of the Qur'ānic context.

As we have seen, the sort of conventional reason which categorises and draws boundaries is for Ibn ʿArabī the culprit, in its failure to curb and to extirpate the exclusivity and prolific differentiation which ineluctably ensue. This is reason as opposed to heart. But we must take care here not to attribute to Ibn ʿArabī an *anti-rational position*. For *qalb* itself, though obviously incorporating 'experiential' elements (as *maʿrifa* of the *ʿārif*) is, upon close examination, in fact a *different sort of reason*. This is the reason of Ibn ʿArabī which transcends the exclusivity, contradictions and linear reasoning of conventional *ʿaql*, as one sees this 'different reason' in his various formulations. The gnostic—here the 'possessor of heart'—does know and understand the truth through a linguistic and ratiocinative process; for in this way he knows the reality of God's unitive immanence in the multiplicity of forms which make up the world around us. But *ʿaql, in its usual workings*, is not a faculty which directs one to this truth; it leads, rather, to the trap of inescapable intellectual constructions which leave us indeed on the very far side of truth—though, in characteristic dialectical fashion Ibn ʿArabī sees even in some of the formulations of ordinary reason elements of truth whose very proponents, in their ignorance, often fail to see and to develop in that way. Thus, for example, the Sophist philosophers among the ancients[43] and the *Ashʿarī* theologians in later Islam[44]—both proponents of ordinary *ʿaql*—did gain a practical grasp of the truth in their respective doctrines of form, accidents and substance and, in the case of the Ashʿarītes,

43. *Fuṣūṣ*, p. 125.
44. *Ibid.*

the notion of continuous creation (*khalq jadīd*). But in both cases the formulations of reason fail to proceed the full way to the complete truth. The Sophists, despite their grasp of continuous transformations in the world, did not understand that the relationship between form and substance can be understood only as one of total unity and mutuality, and 'Had they said that, then they would have achieved the rank of realisation in the matter'.[45] The 'Ashʿarītes in their atomism failed to see the underlying unity of divine immanence under the accidents and atoms in their theory, while, in their associated notion of continuous creation their lapse is similar, here conceived by Ibn ʿArabī as a failure to understand the unitive continuity provided by God's underlying breaths (*anfās*) in the process of continuous creation, destruction and re-creation.[46] But here, too, partial truth *was* gained through conventional reason; and full truth might have been realised, had these practitioners of conventional reason just possessed somewhat more understanding of the absolute unity in things—an understanding achieved through reason as understood by Ibn ʿArabī.

SHUʿAYB

The unitive wisdom of the heart—*ḥikma qalbiyya*—as opposed to knowledge based on conventional reason, should now be clear in its Qur'ānic and metaphysical dimensions for Ibn ʿArabī. But if this *ḥikma* is associated with Shuʿayb, what is the reason for that? The main Qur'ānic citations in this chapter, as we have seen, do not allude to the Shuʿayb story, though one must presume that for Ibn ʿArabī an integral link between this *ḥikma* and Shuʿayb does exist and that a core of Qur'ānic meaning lies within. Ibn ʿArabī in one explicit statement does, indeed, reveal this link and, by implication, this meaning:

45. *Ibid.*
46. *Fuṣūṣ*, pp. 125–126.

> As for the particular relationship of this *ḥikma* with Shuʿayb, because of the branching-out in it, that is, its unlimited branches, because every belief is a branch, thus they—I mean religious beliefs—are all branches. Consequently, when the veil is lifted [truth] will be revealed to everyone, according to his beliefs....[47]

As is so often the case, Ibn ʿArabī here too begins with a 'scholastic', philological explanation: Shuʿayb's root, *sh-ʿ-b*, is the root of *tashaʿʿub*, branching-out, and *shuʿba* and its plural, *shuʿab* (branch, branches), meaning that religious beliefs (*iʿtiqādāt)* are like *branches*, in their unlimited proliferation. Continuing in this figure, the 'tree' from which the branches derive would then be the unitive principle of which the branches form an integral part. These beliefs in 'the created gods', though *on the face of it* unproductive 'dead-ends', leading as Ibn ʿArabī says, only to the encapsulation (for god and believer) in solipsistic exclusivity and spiritual void, when 'revealed' in their depth actually open onto the 'higher principle' in which they are transcended. The believer in a particular 'created god' may, then, through that 'narrow belief' be transported beyond it to a realisation of the full truth. The gnostic is the one who already knows this, for whom the veil has been removed. This is the Qur'ānic 'heart'. From a linguistic beginning in Shuʿayb's name, Ibn ʿArabī has brought us full circle through the presumably unproductive 'gods in the beliefs' back to the unitive principle, God in His essence, with everything here reduced to the same 'one essence' (*ʿayn wāḥida*).[48] If the Shuʿayb story in the Qur'ān is involved here—and it implicitly is—it is most obviously in Shuʿayb's encounter with the 'false' beliefs of his people and his rather restrained approach in that situation. For in this sense, these are, after all, themselves *shuʿab*.

47. *Fuṣūṣ*, p. 123.
48. *Fuṣūṣ*, p. 125.

CHAPTER

8

The Wisdom of Divine Decree in the Word of ʿUzayr

ʿUZAYR, BIBLICAL AND QUR'ĀNIC

Ezra in Biblical and post-Biblical Jewish and Christian tradition is the priest and scribe who is said to have played a role in rebuilding the Temple after the Babylonian exile. He is characterised as a highly learned man who sought to provide a religious foundation for the community.[1] ʿUzayr/Ezra is mentioned only once in the Qur'ān, in 9:30: 'The Jews say ʿUzayr is the son of God and the Christians say Christ is the son of God'. Problematic with respect to its meaning, this verse has been understood by Muslim scholars and exegetes in various ways; they sometimes used extra-Qur'ānic legendary stories in order to explain the meaning and presumed origins of this claim concerning Jewish belief. In any case, some exegetes made little or no comment on the verse, while even for those who did it was not a prime concern.[2]

1. See, for example, *The Blackwell Companion to Judaism*, eds. A. J. Avery-Peck, J. Neusner, pp. 9–10; 61–62.

2. For example, *Tafsīr al-Jalālayn* says little about the verse, while Ibn Kathīr, in his *Tafsīr* (p. 596), provides some commentary with legendary material. See also: Hava Lazarus-Yafeh, *Intertwined Worlds. Medieval Islam and Biblical Criticism*, p. 52 and *passim* and *Shorter Encyclopaedia of Islam*, article, "Uzair', p. 617. The *S.E.I.* article gives an account of 'the commonest explanation of this belief' using legendary sources, as follows: "ʿUzair is one of the *ahl al-Kitāb*, the possessors of the Torah. When they sin, God deprives them of the *tābūt* (sacred ark) and punishes them with a sickness which makes them forget the Torah. ʿUzair mourns. Then a flame from God enters ʿUzair's body so that he is filled with knowledge of the Torah. He teaches his people. God then sends down the sacred ark to Israel again; the Torah is compared with 'Uzair's teaching and they are found to agree; the Jews therefore believe that "ʿUzair must be the son of God.'

If there is any more significant Qur'ānic exegetical place for ʿUzayr, it is in the remarks of various exegetes on another passage in the Qur'ān, a passage in which ʿUzayr is not mentioned at all: in Qur'ān, 2:259, there is a story of an unnamed man who passes by an unnamed town lying in ruins. The man asks, 'How will God revivify this [town] after its death?' God then puts the man to death for a hundred years. When God revives him, the man realises the massive efficacy of God's decree, in certain wondrous effects of the hundred years' lapse; there can then be no doubt about God's potential power in bringing the shattered town back to life. In the mainstream of Islamic exegetical tradition, this man is often identified as ʿUzayr.[3] Ibn ʿArabī seems also to concur with the identification. We shall let Ibn ʿArabī's own words underscore his use of this story in association with ʿUzayr as the referent for 'the wisdom of divine decree' (*al-ḥikma al-qadariyya*), as well as indicating some implicit contexts derived from an Islamic theological notion of God's power and decree (*al-qaḍā' wa'l-qadar*).

THE WISDOM EXEMPLIFIED IN THE STORY OF ʿUZAYR

The wisdom which Ibn ʿArabī will explicate in the name of ʿUzayr, then, is the *ḥikma qadariyya*, the wisdom of divine decree. God's decree, *al-qadar*, strongly implying His absolute power with respect to His creation, was a central issue in the classical tradition of Islamic discursive theology (*ʿilm al-kalām*). In the mainstream of theological opinion, two terms, *al-qaḍā' wa al-qadar*, paired in this way as a matter of theological convention, together mean divine determination and predetermination of things, the *qaḍā'* being God's eternal decree and the *qadar* the temporal implementation and manifestation of the decree (*tawqīt*).[4] Ibn ʿArabī remains here formally within the frame-

3. This may be confirmed by even a cursory survey of the main works of *tafsīr*.

4. For a brief summary of the doctrine, see *Shorter Encyclopaedia of Islam*, pp. 199–200 (articles, '*Ḳaḍā*'', '*Ḳadar*').

work of this most central theological concept, while integrating *al-qaḍā' wa al-qadar* into his comprehensive cosmology in which the notion of 'absolute being', *al-wujūd al-muṭlaq*, serves as unifying principle, encompassing the seeming multiplicity of things in phenomenal, temporal existence. God Himself, says Ibn ʿArabī, abides by the order and organisation of *al-qaḍā' wa al-qadar*, as it is His own order, known to him through His own sources of knowledge (*al-maʿlūmāt*)[5] and thereby necessitating His compliance with it. One aspect of *qadar* is that it performs its function of bringing potential beings into time (*i.e.*, actualizing them) 'according to what they are in their essence'.[6] And their essences are within the divine plan. *Al-qadar*, then, is the 'leading edge' of the *al-qaḍā' wa al-qadar* formulation; it is truly destiny in its full meaning. The 'secret' (*sirr*) of this destiny, says Ibn ʿArabī, is known only to God Himself, but He does sometimes reveal it to certain of His creatures whom He chooses for this. Thus 'the secret of destiny' is for 'one who has heart or will lend an ear while witnessing', says Ibn ʿArabī. He refers here to a Qur'ānic verse about someone who, having heart, might understand the preceding verses which preach the message of paradise for the god-fearing and hell for the hard-hearted.[7]

Ibn ʿArabī goes on to explain more about the *sirr al-qadar*. If it was, as he explained above, the secret of the very nature of divine decree and destiny which God Himself knows 'from what His sources of knowledge give Him', then it is clear that God is in some way 'bound' by this secret and its implementation which are in fact both the metaphysical and the phenomenal nature of reality. This 'binding' is not a true limitation of God but, on the contrary, it is in fact part of His nature and of the world He created. But seen from the 'normal' perspective in which the language of convention compels one to adopt a 'bifurcation'

5. *Fuṣūṣ*, p. 131. Literally: 'Those things that are known'.

6. *Fuṣūṣ*, p. 131.

7. Qur'ān, 50:37; *Fuṣūṣ*, p. 131 and pp. 131–138 for the entire discussion of ʿUzayr.

idea of God as omnipotent creator separated by metaphysical, no less than spatial, distance from His creation, the 'binding' or 'limitation' of God here raises questions. Using his usual sense of irony, Ibn ʿArabī in fact plays on this bifurcation idea. Thus, he says, 'that which is legislated actually legislates over the legislator, in compelling him to legislate over it in a certain way.'[8] Or: what God does, He does because He could not have done otherwise. And this is because His own *qaḍā'* and *qadar* require that. This is divine self-limitation. But would such self-limitation not be a contradiction? The seeming paradox is heightened by Ibn ʿArabī's language in the passage quoted above: '*al-Ḥākim*', 'the legislator,' has the strongest possible connotation of absolute power and authority, while *al-maḥkūm ʿalayhi*, 'that which is legislated', is the *absolute object* of that absolute power and authority, grammatically as well as in its intellectual meaning. How can *al-Ḥākim* be determined by *al-maḥkūm ʿalayhi*?

For the classical theologian using the formulation *al-qaḍā' wa al-qadar*, the problem was one of theodicy and the solution emphasized the divine power *vis à vis* the impotent created world. Whatever the ethical issues involved here, they were handled in ways that maintained that solution.[9] But the formulation of *al-qaḍā' wa al-qadar* as divine determination was of course usually not taken by the theologians as the paradoxical formulation used by Ibn ʿArabī, in pushing the bifurcation idea to its logical extreme.

Ibn ʿArabī approaches the boundary of this logical extreme in his formulation of *al-qaḍā' wa al-qadar* precisely in order *to resolve*, in his way, the seeming contradiction which that formula implies and in so doing he is able thereby to explicate his own notion of ultimate truth. For while Ibn ʿArabī agrees with the theologians on the very basic meaning of *al-qaḍā' wa al-qadar*, as the absolute divine determination of things, he uses the contra-

8. *Fuṣūṣ*, pp. 131–132.
9. See *e.g.*, Watt, W. M., *Free Will and Predestination in Early Islam.*

diction implicit in that, *viz.*, God's own limitation by His own determination, as a way of revealing a deeper reality. Thus, while the theologians remained squarely on the side of divine transcendence in their doctrine of divine determination, Ibn ʿArabī, in taking divine determination to its paradoxical extreme, is then able to resolve the paradox by an appeal to divine immanence. The seeming absurdity of the *Ḥākim* being dependent on the *maḥkūm ʿalayhi* dissipates and the paradox is resolved when one realizes that divine determination has this paradoxical potential only from the perspective of divine transcendence. Thus the 'paradox' dissolves when divine determination is seen through divine immanence. This for Ibn ʿArabī is the 'secret' of *al-qadar* (*sirr al-qadar*), the 'keys to the unknown' (*mafātiḥ al-ghayb*), using a Qur'ānic expression;[10] it is the knowledge of 'the connection between divine power (*al-qudra*) and its object as created being (*al-maqdūr*)'.[11] Seen through immanence rather than transcendence of the divine, the apparent contradiction in the 'limiting' of God which appears in Ibn ʿArabī's thoroughgoing understanding of *al-qaḍā' wa al-qadar* (*i.e.*, the *maḥkūm ʿalayhi* ruling over *al-Ḥākim*) actually points towards its own ultimate resolution.

For Ibn ʿArabī, this is *the truth* of 'the connection of divine power (*qudra*) with its creation, the object of that power (*maqdūr*)' and knowledge of this is 'for God alone';[12] but 'He sometimes teaches some of this to those of His servants whom He so chooses'.[13] The essence of this knowledge lies in that nexus between God and His creation, between *qudra* and *maqdūr*, or in the fact that 'every *ḥākim* is also *maḥkūm ʿalayhi*"—no matter who the *ḥākim* is.'[14] There is no multiplicity. Contradiction and paradox in this sense carry within them their

10. Qur'ān, 6:59; *Fuṣūṣ*, p. 133.
11. *Fuṣūṣ*, p. 134.
12. *Ibid.*
13. *Fuṣūṣ*, p. 133.
14. *Fuṣūṣ*, pp. 131–132.

own resolution; indeed, this is their very rationale and one 'knows' it through inspired insight, *kashf*. Thus, while the theologians' understanding of *al-qaḍā' wa al-qadar*, as divine determination, posits an omnipotent, transcendent God ruling over His creation, Ibn ʿArabī presumes an immanent God whose determination of things represents a reality in which all is He; and no distinctions may be claimed *at this level*.

This, then, is Ibn ʿArabī's first and widest circle of meaning in the chapter devoted to ʿUzayr's wisdom. Here he establishes the sufi metaphysics of the subject. Yet, the prophetic, Qur'ānic side is equally apparent. From his first formulation of the *ḥikma* of ʿUzayr as *ḥikma qadariyya*, with his use of the *al-qaḍā' wa al-qadar* formula, the terminology and associated issues are obviously Qur'ān-derived. This is partly through the broader Qur'ānic background of *al-qaḍā' wa al-qadar* in Islamic theological thought, with all its connotation there of theodicy and ethics. Ibn ʿArabī's transferring of *al-qaḍā' wa al-qadar* from the ethical side of the theologians to his own sufi metaphysical realm did not for him constitute an 'abandoning' of the Qur'ānic tenor of the theological discussion. Rather, the metaphysical dimension was for him the deepest expression of the Qur'ānic truth; so deep and abiding in fact, that there could be no distinction drawn between the two. Thus, Ibn ʿArabī's citing of the passage from Qur'ān 50:38, 'for one who has a heart...', immediately after his first formulation of his metaphysical conception of *al-qaḍā' wa al-qadar*, is so typical of this method in the whole of the *Fuṣūṣ*.[15]

MESSENGERS, PROPHETS AND SAINTS: RELIGIOUS INSPIRATION AND SUFI METAPHYSICS

The second circle of meaning here relates to the subject of messengers (*rusul*), prophets (*anbiyā'*, *nabiyyūn*) and saints (*awliyā'*),

15. This, of course, is the structure of alternating and integrated Qur'ānic and metaphysical elements which makes Ibn ʿArabī's method so distinctive.

as categories and human exemplars of religious inspiration, experience and knowledge. Focusing on the thorny question of the relative status of each of these types with respect to the others, and paying special attention to the quality of their respective spiritual attainments, Ibn ʿArabī treats this issue from the perspective of the metaphysical circle of meaning which he established through *al-qaḍā' wa al-qadar* and sees the whole matter Qur'ānically justified.[16] This is perhaps in contrast to many of the previous explications of the problem by Ibn ʿArabī's sufi predecessors whose approach was more narrowly doctrinal and whose discussion was more descriptive than metaphysical. The goal of legitimating the sufi conception of the *walī* (and *wilāya*), and even showing the primacy though not the superiority of the *walī* over the 'legislating prophet' (*al-nabī al-musharriʿ*), was common to both Ibn ʿArabī and his sufi predecessors, though, again, it was Ibn ʿArabī's metaphysical meaning and emphasis which gave his approach its profound distinctiveness. Both Ibn ʿArabī and his predecessors, however, had an issue here whose terminology, points of reference and general formulation for them were ultimately to be found in the Qur'ān; and neither spared any effort in formulating their respective positions in this way.

Ibn ʿArabī begins his discussion with the Qur'ānic 'messengers' (*rusul*), people who are designated by God for certain communities, bearing legislative directives for the members of those communities. These *rusul* are the same in Ibn ʿArabī's vocabulary as the 'legislating prophets' (*al-anbiyā' al-musharriʿūn*), whom he distinguishes from the 'general prophets' (*al-anbiyā' al ʿāmmiyyūn*). The *rusul*, says Ibn ʿArabī, are also 'saints' (*awliyā'*), and mystically enlightened (*ʿārifūn*); but 'insofar as they are *rusul*' they are at various levels which of necessity correspond to the levels of their respective communities.[17] Thus a *rasūl* possesses knowledge only

16. *Fuṣūṣ*, pp. 133–134.
17. *Fuṣūṣ*, p. 132.

to the extent which his community requires—neither more nor less—and the various communities differ in this respect, some being better endowed than others. The *rusul*, consequently, differ from one another in the extent of the revealed knowledge they possess, by virtue of the innate differences of their communities. This for Ibn ᶜArabī is the meaning of God's words: 'We have set some of the messengers above others'.[18]

What appear, then, to be differences of a qualitative nature between one *rasūl* and another in the Qur'ānic verse cited, in fact reflect within Ibn ᶜArabī's metaphysical framework of *al-qaḍā' wa al-qadar* the metaphysics of differentiation. Though the differences are 'real', they go beyond an ordinary understanding of differences of this kind, as they reflect and are so determined in the 'best of all possible worlds' which is the perfect, inexorable order of the cosmos.

This is further exemplified, says Ibn ᶜArabī, with respect to the knowledge and judgement possessed by the *rusul*. For 'these are derived from the very metaphysical essences of the *rusul*—peace be upon them—making the *rusul* qualitatively different from one another by virtue of their [varying degrees] of metaphysical readiness [for knowledge]'.[19] This differentiation, then, though superficially appearing as 'more' or 'less', 'higher' or 'lower' (which in one sense it is), is more deeply reflective of the inexorable metaphysical order in which evaluations of this sort are *not* to the point; indeed, qualitative evaluations, remaining on the surface as they must, are precisely beside the point, metaphysically. Nor is this the case only for messengers and prophets, for, says Ibn ᶜArabī, it is a universal feature of the world itself. Thus the Qur'ān says, referring to all people, 'God favoured some of you over others, in giving His sustenance'.[20] 'Sustenance' *(rizq)* here means 'the spiritual, like knowledge,

18. *Ibid.*; Qur'ān, 2:253.

19. *Ibid.* Ibn ᶜArabī uses the Arabic term *dhawāt* here for 'their essences', meaning those fixed qualities which give to each individual his fixed identity.

20. *Fuṣūṣ*, p. 132; Qur'ān, 16:71.

and the sensual, like food', says Ibn ʿArabī.[21] And 'God only gives this sustenance in a known measure. This is the just entitlement of the creature seeking it. Consequently, God "gives to everything its unique nature"[22]...and what He wishes is confined to what He knows, according to which He governs. But, as we have already said, what He knows is determined by what [His] sources of knowledge provide Him'.[23]

Messengers, prophets and general humanity are what they are and have what they have, then, because of their metaphysical fixed essences. This is God's act and His decree for creation, reflecting and exemplifying the metaphysical process which in its deepest meaning transcends the personalised religion which we, and God himself in His revelations to us, use to describe the link between God and creation. This meaning is underscored, as it were, in the notion of God's sources of knowledge (*al-maʿlumāt*) determining His acts of creation. This 'determination' is not the seemingly paradoxical situation of an omnipotent God restricted and restrained by His fixed sources of knowledge, but rather a metaphysical gloss on what appears a personalised link between God and Creation.

For Ibn ʿArabī, however, it is not *either* the personalised discourse of revelations *or* the metaphysical truth within them which is the choice of the one who would understand. Both are true, at one and the same time. The Qur'ān, understood as Ibn ʿArabī understands the three passages cited above, embodies and professes for him the metaphysical reality. The background of this reality is ultimately the oneness of all as constituting the immanence of the divine, while the foreground of it is in the variegated phenomenal creation which expresses the underlying metaphysical principle. One aspect of phenomenal creation is the *rasūl, nabī, walī* variegation.

21. *Fuṣūṣ*, p. 132.
22. *Fuṣūṣ*, p. 132; and referring here to Qur'ān 42:27 and citing Qur'ān 20:50.
23. *Fuṣūṣ*, p. 132.

SIRR AL-QADAR

Divine *qaḍā'* is God's creative decree. Here the conception and the general implementation of creation occur. The divine *qadar* is the control and refinement, as it were, of *qaḍā'*. A specific focus of *qadar* is the 'temporalisation' of creation (*tawqīt*). This means the insertion of creation in the time-framework, where it takes on the phenomenal forms which were potential in their fixed essences. *Qadar*, in this sense, actualizes the creative potential in *qaḍā'*, thereby bringing forth phenomenal reality; the variegation of this reality is the actualized aspect of the fixed divine plan. *Qadar*, then, by virtue of its key role in creation, is the decisive component with respect to *qaḍā'*, and, indeed, *qadar*'s, secret (*sirr al-qadar*) 'which God makes intelligible through absolute inspired knowledge (*bi'l-maʿrifa al-tāmma*) to those whom He designates', is 'the most revelatory of knowledge'.[24] For the *sirr al-qadar* represents the truth of that unity and identity of God and man which are so central to Ibn ʿArabī's outlook; it is the exemplification of Ibn ʿArabī's conception of the *al-qaḍā' wa'l-qadar* formula as pointing toward the immanent God. The truth of this secret (*ḥaqīqat al-sirr*), says Ibn ʿArabī, governs all of existence, 'absolute existence as well as conditional existence' (*al-wujūd al-muṭlaq wa'l-wujūd al-muqayyad*).[25] It is the secret of *qadar* which now becomes the focus of Ibn ʿArabī's discussion as he brings together his first two circles of meaning—*al-qaḍā' wa al-qadar* and the messengers, prophets and saints—in his third and final circle of meaning, the special wisdom of the prophet ʿUzayr.

ʿUZAYR: PROPHETIC TEMERITY AND METAPHYSICAL NECESSITY

By way of introduction, Ibn ʿArabī says:

24. *Ibid.*
25. *Ibid.*

> Since the prophets, may God bless them, acquire this knowledge only through the channel of special divine revelation, their hearts are intellectually simple, while they know as well how weak discursive reasoning in fact is, in understanding things as they are, just as oral transmission is likewise weak in knowing what can be known only through taste.[26]

The principle established here is simply an extension of the principle established above, of the necessary hierarchical differentiation existing among messengers, prophets and indeed all ranks of mankind with respect to knowledge and divine benefits. One messenger—or one prophet—is thus 'superior' to another according to Ibn ʿArabī's interpretation of *al-qaḍāʾ wa al-qadar*, much as one wind is stronger than another in the natural order, without, ultimately, any true qualitative distinction of moral or intellectual character being implied. That principle is now applied to the entire category of prophetic knowledge. The issue is not the internal hierarchical differentiation of prophets, but the external differentiation of prophetic knowledge as an epistemological category, distinguishing it from other types of knowledge, particularly that which is acquired through direct experience, or 'taste' (*dhawq*). This is 'the perfect knowledge which exists only through divine disclosure'.[27]

The identity of the rightful recipients of this knowledge, as well as the nature of the knowledge itself, will become the prime concern of Ibn ʿArabī here. Those who possess this ultimate knowledge, which comes through taste, are those whose intrinsic nature predisposed them to receive the knowledge; others may not receive it. And like the differentiation among messengers and prophets (indeed, like the differentiation in everything), the differentiation here reflects the universal principle of *al-qaḍāʾ wa al-qadar*. However, here the stakes are even higher, for the person who possesses this knowledge in fact

26. *Fuṣūṣ*, p. 133.
27. *Ibid.*

possesses the *sirr al-qadar*, which discloses to him the very inner truth behind all the apparent phenomenal differentiation. Though this secret is God's own, He does sometimes share it with some of His creatures, as was already mentioned.

ʿUzayr appears next, abruptly, in the context of this discussion in order to serve as a concrete human example of Ibn ʿArabī's principle. And here we have a prophetic Qur'ānic component which will serve as 'mythological pole' round which everything else argued thus far revolves. Unlike the lone Qur'ānic verses which Ibn ʿArabī previously cited in exemplification of aspects of his views, here a Qur'ānic prophet, whose story is briefly referred to through a number of verses, becomes the main focus of the discussion. This, as we know, is what happens, in one way or another, in much of the *Fuṣūṣ*. And each prophetic story has its own unique order and meaning, consonant with the prophet's personality and life. The consequent type of *ḥikma* which each prophet exemplifies, and the relation of all this to the larger metaphysical truth, constitutes Ibn ʿArabi's central theme. Thus:

> Since ʿUzayr's request was made in the special way [of knowledge accorded only to prophets], he was censured—as tradition has related. Had ʿUzayr sought the sort of mystical unveiling [of the *sirr al-qadar*] which we have mentioned, perhaps he would not have been censured for having sought this [knowledge].[28]

Ibn ʿArabī's first mention of ʿUzayr here serves as a highly compressed and elliptical formulation of the long and subtle thesis which he develops in subsequent discussion. This thesis holds that ʿUzayr requested of God knowledge of *sirr al-qadar*, but this knowledge was inappropriate for him as a legislating prophet (*nabī musharriʿ*), for it may be attained only through the channel of 'taste'; and 'taste' cannot be attained by a legislating prophet *qua* legislating prophet, as he has in this mode no natural

28. *Ibid.*

capacity to receive it (*istiʿdād*). The order and organisation of creation, (*al-qaḍā' wa al-qadar*) do not provide for it. Thus ʿUzayr's request bring upon him God's chastisement. In the further explication of this point Ibn ʿArabī weaves a tapestry of prophetic Qur'ānic skeins with strands of his sufi metaphysics. And thus does ʿUzayr in his Qur'ānic exegetical persona become a focal point of divine *ḥikma*. Let us now see how this all works.

Ibn ʿArabī cites the first few lines of Qur'ān, 2:259 as the gist of the story of ʿUzayr who is presumed to be the subject of this verse. I say 'presumed', because, as said earlier, the verse itself does not mention ʿUzayr; rather, later exegesis often identified the person here as ʿUzayr. This verse comes in the context of the verses immediately preceding it which discuss various types of 'religious sceptics'. Ibn ʿArabī chooses particular passages of verse 259 for comment, presenting them in three parts: 1) The man's question: 'How will God revivify this [town] after its death?' 2) This question, says Ibn ʿArabī, 'necessitated an active answer, through which God responded, as in the words of God, Most High': "Thus did God put him to death for one hundred years, subsequently reviving him". 3) Then, says Ibn ʿArabī, after the revival of the man, God says to him: 'Look at the bones, how We will revive them and put flesh back on them'. The bones, according to most later exegesis, were either those of the man or those of the ass upon which he rode. As another, further, sign of God's power, the man is also told to see how his food had not rotted during his hundred-year death. After this display of divine power, the man finally says, 'I know God is omnipotent over everything'.[29] And this ends the verse.

In identifying the unnamed man as ʿUzayr, Ibn ʿArabī implicitly accepts the predominant exegetical tradition which so names him. This exegetical tradition also identifies the ruined

29. *Fuṣūṣ*, p. 133; Qur'ān, 2:259.

town as Jerusalem in the wake of Nebuchadnezzar's destruction. And sometimes exegesis chooses to comment on the nature of ʿUzayr's request and thereby to draw certain conclusions about his general personality and intent. In such instances, exegesis also sometimes sees ʿUzayr as a somewhat truculent and disobedient person, which was exemplified in his asking of the question in the verse. The reason this question was so inappropriate was, according to some exegetes, because it indicated religious doubt and shaky faith in ʿUzayr's heart or even, perhaps, signified an actual affront to God. Thus the widely-used Qur'ān commentary, *Tafsīr al-Jalālayn*, after identifying the unnamed man as ʿUzayr, says, '... the question, "How can God revivify this [town] after its death?", evinced an attitude of haughtiness here toward the power of God, Most High'.[30] Zamakhsharī in his *Tafsīr, al-Kashshāf*, says that '...the person passing by [the destroyed town] was an unbeliever in the [possibility of the town's] revivification ...',[31] and that, among others, one proof of this person's unbelief is his 'great scepticism, evinced in the phrase, "How [can God] revivify..."'.[32] Zamakhsharī identifies the man as 'ʿUzayr or al-Khiḍr'.[33] The term Zamakhsharī uses to characterise the man is *kāfir*, a strong word indeed, with respect to a person's religious belief.

One could multiply other, similar, examples from the mainstream Sunnī exegetical tradition, where ʿUzayr, understood as being the person referred to in Qur'ān 2: 259 (with the razed Jerusalem as the town, *qarya*), is seen being full of temerity in his questioning—if not worse. Ibn ʿArabī extends the range of this Qur'ānic exegesis, using the story of ʿUzayr as a foundation for making the sufi metaphysical point which is his thesis in the *ḥikma qadariyya* here. Slipping easily and almost imperceptibly

30. *Tafsīr al-Jalālayn*, p. 57.

31. Abū al-Qāsim al-Zamakhsharī, *al-Kashshāf*, p. 389.

32. *Ibid.*

33. For *al-Khiḍr*, see articles in the *Shorter Encyclopaedia of Islam* or the *Encyclopaedia of Islam*, new edition.

between the ʿUzayr of the Qur'ān and exegesis and his ʿUzayr of metaphysical principle, Ibn ʿArabī creates a framework of homologue and analogue between these two dimensions.

Thus, for the Qur'ān–*tafsīr* tradition, the man, ʿUzayr, passing the devastated town, asks an unseemly question. The question concerns knowledge of how God might put the place back together again and it implies, at most, a shaky belief in God's ability to do so. Consequently, as the Qur'ān itself tells it, divine chastisement is quick in coming. So far, this is a tale of exegesis which has an obvious didactic component. For Ibn ʿArabī, there is a sufi metaphysical correlative of this story which, in his view, in fact constitutes the story's deeper meaning.

In telling this correlative story, Ibn ʿArabī works within the main *framework story* of Qur'ān–*tafsīr*, thus maintaining the homology between the two, while constructing the analogue in content which makes the sufi metaphysical point. The man's unseemly question here is, then, simply extended and now involves knowledge of the nature of things in divine creation. And the unseemliness of the question, while still based on the Qur'ān–*tafsīr* point of human limitations (even of a prophet) and the need for faith in God's power, here takes on a metaphysical cast as Ibn ʿArabī argues that ʿUzayr, being a legislating prophet, could not possibly have been eligible for this highest knowledge. As prophet, he did not have the proper natural propensity, *istiʿdād*, in Ibn ʿArabī's sufi metaphysical vocabulary. Again, Ibn ʿArabī's whole point here is the metaphysical extension of the Qur'ān–*tafsīr* story: ʿUzayr, like everything, is a component of the metaphysical universe which is as it is through the metaphysical *qaḍā'* and *qadar*; it could not have been otherwise. Indeed, the highest knowledge of this, which ʿUzayr *illegitimately* sought, would have informed him of this very truth, had he been given it. ʿUzayr is here depersonalized, as his story is transformed into a metaphysical morality play: things are as they are because they are the extension of the perfect divinity. This is the metaphysics of the 'best of all possible worlds'.

From the Qur'ān-*tafsīr* side, ᶜUzayr's request was unseemly because it revealed a temerity and lack of proper faith in God which do not befit a prophet. From Ibn ᶜArabī's sufi metaphysical perspective, ᶜUzayr's request constituted a violation of the natural order which is itself coterminous with the immanent God. The moral component is here transformed into the metaphysical. And the *ḥikma qadariyya* associated with ᶜUzayr as the subject of this chapter is seen now, both morally and metaphysically, to be associated with him paradoxically by virtue of its absence rather than its presence. So the wisdom is defined in the process of explaining the reasons for its denial in this person.

THE ANCIENT RESONANCES IN THE QUR'ĀNIC MOTIF

In incorporating ᶜUzayr's story, which was certainly part of the 'Islamic canon' by his time, Ibn ᶜArabī was also incorporating ancient traditions whose origins and lines of development are to be found in a large body of interrelated Biblical, quasi-biblical, rabbinic, various Christian and Islamic, and perhaps other sources as well, including the great 'cosmopolitan' oral traditions of the Near East. The somewhat diverse and synthetic body of Near Eastern 'religious folklore', in Thackston's terms, is what I refer to here.[34] The Islamic identification in *tafsīr* of the unnamed man and the unnamed town with ᶜUzayr and Jerusalem, respectively, most likely derives from this tradition, in ways which we probably will never know. But, in my view,

34. W. M. Thackston, in the Introduction to his translation of al- Kisā'ī's *Qiṣaṣ al-Anbiyā'* (*Tales of the Prophets*), refers to the oral traditions of 'religious folklore which were not taken directly from the Old and New Testaments ...' (p. xiii). This is a genre, he says, '...which represents much of common Semitic legend and folklore ... and parallels to which can be traced back to the most ancient of Near Eastern mythological literature' (*ibid*). This genre has come down to us in a variety of garbs and guises of religion and language. It is the genre which I think is relevant here.

what is most important is recognising Islam's creative absorption of the elements, *making them Islamic.*[35]

Then, in identifying the prophetic Qur'ānic element here as being central to Ibn ʿArabī's sufi metaphysical thesis, one of necessity recognises that this element represents a very long line of religious culture stretching back into the pre-Muḥammadan past of other traditions. This was a synthesis of cultural interchange in which an Islamic tradition was 'influenced' by predecessors in the most profound manner, while at the same time being unique and creative in what it did with those 'influences'. Such a creative synthesis of cultural interchange was, I believe, relevant to Ibn ʿArabī's own method and understanding in the *Fuṣūṣ*, in particular, but also elsewhere. This is especially true with respect to his vision of a universal esoteric truth of metaphysics lying deep within the prophetic Qur'ānic tales which he interprets. The notion of a direct line of spiritual transmission from the most ancient layers of revealed truth was certainly central to this vision. In Ibn ʿArabī's treatment of ʿUzayr, this phenomenon is perhaps more explicit than in his discussions of some other prophets in the *Fuṣūṣ*, but certain other chapters of the present book do also obviously bear witness to the same principle, if not always with the same degree of explicitness.

35. I am not interested in tracing and finding the *specific antecedent* components of this Islamic ʿUzayr story which Ibn ʿArabī has incorporated; nor am I certain it would be possible. For in the world from whence this story came I imagine a body of sources so numerous with interconnections so extensive and a history so variegated that such ascription, though perhaps sometimes possible, could not often attain to any high degree of probability. 'Pure' lineages must be very hard to come by in this uncertain world of sources. This is Thackston's point, as cited above.

CHAPTER

9

The Wisdom of Divine Sovereignity in the Word of Zakariyyā

ZAKARIYYĀ IN THE QUR'ĀN

Zakariyyā's Qur'ānic story is to be found mainly in 3:35–41 and 19:1–16.[1] In both these chapters, the tale of Zakariyyā is essentially the same: very old, weak, childless and with a barren wife, Zakariyyā supplicates God asking for a child. God responds positively, granting the request in the form of a son, Yaḥyā, who is to be born to Zakariyyā and his wife.[2] Astonished and overwhelmed, Zakariyyā asks how this can be, '... when my wife is barren and I am so advanced in years?'[3] God answers, saying this is easy for Him. Zakariyyā then asks God for 'a sign' which might, presumably, explain His great efficacy. God grants this favour. The sign is that Zakariyyā will not speak to other people for three nights. Zakariyyā emerges from this solitude certain of

1. These are the two most extensive versions of the Qur'ānic story of Zakariyyā. The framework story in both accounts is much the same, with variations in some details. Zakariyyā is also mentioned briefly elsewhere in the Qur'ān, particularly in 8:85, where he is put in the company of John, Jesus and Elias who, according to the verse, were all 'just persons', and in 21:89–91, where there is a more concise version of the longer story found in *sūra* 3 and *sūra* 19. For a general discussion of Zakariyyā in Islam see: T. P. Hughes, *A Dictionary of Islam*, p. 699; and *Encyclopaedia of Islam*, (old edition), art. 'Zakariyyā', p. 1202.

2. Qur'ān, 3:39.

3. Qur'ān, 3:40.

God's favour and power and telling his people: 'Glorify God, morning and night'.[4]

The figure of Mary, mother of Jesus, is important as an associated motif in the Qur'ānic story of Zakariyyā. Where Zakariyyā appears, Mary is often present—not necessarily as an integral part of Zakariyyā's story, but rather as a figure linked in a certain way with Zakariyyā, and seemingly representing a principle which appears in the Qur'ān to characterise the lives of both Zakariyyā and Mary.[5] The immediate personal link between these two individuals in the Qur'ān lies in Zakariyyā's role as the protector and helper of Mary. The common dominant principle in both their Qur'ānic life—stories is that of God's efficacy, mercy and beneficence bestowed upon a most worthy and needy servant. For both of these figures, the divine favour is a son who is a prophet. In both cases, there is a sort of miraculous conception. With Mary, this is an explicit immaculate conception;[6] for Zakariyyā and his wife, there is a divinely aided conception.[7]

The Qur'ānic story of Zakariyyā is, then, a tale of God's power and mercy, His mercy being the main expression of His power. As the second verse of *sūra* Maryam, introducing Zakariyyā, says: 'This is an account of your Lord's mercy to His servant, Zakariyyā'.[8] This Qur'ānic theme of God's mercy is Ibn ʿArabī's foundation in his own discussion of God's power and mercy. And it is his own discussion which for him reveals the true meaning of the Qur'ānic story.[9]

The chapter on Zakariyyā in the *Fuṣūṣ* is titled 'The Wisdom of Divine Sovereignty (*ḥikma mālikiyya*) in The Word of

4. Qur'ān, 3:41.
5. Qur'ān, 3:37.
6. Qur'ān, 3:47; 19:20–21.
7. Qur'ān, 3:39; 19:8–9.
8. Qur'ān, 19:2.
9. Though Ibn ʿArabī's sufi metaphysics is rightly considered his most distinctive creation, the Qur'ān was usually his foundation and the main object of his attention in formulating the metaphysics.

Zakariyyā.'[10] This *ḥikma mālikiyya* of the title refers to God's absolute power and dominion over all, while within the body of the chapter the theme of God's mercy is the main focus, appearing prominently as the universal metaphysical manifestation and agent of His dominion. These are the essential features of the Qur'ānic Zakariyyā in Ibn ʿArabī's view, set out for elaboration and transformation in his particular understanding of the subject.

In developing his interpretation, Ibn ʿArabī organises his discussion according to three themes: 1) the metaphysics of God's mercy 2) the ethical implications of metaphysical mercy and 3) names and attributes, divine and otherwise, in the expression and manifestation of God's mercy.[11] A highly original explication and integration of these themes provides the fabric of Ibn ʿArabī's exegesis of the story of Zakariyyā.[12]

THE METAPHYSICS OF GOD'S MERCY

The metaphysics of God's mercy is formulated through a transformation of the idea of God's mercy found in the Qur'ān. In Ibn ʿArabī's construction, the Qur'ānic connotation of the mercy which a personal God bestows upon those among His creatures whom He chooses acquires a metaphysical face. Through this metaphysical transformation, Ibn ʿArabī universalises divine mercy in a unique and original way, thereby making it a cornerstone of his sufi thought.[13]

10. *Fuṣūṣ*, pp. 177–181.

11. Though Ibn ʿArabī does not explicitly declare this organisation of the chapter, it is constructed in this way.

12. I use the word 'exegesis' in this sense advisedly here and elsewhere. For though Ibn ʿArabī in the *Fuṣūṣ* did not intend an exegesis in the conventional *tafsīr* sense, his intention was clearly explication of a Qur'ānic truth through its integration with his own thought. As we know, again, the latter was for Ibn ʿArabī the complete truth of the former.

13. The transformation of divine mercy which Ibn ʿArabī effects here is a major theme in his thought. On this see T. Izutsu, *Sufism and Taoism*, pp. 116—140.

All have received God's mercy. This is Ibn ʿArabī's claim. It is a claim which is in part deeply Qur'ānic, in spirit and in letter.[14] Indeed, Ibn ʿArabī's opening words in this chapter are a paraphrase of a main Qur'ānic statement of God's universal application of His mercy. Ibn ʿArabī says: 'Know that the Mercy of God encompasses everything'.[15] The Qur'ān—in a close analogue—says in a first-person divine assertion: 'My mercy encompasses everything'.[16] Except for Ibn ʿArabī's formulation 'God's mercy' (*raḥmat Allāh*) in place of the Qur'ānic 'My mercy' (*raḥmatī*), the words used are exactly the same: '*wasiʿat kull shay*'' ('encompasses everything').

But this universal conception of God's mercy is in fact drawn from a broader Qur'ānic context which is a mix of mercy's universal application with a more restrictive notion, making God's mercy available only to those who obey Him. As Qur'ān, 7:156 says: 'He [God] said: My punishment I mete out to those whom I will and my mercy encompasses everything. Thus will I prescribe mercy for those who fear God, who pay alms and who believe in Our signs'.

Ibn ʿArabī, however, has referred only to God's universal mercy and not to the equally Qur'ānic notion of His mercy's restrictive application. Without entering into a discussion of the Qur'ān's 'true meaning' here, it is clear that for Ibn ʿArabī the restrictive and conditional giving of divine mercy is for this discussion irrelevant, though perhaps not untrue. But this apparent disregard of the Qur'ānic conditional mercy is for Ibn ʿArabī not simply part of his sufi predilection for a merciful God; rather, it is also necessary in making the profound transformation of God's mercy effected here. For the metaphysical mercy is nothing if not universal and this for Ibn ʿArabī as well reflected the deepest Qur'ānic truth. However, as we shall later see, in

14. But as we shall see, for Ibn ʿArabī this was the only *relevant meaning* of God's mercy in the Qur'ān.

15. *Fuṣūṣ*, p. 177.

16. Qur'ān, 7:156.

his final summing up, Ibn ʿArabī will bring together the conditional and universal aspect of the Qur'ānic divine mercy, thereby assuring its benefit to all.

Ibn ʿArabī next adds two words to his statement asserting God's universal mercy. These words are the true beginning of his sufi metaphysical rendering of God's mercy in his understanding of Zakariyyā in the Qur'ān. Grammatically adverbial, the two words carry a whole universe of meaning. The first word, '*wujūdan*', may be rendered as 'in its existence-giving nature', while the second, '*ḥukman*', may mean 'in its ontological governance'.[17] These two words thus adverbially qualify God's mercy, suggesting that the mercy in its universal application is both the agent of existence-giving (*wujūdan*) and the process whereby existence-giving is governed (*ḥukman*).[18] In Ibn ʿArabī's redefinition, then, all beings have received mercy *because they exist*, while God's mercy is itself existence or being (*wujūd*). Thus, as mercy is God's overarching attribute for Ibn ʿArabī (exoterically and esoterically), and God is totally identified with it, he later will say 'God is mercy'.[19]

Comprised of nine words in the Arabic original, Ibn ʿArabī's opening statement is his sufi metaphysical gloss on the Qur'ānic idea of God's mercy. From these words, Qur'ānic and metaphysical as one, Ibn ʿArabī develops his particular conception of the universal expression and application of God's mercy. In this development of an idea, Ibn ʿArabī introduces a discussion of God's mercy as prior and superior to His wrath[20]—through the ontological process which is the new meaning of his redefined mercy.[21] Following his opening statement, Ibn ʿArabī says:

17. These words in their nominal forms, *wujūd* (existence, being) and *ḥukm* (determinative or governing force in the ontological process), are key terms in Ibn ʿArabī's thought.

18. It is through these two words that Ibn ʿArabī's transformation of God's mercy is effected

19. *Fuṣūṣ*, p. 179.

20. *Fuṣūṣ*, p. 177.

21. *Ibid.*

'... and [likewise know] that the existence of [His] wrath derives from God's mercy toward His wrath'.[22] The priority and domination of God's mercy over His wrath means here that wrath, like all else, gains its existence from mercy. God as Mercy, rather than wrath, is a notion further transformed from the personal discourse of conventional meaning to Ibn ʿArabī's sufi metaphysical realm. Ibn ʿArabī makes this clear, saying, 'Thus the mercy [of God] precedes His wrath; that is, the connection (*nisba*) of mercy to Him precedes the connection of wrath to Him'.[23] The *nisba* terminology exemplifies the metaphysical dimension of the discussion. The term *nisba* is itself drawn from Ibn ʿArabī's metaphysical vocabulary, as were the qualifiers *wujūdan* and *ḥukman* in his opening statement. It is this 'cushion' of his sufi metaphysical discourse which indicates that Ibn ʿArabī's discussion of God's mercy is different from more usual treatment of the subject. 'Usual' here might mean the language of the Qur'ān itself and post-Qur'ānic religious literature and thought, such as *ḥadīth, tafsīr, kalām* and non-metaphysical, pietistic sufism, where God's mercy essentially means a personal beneficence from Creator to creature.[24]

Ibn ʿArabī then introduces his general metaphysical notion of the 'fixed essences' (*al-aʿyān al-thābita*)[25] which are things in pure form, awaiting their 'descent' into conditional being in the phenomenal world. These essences, says Ibn ʿArabī, in poetic metaphor, 'seek' and 'desire' their phenomenal existence; and

22. *Ibid.*

23. *Ibid.*

24. This is by no means to imply that these various types of thought necessarily have more in common in their conception of God's mercy than what is stated here. They may not. But essential to all of them is God's mercy as something *personal.*

25. *Fuṣūṣ*, p. 177. Generally for Ibn ʿArabī, the *aʿyān thābita* remain in their state of potentiality (*thubūt*) which is the realm of non-existence (*ʿadam*); when they pass over into the realm of phenomenal (conditional) being (*wujūd muqayyad*), they adopt that form which constitutes a new and different state. For a detailed survey of the subject, see: Suʿād al-Ḥakīm, *al-Muʿjam al-Ṣūfī*, pp. 831–839.

the mercy then fulfils that desire.[26] As there is an essence (ᶜ*ayn*) for every thing (*shay'*), the mercy, as 'existentiating force', of necessity touches everything. In Ibn ᶜArabī's words:

> Since for every essence there is an existence which it seeks from God, consequently God's mercy encompasses every essence. Thus God, through His mercy, by which He is merciful to an essence, receives that essence's desire for its [phenomenal] existence. Then He creates it. We say, therefore, that God's mercy encompasses everything, in its existence-giving nature and in its ontological governance' (*wujūdan wa-ḥukman*).[27]

This explanation, clarifies, among other things, how God's mercy, *as agent of being*, is, by virtue of that characteristic, more important than and prior to God's wrath, since the wrath—like all other things—is brought into being by the mercy and consequently depends on it.

At first glance, a binary structure seems implied here: mercy as metaphysics and mercy as personal favour; God as the personal, Qur'ānic God, and God as Principle of Being. Which God and which mercy now take pride of place? The personal or the metaphysical? As elsewhere, Ibn ᶜArabī's formulations leave no doubt as to the answer: any distinction between the two becomes a moot point.[28] They are as one—though this one must now be seen from a perspective provided by the metaphysical. The 'addition' of the metaphysical to the personal irrevocably changes the personal and establishes a new realm of meaning and a new way of discussing the issue. Once the transcendent core of a Qur'ānic or traditional concept has been thus determined and invoked one cannot again completely restore its full exoteric meaning. The shift in perspective must

26. *Ibid.*

27. *Ibid.*

28. As with most issues of religious thought, here too for Ibn ᶜArabī the either/or formulation serves as a basis for its own resolution in some formulation that transcends the apparent contradiction.

remain.[29] Ibn ʿArabī next explores the meaning of this shift in its ethical implications and, later, in the perspective of God's (and other) names and attributes. Thus will his initial thesis be brought to fruition and its full message made explicit.

THE ETHICAL IMPLICATIONS OF METAPHYSICAL MERCY

Islam as an 'ethical religion' is, in its own view, a system expressing a divine order and organisation for human life on this earth, individual and communal, linked to salvation in the next world. From the Qur'ān onwards, the very rationale of human existence in this world (*al-dunyā*) is as preparation for life in the next (*al-ākhira*). The whole foundation of the revealed principles and laws for human life, individual and collective, is to be found in the scheme of the Day of Judgment (*al-sāʿa, yawm al-qiyāma, yawm al-dīn*), punishment and reward.[30] Given the centrality of this theme in Islamic thought, the question whether God was more merciful than wrathful obviously was of great import.[31]

Sufism in general took a pronounced stand in favour of God as essentially merciful.[32] Prior to Ibn ʿArabī, however, in this as in so many other matters, the God–Man relationship was mainly understood in sufism in more personal and pietistic terms. Mercy, God's most prominent characteristic for much of sufism, was the gift of a loving God to His beloved creatures. The depth of mystical experience often both confirmed and made possible

29. The new perspective in fact becomes the criterion of thought for other issues.

30. For a good discussion of these issues, see: T. Izutsu, *The Structure of the Ethical Terms in the Qur'ān.*

31. Although many different opinions were expressed on this matter, the central view—if one can speak in such terms—was that God's mercy and wrath coexisted in a sort of balance; and that God's mercy was related to the servant's obedient behaviour for which mercy was given. See Da'ūd Rahbar, *God of Justice: A Study in the Ethical Doctrine of the Qur'ān*, p. 226 and T. Izutsu, *The Structure of Ethical Terms in the Qur'ān, passim.*

32. See, *e.g.*, A. Schimmel, *Mystical Dimensions of Islam, passim.*

this truth. And the mystical meaning of God's mercy often swelled into a monolith of divine merciful comportment, with the God of mercy totally negating and effacing the God of wrath. In order to make the point, sufism sometimes even drew it out to a paradoxical—if not antinomian—extreme. Abū Yazīd al-Bisṭāmī, for example, whose *shaṭahāt* or 'theopathic utterances', pushed the conventions of Islamic doctrine to their outer limit, was reported to have chastised God for presuming to punish any of His creatures and claimed for himself the power to intercede for all of mankind on Judgement Day. In this way only would God close the gates of Hell and ensure that all would be saved.[33]

Though not all of sufism traded in such notions, the theme of the overarching divine mercy was central. Divine forgiveness and love outweighed all. One day all would receive God's mercy and all would be saved.[34] Though by no means *automatic*, because of conventional doctrinal stipulations to the contrary, God's bestowing of mercy was still in this view somehow *universal*. For though still within the conventional referential context of trial, punishment and reward, the sufi perspective on these matters usually saw God's mercy somehow as overcoming all, including His wrath. With Ibn ʿArabī, convention was shifted somewhat further, as the move to the metaphysical realm was effected. Here, the sufi universalisation of God's mercy was extended beyond the realm of the individual and personal, becoming synonymous with being itself and, thereby, in Ibn ʿArabī's terms, with God Himself.

Ibn ʿArabī raises the ethical issue by way of extending his explication of God's mercy as metaphysical process. He carries his logic here to its conclusion in asserting that the mercy touches all things, including even God's wrath and His names.[35] Having achieved this, Ibn ʿArabī then says that:

33. See, M. ʿAbdur Rabb, *The Life, Thought and Historical Importance of Abū Yazīd al-Bisṭāmī*, pp. 160–163.

34. See, *e.g.*, R. Nicholson, *Studies in Islamic Mysticism*, pp. 1–149.

35. *Fuṣūṣ*, pp. 177–178.

> Within mercy's application there is no consideration of achieving any goal; nor is there consideration of what is "suitable by nature". Rather, the "suitable" and the "unsuitable", all of it, is touched by divine mercy, in mercy's giving of existence... Thus everything mercy has remembered is "happy"—and there is nothing it has not remembered. Every existing thing, has, then, been touched by mercy.[36]

With this ontological universalisation of mercy's function, Ibn ᶜArabī has provided a foundation in ethics for his next move in the transformation of mercy from the personal to the metaphysical realm. For God's metaphysical mercy has now been shown to be structurally and ineluctably related to the ethical. Thus:

> Oh friend, do not shrink from understanding what we have said in relation to your thoughts concerning those who are suffering and what you believe concerning the pains [of hell] in the world to come—pains which [seemingly] provide no respite from suffering to those on whom they are inflicted. Know first, then, that mercy is universal in its mode of bringing [things] into being. Through mercy to the pains [of those suffering] the pains [themselves] are brought into being.[37]

Even the afflictions of those punished in hell, then, are the object of God's mercy—because the afflictions 'exist'. Thus if existence, being (*wujūd*), is the main criterion in divine mercy's nature and application, and if the application of mercy as being is of necessity universal, then what indeed are we to think of the torments of those in hell? And how are we to see the conventional standards and systems of commands and prohibitions, rewards and punishments, with their resolution in the world to come, in heaven and in hell?

Hell is real but 'irrelevant' from Ibn ᶜArabī's new perspective. For even if one is there and suffering, one is still the recipient

36. *Fuṣūṣ*, p. 177.
37. *Fuṣūṣ*, p. 178.

of God's mercy. Suffering and punishment have been redefined, so that the sting has been taken out of them. Ibn ʿArabī has not mentioned paradise and reward, for though his understanding of them would also not be a wholly conventional one, the ethical crux for him is in the issue of punishment in hell. A certain conventional sufi notion of God's mercy can obviously take the force out of the fear of hell, but Ibn ʿArabī's transformed metaphysical mercy virtually neutralises it. Heaven and hell have been made 'equal' with Ibn ʿArabī's great shift into mercy's ontological meaning.[38]

Both heaven and hell are now aspects of God's ontological mercy—like all created things. And—to make the point more sharply—even the afflictions felt by the denizens of hell are themselves acts ontologically of divine mercy. We have come full circle here in Ibn ʿArabī's transformation of God's mercy—and thereby of His wrath. This transformation of mercy creates a superficial exoteric paradox of the first order: the 'sameness' of His mercy and His wrath. How can the seeming intrinsic and natural *opposition* of God's mercy and His wrath be reduced to the *sameness* implied in Ibn ʿArabī's claim that the sufferings in hell are in fact the application and expression of divine mercy? The mercy as ontological principle resolves and reveals the inconsequential and putative nature of the 'paradox'. To those who 'know'—the gnostic adepts—this is what they imagine when they ask God for mercy. For others, the matter remains in its superficial, literal formulation.[39]

Ibn ʿArabī asserts further that the 'twofold' nature of God's mercy—the conventional and the metaphysical—has its correlative in a corresponding 'two-tier' human understanding of mercy. Thus the deep metaphysical mercy ('the essential', *bi'l-dhāt*)[40] is

38. Sometimes Ibn ʿĀrabī virtually denies the literal existence of hell and views it as a metaphor for the state of spiritual impoverishment. See, *e.g.*, the chapter on Hūd in this book.

39. *Fuṣūṣ*, p. 178.

40. *Ibid.*

known to be the true mercy by the *ahl al-kashf*[41] (gnostics), while the conventional, personal mercy is that which the 'unenlightened', still-veiled people, *al-maḥjūbūn*,[42] think is the true mercy. The veiled folk, then, simply, 'ask God to be merciful to them in their belief....' But *ahl al-kashf* '... ask mercy *to inhere in them*...'[43].

The veiled folk, then, in their limitation seek the personal mercy of a personal God and are unaware of the deeper truth of their pleas and imprecations. For there is a difference between asking the mercy *to inhere in one* and asking God *to be merciful to one*. In the former case, one is (rhetorically, in the formulation here) seeking or acknowledging the occurrence of a metaphysical process. Ibn ʿArabī's language clearly indicates this: the enlightened folk want mercy to inhere in them (*an taqūma bihim*). In other Islamic intellectual contexts, forms of the verb *qāma bi* were commonly used to denote the metaphysical process of an attribute inhering in a substance.[44] A conventional pious cry for divine mercy would, of course, not normally be couched in such abstract language. It would, rather, be done in exactly the manner which Ibn ʿArabī characterised as the way of the veiled folk: asking God *personally* to be merciful to them. Here the language of pious plea is the usual one. But its very formulation is a sign of the epistemological incompleteness and spiritual inadequacy of the one who voices it. Such pleas, though profoundly spiritual, and part of the fabric of tradition, for Ibn ʿArabī bespeak also an ignorance of the reality one is presumably addressing. For though people may say, 'Oh God, be merciful to us', in reality, says Ibn ʿArabī, 'Nothing is merciful to them except the mercy's inhering in them (*wa-lā yarḥamuhum*

41. *Ibid.*

42. *Ibid.*

43. *Ibid.*

44. As is often the case with Ibn ʿĀrabī, here too his borrowing of ideas and methods from other Islamic sciences renders the borrowed item suggestive in its former sense while at the same time being integrated in Ibn ʿĀrabī's own system.

illā qiyām al-raḥma bihim)'.[45] Those who know this may indeed even beseech God for His mercy and this is not at all misplaced; for they know the reality behind their words. But for the veiled folk, their words and the pious emotion which gave rise to them are the full reality. Whatever the feelings and phrases of the veiled folk, however, the truth is that metaphysical mercy already inheres in them, as it does in everything else. Not knowing this, they are spirituality stunted and their ethical understanding, in particular, is rendered shallow.

Though the metaphysical mercy makes 'inadequate' the conventional notion of God's mercy and wrath and the whole ethical framework surrounding them, it does not necessarily follow from this that there is an implicit true antinomianism here. For Ibn ʿArabī is not in any sense rejecting the traditional ethics, in behaviour or in conception, but he is, rather, placing it in a perspective which must radically alter one's understanding of it. Doing the good and avoiding doing the bad, as the Law dictates, remains central and constant for Ibn ʿArabī; but his understanding of this is subsumed in the truth of universal divine mercy. In the baldest formulation, then, whatever their behaviour, all will be 'saved'. Here the intertwining of the traditional ethical and Ibn ʿArabī's sufi metaphysical outlooks is total. Each appears entangled with and reflecting the other. The focal point is in the Qur'ānic term *raḥma* itself, which in its metaphysical transformation still resonates with traditional meanings. Ibn ʿArabī puts a final gloss on the issue at the end of his discussion of the third aspect of mercy: names and attributes.

NAMES, ATTRIBUTES AND MERCY

Names and attributes, naming and attributing, figure prominently in Ibn ʿArabī's discussion of God's mercy. As elsewhere in Ibn ʿArabī's thought, in general, and in the *Fuṣūṣ*, in particular, the

45. *Fuṣūṣ*, p. 178.

issue of names and attributes is intrinsically related to the over-arching theme of the remote God and the manifest God. And as in other discussions of this issue, here also Ibn ʿArabī's purpose is to reveal the ultimate identity of God and man in the universal principle of absolute being (*al-wujūd al-muṭlaq*). But because of divine mercy's unique position in the traditional Islamic system of values and concepts, especially in its ethical significance, its metaphysical role here is correspondingly great. Explicating God's mercy in the realm of the names and attributes provides Ibn ʿArabī with another focus for conveying this significance. Here we shall find Ibn ʿArabī's ultimate answer to the ethical question which arose from his metaphysical rendering of God's mercy.

Having established this metaphysical redefining of God's mercy at the outset, as well as raising the derivative ethical questions, Ibn ʿArabī embarks on a long, sometimes obscurantist, and often disjointed treatment of names and attributes, in connection with God's mercy. His argument utilises concepts, terms and doctrine from the Islamic theological tradition. The main thrust of Ibn ʿArabī's thought here concerns the ways in which names (*asmā'*) and attributes (*ṣifāt*) are related to the beings and things which are defined by them. Though his obvious focus is on God's and man's relationship, especially with regard to mercy, and particularly God's designation as Merciful and Compassionate (*al-Raḥmān, al-Raḥīm*), Ibn ʿArabī first explores more general approaches to the issue. Echoing the theories of certain Muʿtazilī theologians, in particular in their discussion of the divine attributes (*ṣifāt Allāh*), Ibn ʿArabī argues that names and attributes do not exist as discrete entities attached to the things characterised by them. They are, rather, 'relational' (*nisab*) and the fact of someone's being described as, for example, 'knowing', because of the inhering of knowledge in that individual, is really a 'modal condition' or 'state' (*ḥāl*) of that one.[46]

46. *Fuṣūṣ*, p. 179. For a good history and discussion of the general issue see: R.M. Frank, *Beings and their Attributes: The Teachings of the Baṣrian School of the Muʿtazila in the Classical Period.*

If this be the general case, and on this example, then Ibn ʿArabī can say that mercy possesses a 'determinative force' (*ḥukm*).[47] This means mercy, by inhering in something, renders that thing merciful (*rāḥim*) as well as making it the recipient of mercy (*marḥūm*), just as having knowledge (*ʿilm*) inhere in one makes one knowledgeable (*ʿālim*).[48] Thus mercy's inhering in something means that thing is 'merciful' as well as 'mercy-full', *i.e.*, it evinces the active, giving, characteristic of mercy, as well as being the object or passive recipient of mercy. Also, the 'mechanism' of mercy, or any other attribute, inhering in something (*i.e.*, in God or in man) is, through the *ḥāl*, again 'modal' rather than 'positional'. For in the case of God, it is clear 'He is not a locus for created things' (*laysa bi-maḥall li'l-ḥawādith*).[49] Nor is God 'a locus for the creation of mercy [in the recipient of it]' (*fa-laysa bi-maḥall li-ījād al-raḥma fīhi*).[50] This sort of language, says Ibn ʿArabī, is characteristic of those discursive theologians who see the naming/attributing phenomenon as one in which some kind of entity—the attribute—is 'placed' in a substance (locus, *maḥall*). This cannot be true of God, either in His mercy-giving or in His being intrinsically merciful; nor could it be true for man as 'mercy-full', for the attributing process works here as it does universally.[51] Thus 'God is compassionate (*Raḥīm*) by virtue of the mercy's inhering in Him. It may, consequently, be affirmed that God is in fact Mercy (*annahu ʿayn al-raḥma*)'.[52] The attribute and its locus, then, are as one; the locus reflecting the attribute—indeed, *being the attribute*, as an aspect of its nature.[53]

47. For various aspects of Ibn ʿĀrabī's use of *ḥukm*, see W. Chittick, *The Sufi Path of Knowledge*, pages 8, 39, 48.

48. *Fuṣūṣ*, pp. 178–180.

49. *Fuṣūṣ*, p. 179.

50. *Ibid.*

51. *Ibid.*

52. *Ibid.*

53. *Ibid.*

These are the bare bones of Ibn ʿArabī's highly complex argument here concerning names and attributes. What does it mean for his central thesis on God's mercy as absolute being (*wujūd muṭlaq*)? Most prominently, it means that if God is mercy, and mercy, redefined as absolute being, is all creation, then creation is identified with God. Ibn ʿArabī, in a slightly different formulation earlier, alluded to this where he says, 'Everyone whom Mercy has remembered has thereby become merciful (*rāḥim*).'[54] This is striking. For not only is mercy's recipient *marḥūm* the object of Mercy, but it is merciful as well—like God, who is merciful because mercy is an attribute of His. God's creation is, then, truly in His own image. For if having mercy means one is merciful, then all creatures are merciful—not just God. And if mercy is now transformed absolute being, then being merciful (*i.e.*, having mercy) is to be part of that absolute being. And if God is mercy, *i.e.*, absolute being, then all the merciful (all creation) are God. God is all, and all are God. And here the question of the remote essential God and the manifest God of the names would seem to have been resolved, in their reduction to absolute being.[55] Ibn ʿArabī elaborates more on this point toward the end of the chapter, in his final clarification of the ethical issue.

With respect to the whole range of God's names and attributes, Ibn ʿArabī voices agreement with the sufi thinker Abū'l-Qāsim b. Qasī.[56] In addition to the determinative force of names and attributes (*ḥukm*) being expressed modally in their relation to the thing which they define, Ibn ʿArabī transmits from al-Qasī the notion that 'all the names indicate one essence.'[57] Here, Ibn ʿArabī can resolve the one/many conundrum with respect to God, by reducing the *many* to the *one*. Mercy plays a special role here as well, for the notion that each name is formally

54. *Ibid.*
55. *Ibid.*
56. *Fuṣūṣ*, p. 180. Abū'l-Qāsim b. Qasī, a twelfth-century sufi.
57. *Ibid.*

distinguished by some special quality of God which sets it apart from all the others would still seem to imply some difficulty in reducing the *many* to the *one*. But in Ibn ʿArabī's view, God's mercy, having its special status, may be sought and addressed *through any divine name*—even those which, on the face of it, would appear to have meanings opposed to, or radically different from, mercy. For example, if one seeks mercy from God in his role as '*al-Muntaqim*', the Retributive, this is quite in order, because God's attribute of retribution is (like all things) subsumed under mercy and is thereby ultimately reducible to mercy—at least to mercy *as absolute being*.[58] And here the reduction of the names to one essence is most profoundly expressed in its ontological meaning. Mercy subsumes and absorbs all the other attributes. Thus God's mercy in its metaphysical mode is absolute being, and so too are all the other divine names and attributes absolute being in their reduction to the one divine essence which is coterminous with His mercy.

A RETURN TO THE ETHICAL

From this special treatment of the issue of names and attributes, Ibn ʿArabī concludes the chapter on God's mercy exemplified in Zakariyyā's tale with a return to the ethical aspect. This return to the ethical here is not arbitrary on Ibn ʿArabī's part. Indeed, in making this shift his language itself is indicative of that: The return is indicated by the word '*thumma*', 'and again'.[59] The discussion will indeed affirm the ineluctable nature of the ethical conclusion to be drawn from Ibn ʿArabī's metaphysical transformation of God's mercy and the consequent view of the ethical as another side of the God/Man metaphysical unity.

The final form of Ibn ʿArabī's ethical discussion here recapitulates his earlier version of it as a twofold nature for mercy:

58. *Fuṣūṣ*, pp. 179–180.
59. *Fuṣūṣ*, p. 180.

the personal, conventional mercy of a personal God and mercy as absolute being (*wujūd muṭlaq*) and the process by which that being brings all things into conditional existence (*wujūd muqayyad*). In the earlier discussion, Ibn ʿArabī indicated that for those who 'know' (*al-ʿārifūn, ahl al-kashf*), the torments of hell may not be exactly as exoteric hearsay would have it. For God's mercy, as the process of being, is universal, touching even the pains of hell themselves. It is the unenlightened who are ignorant of this truth. But the real, though implicit, problem here is left unresolved: if God's mercy is in truth universal being and if in the nature of things all are of necessity touched by that being—even the 'damned'—then what of the requirements of the Law? If all are ultimately reduced to a total identity with God, and He is redefined as absolute being, and the source of conditional being, and His mercy—among all His other attributes—is rendered in the same way (creating a total identification of God and His mercy), then what place, if any, is left for the importance of what His servants do? This was, after all, the main concern in the established Islamic religious–legal traditions.

Ibn ʿArabī explicitly—though without giving all away—thus addresses the issue: God's Mercy may be attained in two ways, that of meeting the divinely enjoined ethical–legal obligations, *ṭarīq al-wujūb*, and that of divine grace, *ṭarīq al-imtinān al-ilāhī*, 'which is not connected with any [human] action'.[60] We have the same personal and metaphysical mercy in this formulation as earlier, called respectively there, 'mercy through asking' (*bi'l-su'āl*) and 'essential mercy' (*bi'l-dhāt*). But here Ibn ʿArabī will go beyond his earlier words, by putting the two types of mercy in a specific Qur'ānic and *ḥadīth* context. This both serves to validate Ibn ʿArabī's dichotomy of mercy in Islamic traditional terms and proposes an answer to the ethical question. The ethical answer, stated most succinctly in a *ḥadīth*, is in turn

60. *Ibid.*

supported by Ibn ʿArabī's Qur'ānic validation of the twofold mercy.

The human attainment of God's mercy through good acts which bring mercy as their reward (*ṭarīq al-wujūb*) is exemplified, says Ibn ʿArabī, in the passage in 7:156 where God says: 'I will give mercy to those who are God-fearing and who give alms.'[61] This is a conception of a personal God bestowing a personal boon of mercy on those of His creatures who obey Him through proper comportment. Human acts have pride of place here. One's destiny is to a great extent in one's own hands. This is a foundation of the conventional Islamic worldview, providing the rationale for Islam's behavioural demands.

The universalisation of God's mercy (*ṭarīq al-imtinān al-ilāhī*), which for Ibn ʿArabī means the metaphysical mercy as absolute being, he also finds in 7:156, from which he cites the passage: 'My mercy encompasses everything.'[62] Ibn ʿArabī says that this way of attaining God's mercy 'is not connected with any [human] action' (*la yaqtarinu bihi ʿamal*).[63] This is also exemplified for him in another Qur'ānic passage, 48:2, which Ibn ʿArabī cites for this purpose: 'In order that God might forgive you your sins, past and future.'[64]

If, then, Ibn ʿArabī's initial distinction between mercy which is effective (*lahā athr*) through supplication or human entreaty (*bi'l-su'āl*) and that which works 'essentially' (*bi'l-dhāt*), as metaphysical process, is reflected and paralleled here in his final formulation of mercy which is attained (*tunāl*) by way of 'obligation' (required acts, *wujūb*) and 'divine grace' (metaphysically, *al-imtinān al-ilāhī*), one may say further that these are obviously, in effect, the 'same' categories. There are, however, some striking differences. Earlier, Ibn ʿArabī explained how these ways worked and what they meant, raising the ethical issue in

61. *Ibid.*
62. *Ibid.*
63. *Ibid.*
64. *Ibid.*

this context, but not attempting in any way to resolve it. Also, though the Qur'ānic and traditional issues obviously loomed large, Ibn ᶜArabī did not at that point provide explicit textual reference and connections. He also gave the impression that those who sought God's mercy in the conventional way were somehow benighted. Here it is now different. The new formulation asserts, *in Qur'ānic words*, first that those who behave as commanded *will* reap the reward of God's mercy. This is mercy attained through obligation, whereas its original counterpart, mercy having its influence through supplication, was portrayed as the mistaken way of the ignorant, unenlightened folk who do not understand that in any case God's metaphysical mercy has already visited them. The position has thus been profoundly refined. For the 'unenlightened' now *do* receive God's mercy for their meritorious acts. This way—enjoined in the Qur'ān—*does* yield results, but in a conventional manner. By implication, this 'ordinary' mercy does exist. But so does the metaphysical mercy, on the other hand, which Ibn ᶜArabī also sees in 7:156: 'My mercy encompasses everything.' Unlike the rather stark contrast drawn initially between the two types of mercy and their recipients, Ibn ᶜArabī's formulation here seems to provide a link which softens this division. Further, although the conventional mercy in Qur'ān, 7:156 is attained by the morally upright, the broader context for 7:156, which is found in 7:155, where Mūsā alleges God's hand to be present in the acts of the wrongdoers, does imply that perhaps mercy is indeed deserved by all, 'good' and 'bad'.[65] For though the Qur'ān is not a systematic theological treatise—being rather a text expressing a range of

65. In 7:155 we have the story of Mūsā and his followers who in their disobedience provoked God. God, in turn, in His mercy, withheld from them the punishment of destruction. This passage is thick with themes of theodicy. Perhaps most important for our concerns in this context is Mūsā's peroration before God:

> '... Will you annihilate us because of what the impudent among us have done? But certainly this is only Your trial through which You lead astray those whom You will and guide those whom You will. You are our friend.

interwoven layered motifs—implicit intellectual frameworks are obviously present. One which is certainly present in 7:155 is the 'opposition' between God's ability to determine his servants' acts and His just nature which logically must preclude His punishing of those servants who do wrong at His direction. Thus here, 7:156, 'My mercy encompasses everything', may well resolve the 'contradiction' without, in systematic fashion, explaining exactly how this might occur. The Qur'ānic ideas are so layered here that they could provide such a resolution, if it should be sought. Ibn ʿArabī would, then, seem to have found a specific Qur'ānic 'proof-text' (and context) for his main assertion of the universal giving of divine mercy, *whether seen exoterically or esoterically*. Indeed, in Ibn ʿArabī's eyes that distinction may now have been effaced. For if God's mercy may be shown to have universal presence *according to the Qur'ān*, then its esoteric—metaphysical—universal dimension, as argued here, may in consequence be seen as being on a Qur'ānic continuum. The metaphysical would in this case be seen in the Qur'ān as God's mercy which encompasses everything—an implicit reference already made by Ibn ʿArabī at the outset.

The connection between these 'two truths' is integral and organic—indeed, ideally, as mentioned earlier, there is for Ibn ʿArabī only one truth, certainly for the spiritually adept. Even the most literalistic reading of the Qur'ān in those verses which Ibn ʿArabī adduces here does reveal at the least a 'creative ambiguity' between God's strict and narrow giving of mercy to those who 'deserve' it and His universal bestowal of mercy. Ibn ʿArabī

> Forgive us and be merciful to us. You are the best of the forgiving. Ordain for us good in this world and the next. We turn toward You'.

Mūsā, then, affirms God's power to exercise mercy or wrath and asks Him for mercy. At the same time, Mūsā says that the misbehaviour of his companions was only God's trial '...through which You lead astray those whom You will'. The logic of Mūsā's statements is that God may hold people responsible for their acts and thereby reward or punish them as the case may be, while He also, in some way, determines those acts.

conveys this very well in adducing two additional 'proof-texts', as his concluding words. The first is Qur'ānic, from 48:2: 'In order that God might forgive you your sins, past and present'; and the second, even more directly to the point, is the well-known *ḥadīth qudsī*, 'Do what you will, God has already forgiven you.'[66] For what is quite clear now is that God's mercy, as Zakariyyā and Maryam knew it, and as it is expressed universally through God's dominion over all, is for Ibn ʿArabī universal because of its metaphysical meaning. Here all possible Qur'ānic understandings of God's mercy come together in ontological unity.

66. Aḥmad b. Hanbal, *Musnad*, Volume 2, p. 492.

CHAPTER

10

The Wisdom of Singularity in the Word of Muḥammad

The chapter on Muḥammad is the final chapter in the *Fuṣūṣ*. This placement obviously reflects Ibn ʿArabī's assumption of the finality of Muḥammad's prophecy. The idea that no prophet would come after the Prophet of Islam was a received truth for Muslims. Based on references in the Qur'ān to Muḥammad as 'seal of the prophets', this doctrine foreclosed the possibility of further prophets and prophecy subsequent to Muḥammad.[1] The 'singularity' associated with Muḥammad's particular wisdom in Ibn ʿArabī's title for this chapter,[2] as well as the chapter's position in the *Fuṣūṣ*, thus provides an implicit framework of traditional veneration toward the Prophet. Within this, Ibn ʿArabī interprets the singularity of Muḥammad from his own particular perspective.

SINGULARITY AND TRIPLICITY

Ibn ʿArabī begins by couching Muḥammad's singularity in terms which situate the Prophet in a certain broad context: 'His wisdom is singularity, because he is the most perfect being in this human species. Thus was everything begun with him and thus was it sealed. Indeed, Muḥammad was already a prophet when Ādam was still between water and clay; and he

1. Qur'ān, 33:40.

2. The term IbnʿArabī uses is *ḥikma fardiyya*, which I have rendered as 'the wisdom of singularity'. *Fuṣūṣ*, pp. 214–226.

then, through his elemental nature, became the seal of the prophets'.[3]

Here is a Prophet Muḥammad who is singular in his nature and the 'seal of the prophets'—ideas which, again, are central within the realm of the traditional portrayal of Islam's Messenger—but Ibn ᶜArabī's Muḥammad is also 'the most perfect being in this human species'.[4] Everything 'was begun with him and thus was it sealed'.[5] His prophethood was already established when Ādam—progenitor of humanity and himself a prophet—'was still between water and clay' (not yet even fully-formed). And then, through his 'elemental nature' (*al-nash'a al-ᶜunṣuriyya*) did he become 'seal of the prophets'.[6] All of this constitutes some of the core features of Ibn ᶜArabī's gloss on the explicit Muḥammad of Qur'ān and tradition, a gloss which already has distinctly metaphysical overtones infused with metaphysical meaning: as the most perfect being (*mawjūd*), Muḥammad is the Perfect Man (*al-insān al-kāmil*). This for Ibn ᶜArabī renders the Prophet of Islam a manifestation of metaphysical unity. Embodying such ontological significance, Muḥammad is the beginning and the end, the circle of creation and existence being represented in him. Thus was he already a prophet when Ādam was not yet fully formed. Muḥammad's ontological status has here situated him within an *eternal* and a-temporal dimension. Like all manifestations of *al-insān al-kāmil*, Muḥammad transcends the phenomenal world. His appearance in time constitutes an embodiment of the eternal. Thus did Muḥammad become 'seal of the prophets' in this world 'through his elemental nature'.[7] This 'elemental nature'—the composite

3. *Fuṣūṣ*, p. 214. The post-Qur'ānic legendary tradition concerning Ādam contains numerous stories about his creation from clay and other compounds over a long period of time. See the article 'Ādam' in the *Encyclopaedia of Islam*, new edition, Vol. I, pp. 176–179.

4. *Fuṣūṣ*, p. 214.

5. *Ibid.*

6. *Ibid.*

7. *Ibid.*

of physical elements, *ᶜunsurī*—provides the 'bodily form', the 'shell' containing the eternal presence which has come into this world. The Qur'ānic and traditional singularity and primacy of Islam's Prophet over all others has, then, been given Ibn ᶜArabī's special interpretation.[8] This 'metaphysical Muḥammad' serves as the overriding characteristic of the Prophet which Ibn ᶜArabī will elucidate in a tripartite explication. And here, Muḥammad's religious significance is exemplified in a unique way.

THREENESS

Ibn ᶜArabī gives his tripartite framework as a gloss on his opening remarks:

> The first odd prime number is three; the prime numbers [after three] themselves are derived from that primacy [of three]. Thus was he (peace be upon him) the most perfect proof of his Lord, for he received the whole array of the words which are the referents of Ādam's names. In his triplicity, then, he is virtually his own proof. And as his reality assumes its primal singularity through that which is tripartite in [its] constitution, he consequently said concerning the realm of love, which is the source of existing things, "Three things are beloved to me in this world of yours". [He said this] by virtue of his triplicity. Then he mentioned women and perfume, [saying also that] prayer provided him [full] satisfaction.[9]

Thus, Muḥammad's primacy and singularity, metaphysically and as prophet and metaphysically, are here related to the number three as the first odd prime number and to threeness (*tathlīth*), with a final reference to the *ḥadīth* about the three things which the Prophet loved. 'The first odd prime number is three', then, refers to Muḥammad himself, for the number three thus defined is unique and primary in a way that no other

8. But again, as in other Qur'ānic/metaphysical meanings, for Ibn ᶜArabī the 'two sides' of meaning are in fact one.

9. *Fuṣūṣ*, p. 214.

number can be—and he is unique and primary in a way that no other prophet can be. These are Muḥammad's most salient characteristics, as Ibn ʿArabī has here described him.[10] In this perfection, Muḥammad most perfectly points toward God ('his Lord') through 'the words which are the referents of Ādam's names'. These 'names' are, of course, not Ādam's own names, but, as the Qur'ān says, they are the names of all things which God taught to Ādam and, as such, for Ibn ʿArabī they are the divine names.[11]

ĀDAM AND MUḤAMMAD

As we have seen in the chapter on Ādam, he, like Muḥammad, constitutes a point of theophany in the phenomenal world; he too is a '*quṭb*' round which the whole of creation revolves and through which it is sustained; and he too is a *maẓhar* of absolute being in a sea of conditional being. All of this is despite what Ibn ʿArabī has said here, in the discussion of Muḥammad, referring to Ādam as still being 'between water and clay' when Muḥammad was already a prophet. Much of Ādam's status as ontological principle seems for Ibn ʿArabī, as we know, to be related to his possession of the divine names which God gave to him. Now Muḥammad's ontological status here is, in a somewhat parallel relationship, also related to these names which Ibn ʿArabī refers to as 'Ādam's names'. However, there is a difference: Ādam's status is based on his possessing from God the names themselves. Muḥammad, though, 'received the whole array of the words which are the referents of Ādam's names'.[12] These

10. Again, there is an interesting interweaving here of the traditional components and Ibn ʿArabī's own gloss on them.

11. Qur'ān, 2:31.

12. Though Ibn ʿArabī uses the term 'words' (*kalim*) here in its particular context and meaning for the *Fuṣūṣ*, as indicated above, there is an implicit Qur'ānic Ādamic reference to Qur'ān 2:37, 'Then Ādam learnt words (*kalimāt*) from his Lord,' which provides further confirmation of the Ādam–Muḥammad connection and relationship for Ibn ʿArabī.

words (*kalim*) in the *Fuṣūṣ* are the very personification of truth in all of the prophets. They are here also 'the referents of Ādam's names' (*mussamayāt*), to be understood as the *meanings* of Ādam's names, meanings as in the *sense* of the names, and not just what they *refer* to. In the more specific context of the *Fuṣūṣ*, if in a particular chapter of the *Fuṣūṣ* the prophet who is its subject has a certain 'wisdom', *ḥikma*, represented in the 'word' (*kalima*) associated there with him—Ibn ʿArabī's usual formulation for introducing the prophets in the chapter titles—then this 'word', embodying the 'wisdom', is the very essence of that prophet's being as a divine truth, embodied and personified in the prophet. Each individual prophet, then, *is* a particular *kalima*—or, each *kalima* a prophet. This, as we know, is the standard formulation in the *Fuṣūṣ*. There is an exception, however, in the case of Muḥammad. Here, this prophet has been given 'all of the words, which are the referents of Ādam's names' and, therefore, he incorporates in himself the entirety of meanings of the divine names. The whole prophetic corpus of wisdom and words is thus his. Muḥammad is here, then, the repository and expression of the full metaphysical truth, just as in the more obvious sense he is 'seal of the prophets' (unique in his *finality*). Indeed, from Ibn ʿArabī's perspective, 'seal' might be seen in both ways, representing both the exoteric and esoteric meanings of this idea. If Ādam is 'inferior' to Muḥammad in Ibn ʿArabī's scheme, it is in this sense, and it is of obvious significance for an understanding of Ibn ʿArabī's esoteric 'tracking' of the Qur'ān. Ibn ʿArabī will go on to explore Muḥammad's esoteric metaphysical side with further thoughts on the Prophet's 'triplicity'. It is in the exposition of this triplicity and associations with the notion of three or threeness that Ibn ʿArabī finds the proper context for a full understanding of the Prophet's truth. Here the *ḥadīth* of the three things dear to the Prophet will play a central role.

Muḥammad's perfection for Ibn ʿArabī, as we have seen, is in and through his rather abstract identification with 'the first odd prime number', three. Ibn ʿArabī's explication of this idea begins with the concrete, and not at all abstract, *ḥadīth* that the Prophet said three things were beloved to him in this world: women, perfume and prayer.[13] This particular tradition is highly amenable to Ibn ʿArabī's typical sort of explanation of something which may on surface appear a juxtaposition of 'incompatible'—even 'contradictory'—elements. Thus will he be able to make his point in explaining what Muḥammad could have meant in declaring his favourite things in this world to be women and perfume before prayer. Ibn ʿArabī's explanation of the narrative provides a varied collection of ideas in the explication of Muḥammad's *ḥikma.*[14]

WOMEN

'Thus did [Muḥammad] begin by mentioning women and then ending with prayer. That is because woman is part of man in her own very creation. And man's knowledge of himself precedes his knowledge of his Lord'.[15] Muḥammad's professed preference for women over all other things, is then, not due to any compelling concupiscence on his part; it seems, rather, to be explained in the Biblical/Qur'ānic account of the creation of woman (Eve) from the rib of man (Adam).[16] Man (epitomised

13. Nasā'ī, 36:1, for the *ḥadīth.*

14. The main point, again, of course, is the metaphysical transformation of tradition.

15. *Fuṣūṣ*, pp. 214–215.

16. In the Bible, this is found in Genesis 2:21–23, where God causes man (Adam) to sleep and then from one of Adam's ribs He makes woman. In the Qur'ān (4:1), it says: 'Your Lord who created you from a single individual (*nafs wāḥida*) and created from that individual its wife (*zawjahā*)'. The Qur'ān does not specify the identity of that individual or the way in which God created from him his wife. In much of the Islamic exegetical tradition, however, the *nafs wāḥida* is named as Ādam and God created his wife from one of his ribs on his right side, in some accounts while Adam was asleep. See, for example, *Tafsīr al-Jalālayn*, p. 97, and *Tafsīr Ibn Kathīr*, p. 286. Through the disseminated *tafsīr* tradition this story had obviously gained broad exposure—hence Ibn ʿArabī's natural reference to it.

here in Muḥammad) loves woman because her very physical origins were in him (literally, from a piece of him)—and not *primarily* in sensual thrall over her. Indeed, by clear implication one may say Ibn ʿArabī's logic is that man first and foremost loves woman *as an act of self-love*: he is attached to 'a piece of himself'. This is clearly Ibn ʿArabī's unfolding argument, in an attempt to use the Prophet's reported profession of a great love for women, as another expression of the unitive truth of Creator and creation.

Thus, if 'man's knowledge of himself precedes his knowledge of his Lord', as above, then his 'knowledge' of woman may surely be seen as a basis of his knowledge of his Lord; for self-knowledge here has implicitly been defined as knowledge of woman, and, to continue, 'man's knowledge of his Lord is a result of his knowledge of himself'.[17] Therefore, says Ibn ʿArabī did the Prophet say, 'he who knows himself knows his lord''.[18] There are two meanings inherent in this tradition, according to Ibn ʿArabī: either that knowledge of the self is not possible or that it is possible. In the first instance, the realisation of knowing one's Lord is thwarted, while in the second it is fulfilled. But knowledge of one's Lord *is* possible for Ibn ʿArabī and 'thus is Muḥammad the clearest proof of his Lord, for every part of the world is a proof of its origin, which is its Lord. Understand!'.[19]

Ibn ʿArabī has established an implicit 'comparative model' here, juxtaposing the relationship between source and derived part in the realm of God and creation and in the dimension of man (read: Muḥammad) and woman. Every part of the created world points back towards its origin, God, *if one has understanding*; likewise does woman, made of a piece of man, in her very

17. *Fuṣūṣ*, p. 215.

18. This is a standard and widely-known and used sufi saying. Sometimes considered a Prophetic saying (*ḥadīth*) and sometimes a first-person saying of God reported by the Prophet (*ḥadīth qudsī*), its importance from different sufi perspectives is obvious.

19. *Fuṣūṣ*, p. 215.

being serve as a proof of her own origin. In each case the part informs us of the whole—the part is a *dalīl* or 'proof', indicating the presence of its origin, the whole. Thus does Muḥammad, as the most exemplary piece of God's creation, most perfectly point back towards his divine origin; and so too does woman, created from man, serve as most perfect 'proof' of her origin. Further, in each case, the source, or origin—God or man—is enhanced and informed by its part; the relationship is reciprocal in that the source is as much in need of it as the part. In the case of man and woman, then, man truly knows himself through the encounter with woman. But as knowing oneself—if possible—is the path to knowing God, then man's knowledge of God is a direct function of his relationship with woman. In man's knowing himself through woman, he is then able to know God; and in knowing God comes the realisation and completion of one's ontological standing. Ibn ᶜArabī continues further with this theme, tending toward his ultimate goal in the principle of metaphysical unity.

Ibn ᶜArabī now diverts his emphasis from the side of man, in his longing for God through woman, to the divine side, in God's longing for man—on the model already constructed and with Ibn ᶜArabī's usual rigorous insistence on mutuality and parity in the divine–human relationship. Thus, in speaking of Muḥammad:

> Therefore were women beloved to him and did he yearn for them, because this is by way of attraction of the whole for its part; and thus did [the Prophet] with that explain this matter, from God's perspective, in God's words, concerning the elemental human constitution: "And I breathed into man from my spirit".[20] Then God characterised Himself in the strength of this longing to meet man, saying to those who long [for Him]: "Oh David, I yearn more for them",[21] that is, for those who yearn for Him. This would be a special meeting.[22]

20. Qur'ān, 15:29.
21. This is obscure and does not appear in the standard collections.
22. *Fuṣūṣ*, p. 215.

In so animating man, God created with his breath another for whom He longs. God, 'in seeing them',[23] says Ibn ʿArabī, wants very much that they see him. But 'the situation prevents that',[24] for as the well-known *ḥadīth* relates in God's own words: 'No one among you will see his Lord until he dies'.[25] Though the relationship is symmetrical and equal in mutual longing for contact with the other (indeed, God's longing is even greater), man cannot fully achieve the contact in 'seeing' God, which they both so desire, until he dies and enters the next world. God must, then, bring each human life to an end in death, thus 'consummating' the relationship. God, in His mercy, however, suffers pangs of remorse at having to do this, knowing what great terror death will strike in the heart of his servant. There is, though, no other way to achieve the desired goal. Ibn ʿArabī conveys this meaning in citing the haunting and poignant '*ḥadīth* of hesitation', stated, once more in God's own words: 'I do not hesitate in anything I do as much as I hesitate in taking my believing servant who loathes death—and I loathe harming him, but it is necessary for him to meet Me'.[26] Thus, says Ibn ʿArabī, God in His mercy 'merely announces glad tidings [to the servant] and does not tell him that he must die, lest He pain him by mentioning death'.[27]

Ibn ʿArabī continues this tale of poignant divine longing for man and man's insistent yearning for God with a verse of love poetry, expressing the pathos and power of this mutual attraction: 'My beloved yearns to see Me, while I yearn still more [to see him]. [Our] very beings grow impassioned in anticipation [of our meeting], but fate does prevent it. Thus do I wail in complaint, as does he'.[28]

23. *Ibid.*
24. *Ibid.*
25. *Ibid.*, *Muslim*, LII:95.
26. *Fuṣūṣ*, p. 215; Bukhārī, *Ṣaḥīḥ*, LXXXI:38.
27. *Fuṣūṣ*, p. 215.
28. *Fuṣūṣ*, p. 216.

This strong frustration of the 'unconsummated' desire of God to meet his servant, as the servant yearns to see Him *before death*, is situated well within the conventional Islamic doctrinal boundaries of the relationship between God and man, if somewhat fervent in tone and expression.[29] For Ibn ʿArabī this is a point strongly made, in the context of the general issue of the love of man for woman (and *vice versa*), as a model for divine–human love. Ibn ʿArabī's conception of the frustration in this loving relationship between God and His servants before death will be seen to have a clear purpose in his resolution of the main concerns in this chapter. Before proceeding further toward this resolution, and as preparation for it, one might ask why is God so eager, indeed, to meet his servants and for them to *see* Him—so insistently eager that He, like the servant, strains and flails at the impediment of this physical, earthly life before death? The answer to this question will emerge from Ibn ʿArabī's further discussion of the main issues relating to the Prophet and women, and male–female relationships in general, where for him some semblance of the divine–human relationship after death may be found here before death in this 'mundane' relationship.[30]

Ibn ʿArabī thus continues with the Qur'ānic theme—here reiterated—of God's breathing into His prime creation (man, Ādam). This, says Ibn ʿArabī, means that in vivifying His creature in this way, God is only longing for himself: 'Do you not see [God] creating man in His image, because this is from His spirit?'[31] Indeed, a man's very constitution, says Ibn ʿArabī, has a special quality relating it to fire and this results from his being inflated with God's breath, as that commingles with the four Galenic elements of blood, phlegm, yellow bile and black bile, which, in this theory, are basic to the human bodily

29. Indeed, 'the *ḥadīth* of hesitation', Ibn ʿArabī's point of departure here, is obviously from within central sources, while his absorption of it is through the filter of his own principles.

30. It is, of course, never 'mundane' except for those who cannot see.

31. *Fuṣūṣ*, p. 216.

makeup. This quality of fire attached to the human constitution is extraordinary and unique, says Ibn ᶜArabī; it is in some sense 'preternatural', for if it were 'natural' it would be represented in 'a burning which was light, not fire'.[32] Thus, for example, 'did God speak to Mūsā only in the form of fire',[33] says Ibn ᶜArabī, obviously referring to the Biblical/Qur'ānic story of Moses and the divine voice emanating from the burning bush. The divine breath (*nafas al-Raḥmān*, breath of the Merciful) which inflates man is the source of this divine fire which inhabits and typifies man, in contrast to the rest of creation which is not a recipient of the divine breath and is instead characterised by 'light'.[34] Most strongly put: 'The divine breath is implicit in the very stuff by virtue of which man is man'.[35] Man and God come together here *within man*. This divine–human nexus is the source of man's finding God *within himself*. With this foundation, God then 'produced from man a person in the image of man which He called "woman". She then appeared in his image and man, then, consequently, yearned for her as something would yearn for itself, and she longed for him with the longing of something for its origin. Thus is woman loved by man'.[36] For Ibn ᶜArabī, this explains why 'God loves the one He created in His own image, to whom He compelled the illuminated angels to prostrate themselves, despite the angels' great status, their position, their rank and their lofty natural constitution'.[37]

The God/man and man/woman analogue is now quite clear. For in Ibn ᶜArabī's words, it is 'here the relationship [between God and man] occurs'.[38] The form or image (*ṣūra*) which this relationship takes is for him 'the greatest relationship, the clearest

32. *Ibid.*
33. *Ibid.*
34. *Ibid.*
35. *Ibid.*
36. *Ibid.*
37. *Ibid.*
38. *Ibid.*

and the most perfect'.[39] It is in the form of a pair, says Ibn ʿArabī, as 'it makes a duality of the existence of God, just as woman, through her existence, makes of man a duality, splitting him into a pair'.[40] Then, says Ibn ʿArabī, does 'the triplicity appear: God, man, woman'.[41]

The *unity* of God and man through man's yearning for woman has evolved now through *duality* to Ibn ʿArabī's starting point in *triplicity*. But these are all variations on the same theme of the divine–human encounter and intertwining in a curious 'paradoxical twist': where the one (either God or man, on the divine model) is 'split' in two, with another being formed from a part of him, with this 'split' providing a path to 'reintegration' of the 'two' parts (through the intermediary of God, in the case of the male/female pair).[42] The 'split', then, rather than indicating any detraction from unity, exists as *a means of effecting and enhancing it*—and as a metaphor for the 'split' between God and His creation its resolution points toward resolution of the larger 'split'. Ibn ʿArabī brings it all to a prominent head with an intensified discussion of man and woman, in a more frankly sensual manner. He will then proceed to the subject of perfume, the second member of the 'trinity' of things said to have been beloved to the Prophet.

God 'made woman loveable for man',[43] says Ibn ʿArabī, 'just as God loves the one [made] in His own image'[44] (*i.e.*, man). Indeed, 'love occurs only for the one who was made from [the lover]—man's love itself being for the One from whom he was formed and that is God'.[45] Man, then, in loving woman is in fact loving the one from whom he was made, *viz.*, God, in His

39. *Ibid.*
40. *Ibid.*
41. *Ibid.*
42. *Fuṣūṣ*, pp. 216–217.
43. *Ibid.*
44. *Ibid.*
45. *Fuṣūṣ*, p. 217.

'pneumatic creation' of man, woman being a part of God created from man. 'He who knows himself knows his Lord' here would mean that woman *is man's self*, as she was constructed from a part of him by God and in 'knowing' her, man literally knows himself, thus knows God.[46] This is an inexplicable, natural process, not occurring through premeditation on the part of man. Thus: '[The Prophet] said [women] "*were beloved*" [to me, in the passive voice], and he did not in an active voice say "I love" [women]. This is because man's love is really for his Lord in whose image he was made, even in loving his wife. He loves his wife, then, through God's love for him, manifested in a divine fragrant creation'.[47] Women, as this 'divine fragrant creation', are God's gift to man in His love for him and in His own desire thereby to be known to him, as again, in its highly intricate way, the attraction is always mutual.[48]

Man's compelling attraction for woman now becomes more focused in Ibn ʿArabī's formulation through a frank vocabulary of physical attraction and Islamic legal regulations concerning sexual relations:

> When man loves woman, he seeks union [with her]—that is, the ultimate union which is to be found in love. Indeed, there is no greater union than marital union within the elemental human constitution. For physical desire pervades all of man's organs and for this reason was he commanded to perform the required ritual ablutions [after sexual relations]. Purification in this way becomes complete, as is man's physical extinction in woman at the moment of desire's consummation.[49]

But because not all men will understand the deeper spiritual element of physical relations, 'God is jealous that his servant might think he actually derives pleasure from someone other than

46. In Ibn ʿArabī's terms, this is the meaning of the saying.
47. *Fuṣūṣ*, p. 217.
48. This for IbnʿArabī reflects the general metaphysical unity.
49. *Fuṣūṣ*, p. 217.

God'.[50] God thus 'purifies man through the required ablution, in order that man should return his gaze toward God. For within the one in whom man is consumed in desire there is indeed nothing other than that [pleasure]'.[51]

Though man may witness and experience God's presence without reference to woman by looking within himself in the absence of any intermediary (*bi-lā wāsiṭa*), the best vision (*shuhūd*) of God which man may attain, says Ibn ʿArabī, is still that which is achieved in relations with woman: 'Thus is man's vision of God in woman the most complete and the most perfect'.[52] This perfection in man's vision of God through woman occurs through an incorporation of both the *passive* and *active* modes of God's amenability to man's visionary experience of Him.[53] Thus is the vision 'complete' and 'perfect' and thus does '[the Prophet], may God bless and preserve him, love women because of the perfect vision of God [to be found] in them'.[54] This indeed, for Ibn ʿArabī, is the *only* way man may 'see' God this side of the eternal divide, for 'God essentially is totally divorced from all forms..., so when in this way the issue [of seeing Him] becomes impossible, but [at the same time] seeing Him may only occur [in this world] in material form, then seeing God in woman is the greatest and most perfect vision'.[55] Also, the 'greatest union', says Ibn ʿArabī, between God and man, using the term '*wuṣla*', which has the meaning of sexual relations as well, is 'marital union which is like the divine approach to the one He created in His image, so that He could appoint him [man] as His successor. Then does God see Himself in man ... for man in his manifest side is creation, while in his inner aspect he is God'.[56] The reciprocity of the divine—human

50. *Ibid.*
51. *Ibid.*
52. *Ibid.*
53. *Ibid.*
54. *Ibid.*
55. *Ibid.*
56. *Fuṣūṣ*, pp. 217–218.

relationship is again clear here. A man who cannot recognise all this in his relationship with a woman, says Ibn ʿArabī, is not engaged in 'divine love' (*ḥubb ilāhī*), but rather he is pursuing mere 'natural desire' (*al-shahwa al-tabīʿiyya*).[57]

Before introducing the second of the most beloved things for the Prophet, perfume (*ṭīb*), Ibn ʿArabī 'digresses' in a bit of rambling, but very interesting, discussion of masculine and feminine from the grammatical and linguistic perspectives in the time of the Prophet. This discussion includes as well related aspects of Ibn ʿArabī's sufi metaphysics and develops into a sort of introduction to both the second and third of the three beloved things, perfume (*ṭīb*) and prayer (*ṣalā*):

> Then he (peace be upon him) gave priority in this tradition to the feminine over the masculine, because he intended [to reveal] an interest in women. Thus he said three [in feminine form] and he did not say three [in masculine form] with the *hā* [ending], though among those three things, he does mention perfume which is [grammatically] masculine in gender. The custom of the Arabs certainly was to give priority to the masculine over the feminine [in this sort of situation]. Thus would they say, "The Fāṭimas and Zayd returned" [using the masculine plural form for "returned"], but they would not use the feminine plural form for "returned". In this way, then, did they give priority to the masculine [in verbal sentences] over the feminine, though [the masculine word] might be singular [as in this case] and the feminine 'you' [for example], might be a plural. The Prophet was an Arab and thus did he (peace be upon him) recognise particularly the meaning which was intended [in the saying] concerning the love imposed on him, as he did not himself play a part in causing his [particular kind of] love [for women]. Rather did God teach the Prophet what he had not known—and God's favour toward him was great. For this reason did the Prophet favour the feminine over the masculine in his saying "three" without [the masculine pronominal suffix] *hā'*.[58] How wondrous is his knowledge—

57. *Fuṣūṣ*, p. 218.
58. *Fuṣūṣ*, pp. 219–220. Ibn ʿArabī means here, of course, the *tā' marbūṭa*.

> Peace be upon him—of the realities and how strong his concern for the verities. Then he made the final part of the statement similar to the first part in [its] femininity, while he situated the masculine between them. The Prophet, therefore, began [the saying] with women and ended [it] with prayer. Both of these are feminine [grammatically], and perfume is between them, as is the case with [man's] very being. For man is situated between the [divine] essence from which he emerges and woman who emerges from him. He is thus [like the perfume] between two feminines: the feminine of [the divine] essence (*dhāt*) and the really feminine. Women are the really feminine while prayer is something other than that. And perfume is located between them, like Ādam between the [divine] essence from which he came and Eve whose existence was from Ādam. If you wish, say [for example] "attribute" (*ṣifa*) which is also [grammatically] feminine. Or, if you wish, say "capability" (*qudra*) which is also [grammatically] feminine. Whichever [intellectual] trend you wish to belong to, you will find only the feminine [terms] appearing, even among the adherents of "causality" who make God the cause of the existence of the world. [The word] "cause" (*ʿilla*), then, is [also] feminine'.[59]

Apart from Ibn ʿArabī's case for the Prophet's linguistical emphasis on the feminine (against the grain of linguistic usage in Muḥammad's time), the most important feature here is his related use of the grammatical gender distinction in the Arabic language to develop his argument. This is the central *structural aspect* of his discussion in which serious specific themes are mooted and treated.[60] Thus does Ibn ʿArabī make much of the fact that in Arabic feminine nouns usually are identified by the presence of a particular ending (*tā' marbūṭa*). The majority of the substantive nouns in the Islamic religious intellectual sciences are, according

59. *Ibid.*

60. In doing this, Ibn ʿArabī is following a well-established medieval scholastic tradition. The Arabic grammarians, for example—to cite a most prominent case—often went so far as to make structure dominant over content in their analysis of Arabic grammar and syntax. See, for example, *Sharḥ Qaṭr al-Nadā wa-Ball al-Ṣadā* of Abū Muḥammad ʿAbdullāh Jamāl al-Dīn b. Hishām al-Anṣārī.

to him, of this type.[61] The very truth which the scholars of these sciences seek, then, must be 'feminine' for Ibn ᶜArabī, the masculine conceptual elements in their quest never taking pride of place in their main formulations. Be this as it may, Ibn ᶜArabī's approach here can be illuminated also by reference to the general medieval Islamic 'scholastic' method and attitude, where the *formal* grammatical, syntactical and intellectual structural features are considered to carry substantial meanings. Thus apart from examples already referred to, Ibn ᶜArabī also clearly indicates the notion that God exemplifies the feminine: for if, as above, man is situated between two feminines, the first being 'the essence from which he came', this 'essence', the grammatically feminine *dhāt,* can be no other than God, as God is obviously man's origin. This notion is further developed when Ibn ᶜArabī posits man's origin in God's essence by referring to the feminine grammatical status of the word 'essence' (*ta'nīth dhāt*).[62] Grammatical structure and form would seem here, again, in that quintessentially medieval scholastic way, to indicate *a substantive theological reality*, though not, one must add, without that reality for Ibn ᶜArabī having already been deeply present in the thought.[63]

PERFUME

Perfume, following on from women, is Ibn ᶜArabī's next subject. In addition to being the masculine 'sandwiched' between the two (more important) feminines, perfume may also be seen thus: 'As for the wisdom [associated with perfume] and the Prophet's putting it after women, this is because of the scents of creation in women, for the sweetest perfume is the embrace of the beloved, as it is said in the well-known adage'.[64] But these 'scents of

61. One may, of course, recognise this as a *fact* (if indeed it is) without drawing Ibn ᶜArabī's intellectual conclusions.

62. See above and *Fuṣūṣ*, pp. 219–220.

63. In this sense, for Ibn ᶜArabī *form* and *content* were fused.

64. *Fuṣūṣ*, p. 220.

creation' (*rawā'iḥ al-takwīn*)[65] here are more than a poetic metaphor for the closeness of women to God. In an extended discussion of these scents, Ibn ʿArabī deepens his conception, relating them in a very complex and nuanced manner to the intertwining of metaphysics and ethics so central to his thought. Thus, says Ibn ʿArabī, was Muḥammad at first a mere passive servant of God, with no desire to lead, until God gave him a special, active role in the realm of the divine 'breaths' (*anfās*), 'which are the wonderful scents. In this way was perfume beloved to the Prophet'.[66]

In identifying the divine *breaths* with the *scents*, Ibn ʿArabī has implicitly entered the realm of metaphysics, for the Qur'ānic 'breath of the merciful' (*nafas al-Raḥmān*) is, as we know, the 'emanation' of being and its permeation 'downwards'. Here, as we have seen elsewhere, God's mercy as personal is transformed into being (*wujūd*) and God as merciful (*al-Raḥmān*) becomes God as source of being—and this with all the attendant ethical implications.[67] Ibn ʿArabī, therefore, continues, drawing out these implications:

> The Prophet, then, understood the ranks [of being] associated with God, in God's words [describing Himself], "Lofty of Rank, Possessor of the Throne",[68] because of His sitting on it by virtue of His name, the Merciful. Thus there remains nobody around the throne who is not touched by divine mercy, as in God's words: "My mercy encompasses everything"; indeed, the throne encompasses everything and its occupant is the Merciful. Through His reality, then, does [His] mercy permeate the cosmos....[69]

65. This expression serves Ibn ʿArabī's purpose well, implying, as it can, a blending of the earthy and the metaphysical.

66. *Fuṣūṣ*, p. 220.

67. The chapter on Zakariyyā most clearly addresses these points in detail.

68. Qur'ān, 40:15.

69. *Fuṣūṣ*, pp. 220–221. The Qur'ānic 'My mercy encompasses everything' (7:156) is for Ibn ʿArabī a virtual Qur'ānic proof text for his sufi elevation of God's mercy to His highest attribute and, most importantly, the transformation of personal divine mercy into an ontological process.

Women, perfume, the sweet scents of women's perfume, the divine breaths of the Merciful God (*al-Raḥmān*), the mercy of the Merciful in its universal application—all of these, intertwined with, reflecting, and indeed identified with one another, create a story of profane and sacred love of physical and metaphysical import. The main motif in this story is that of human physical union as microcosmic model of the divine union with His creation, in His very breathing into it as His act of ultimate mercy. In dramatically encompassing both the earthy and the cosmic in its universal sweep, this story so well serves Ibn ʿArabī's purpose in revealing his truth to Everyman. The traditional story of the Prophet's greatly beloved third wife, ʿĀ'isha, in her trial of unfounded allegations of improper sexual behaviour,[70] is context for Ibn ʿArabī's final remarks in the realm of perfume. Here the ethical dimension in its earthy personal side, combined with its larger metaphysical meaning, is emphasised.

In light of all the above, then, says Ibn ʿArabī, 'did He, Most High, make perfume a factor in exculpating ʿĀ'isha, where He said, "Bad women are for bad men and bad men are for bad women, while good women are for good men and good men are for good women and these [good ones] are innocent of what is said [against them]"'.[71] This verse (Qur'ān, 24: 26) was traditionally identified as part of God's statement exculpating ʿĀ'isha from the grievous and irresponsible allegations of infidelity brought against her by vicious gossip-mongers, chief among them ʿAbd Allāh b. Ubayy.[72] But what does this have to do with the Prophet and perfume? The *basic* connection for Ibn ʿArabī, it seems, is, again, linguistic and formal: the Qur'ānic adjectival term for 'good' as applied both to women and men

70. For a general account of this story, see: *Encyclopaedia of Islam*, new edition, volume 1, pp. 307–308.

71. *Fuṣūṣ*, p. 221.

72. A mainly negative figure in early Islamic historiography. For a general account of ʿAbd Allāh b. Ubayy, see: *Encyclopaedia of Islam*, new edition, volume 1, p. 53.

in 24: 26 is *ṭayyib* (also 'sweet', 'pleasant') which is the same root and has the identical consonantal spelling as *ṭīb*, perfume (though it obviously has different vocalisation). But the 'linguistic' and 'formal' here, as we know, like all such 'scholastic' features, may indeed be substantive as well: perfume is sweet *and* good. Thus, says Ibn ʿArabī, taking it further: 'God, then, made the scents of the good people sweet, because speech is breath and is virtually the same as scent. Speech issues in the good and the bad according to its content in the particular form it takes. When seen in its divine origin, it is all good, for He is good; when seen as praised or blameworthy, it is good and bad'.[73]

Speech (words) and breath have here been identified one with the other, with speech having two aspects: one all good (from the divine side) and the other good and bad (in creation). Perfume is good through its identification with the divine breath and with the good (*ṭayyib*). Ibn ʿArabī finishes this very complex discussion with an extension of the ethical points above: the good and the bad—the *ṭayyib* and *khabīth* of Qur'ān 24:26—are basic to this world, as are the sweet and the putrid. The Prophet was reported to have proclaimed his dislike for the odour of garlic, while the angels abhorred what seemed to them the putrid smell of human beings. But the Prophet, says Ibn ʿArabī, was by his nature inclined generally to see the good in things (*e.g.*, the *ṭīb* and *ṭayyib)* and not the bad. Even when he acknowledges the bad in something, he does not abjure the thing itself but rather only its objectionable quality, as in the case of garlic whose *odour* he detests but not the garlic itself. There is good and bad in this world, sweet and putrid, says Ibn ʿArabī, and one cannot deny the presence of the bad and the objectionable, for this is the phenomenal world of differentiation. But the Prophet, in his natural proclivity for the good, saw that underlying the categories of good and bad, all things were acceptable in their deeper reality, for 'God's mercy is in the bad and good. The bad in itself is good and the good

73. *Fuṣūṣ*, p. 221.

in itself is bad'.[74] We have now been returned to the metaphysical realm of unity, where all differentiation is lost. This is the world of union between God and man through woman. In its surface manifestation this union 'paradoxically' began with that very differentiation which enabled the Prophet to declare that women had become for him the most beloved thing.

PRAYER

Ibn ʿArabī concludes with his discussion of 'prayer' (*ṣalāt*). Central here for him is the notion that Muḥammad found total satisfaction in prayer, as it constitutes for man a direct experience of God in 'seeing' Him (*mushāhada*) and a private conversation between man and God (*munājāt*). Ibn ʿArabī illustrates this mutuality and experience of God in prayer with an engaging 'exegesis' of *sūrat al-Fātiḥa*, whose recitation is integral to the *ṣalāt*. He argues in 'point-counterpoint' fashion and invokes both Qur'ān and a particular *ḥadīth* source, showing an alternating focus between God and man in the prayerful recitation of the *sūra*. Thus:

> [*Ṣalāt*] is a private conversation between God and His servant, as He said, "Thus, remember Me, I will remember you".[75] *Ṣalāt* is divided between God and His servant in two parts, its first part for God and its [second] for the servant, as it was transmitted in the sound narrative, from God, Most High: "I divided *ṣalāt* between Me and My servant into two parts, one part for Me and one for My servant and for My servant is whatever he asks".[76] When the servant says, "In the name of God, the Merciful, the

74. *Fuṣūṣ*, p. 222.

75. Qur'ān, 2:172.

76. Ibn ʿArabī's recitation, beginning here and following, of God's words asserting His division of the prayer, and in particular its *Fātiḥa* components, into two parts, one for Himself and one for His servant, is directly taken, verbatim and in paraphrase, from a well-known *ḥadīth qudsī*. This narrative is usually cited as being in Muslim, IV:38, which is perhaps its most prominent location, but it appears also in several other *ḥadīth* collections, as well as elsewhere in Muslim. For a list of references, see William Graham, *Divine Word and Prophetic Word in Early Islam*, pp. 182–184.

> Compassionate", God says "My servant praises Me". When the servant says, "Praise be to God, Lord of the worlds", God says "My servant has praised Me". When the servant says, "the Merciful and Compassionate", God says, "My servant has extolled Me". When the servant says, "King of the Judgement Day", God says, "My servant had praised Me and given full authority to me". This first part [of the *Fātiḥa*], all belongs to God, Most High.[77]

Thus for Ibn ᶜArabī God's part of the *Fātiḥa*, in the context of *ṣalāt*, comprises the reciprocal assertions of man in reciting the *Fātiḥa* and God's responses in and to the recitation of these first four of the *Fātiḥa*'s seven verses. These are 'God's verses',[78] for Ibn ᶜArabī, as they all, in various formulations, praise, extol and make obeisance to Him. God's response to the statements in the verses reaffirms these laudatory tributes to Him. However, His reaffirmation is also *His response*, indicating not only His agreement with the content of His own revelation, but, most importantly for Ibn ᶜArabī, *the mutuality* of the divine–human encounter in the *ṣalāt's* central Qur'ānic recitation, the *Fātiḥa*. Not only is the *ṣalāt* 'divided' (*maqsūma*) into two parts, for God and man, but *within* each part the reciprocality of human assertion and divine response weaves a tight fabric of divine–human intercourse which is Ibn ᶜArabī's main point here. God's servant is not merely 'praying' and 'worshipping', but communicating with and 'meeting' God. This will operate similarly with respect to the 'servant's part' of the *Fātiḥa,* as recited in the *ṣalāt.*

Verse five of the *Fātiḥa* constitutes for Ibn ᶜArabī a sort of transition or 'reciprocal link' between God's part and man's:

> Then the servant says "You do we worship and from You do we seek aid", and God says, "This [verse] is between Me and My servant and My servant may have whatever he wishes". Thus does God here [in His response] adduce the co-operation [between Himself and man] in this verse.[79]

77. *Fuṣūṣ*, p. 222.
78. *Ibid.*
79. *Fuṣūṣ*, pp. 222–223.

Verses six and seven are man's part of the *Fātiḥa*:

> When the servant says 'Guide us on the straight path, the path of those upon whom You have cast Your favour, not the recipients of your wrath nor those who have gone astray', God says, 'Thus these [verses] are for My servant and My servant may have whatever he wishes'. These [verses], then, belong to God's servant, just as the first ones belonged to Him, Most High.[80]

With this reciprocity and mutuality in reciting the *Fātiḥa* during the *ṣalāt*, Ibn ʿArabī has a foundation for deepening his conception of the divine-human encounter in prayer.

At its highest and best, says Ibn ʿArabī, the encounter of God and man in *ṣalāt* produces a human being who is 'possessed of vision' (*dhū baṣar*) and therefore 'sees his partner',[81] *i.e.*, God. For such a person the experience of *ṣalāt* is 'seeing' (*mushāhada*) and 'vision' (*ru'ya*) of God: 'If one is not possessed of vision, one then does not see God'.[82] But for Ibn ʿArabī, one may *hear* God, as appears in Qur'ān 50:37: 'One who lends an ear and bears witness'. Such a person performs *ṣalāt* 'with belief'[83] (*īmān*) and 'as if he saw God'.[84] While this is not as good as the first rank of experience, seeing, which is akin to *gnosis*, it is close and represents a high spiritual state. But the 'total satisfaction' which accrued to the prophet (*qurrat ʿayn*) from *ṣalāt* and which comes only with 'seeing', is the 'true goal' of *ṣalāt* (*ghāyatuhā*).

Ibn ʿArabī then universalises this conception of *ṣalāt*, putting it in a cosmological context by addressing the main bodily movements in prayer:

> As being (*wujūd*) is from an intelligible movement which transforms the world from a [state of] non-being to being, prayer encompasses all the movements [invoked]; they are three in

80. *Fuṣūṣ*, p. 223.
81. *Ibid.*
82. *Ibid.*
83. *Ibid.*
84. *Ibid.*

number: vertical movement, which is the vertical state of the worshipper at prayer; horizontal movement, which is the state of the worshipper in bending down; and movement downwards, which is the state of his total [ritual] prostration [in the *ṣalāt*].[85]

These three movements, ritually essential to the Islamic legally-enjoined worship (*ṣalāt*), correspond, says Ibn ʿArabī, to the basic life-forms in the created universe: the first corresponds with man, the second with animals and the third with plants and inanimate objects which have no internally generated movement of their own, as they must be moved by something else.[86] Prayer here, then, in addition to being the point of visionary encounter between God and man, becomes a microcosm, in the human sphere, of the macrocosm of the created world in its emergence from non-being (*ʿadam*) to being (*wujūd*). The worshipper, in performing the required movements during *ṣalāt,* is engaged in a symbolic recapitulation of the 'creation' or emergence of the world. When it is the perfect (gnostic) worshipper who is involved, then 'seeing' God completes the process, effecting a total unity of man, God and creation. This seems for Ibn ʿArabī the obvious source of the Prophet's reported total satisfaction with prayer. The significance of these deeper meanings of *ṣalāt,* as Ibn ʿArabī has expounded them, is indeed great. Why, then, one may ask, is *ṣalāt* third among the three things beloved by the Prophet (though, as we have seen, it *is* grammatically feminine and in that sense 'superior' to perfume)? An answer may be found, I believe, in Ibn ʿArabī's final discussion, on the *kind of God* man encounters in prayer. Of value in its own right, this discussion may also help to answer our questions, as well as providing a useful focus for resolution of all the issues raised here.[87]

85. *Fuṣūṣ*, p. 224.

86. *Ibid.*

87. It is clear that Ibn ʿArabī himself sees this final part of the chapter on Muḥammad as a sort of summing-up.

In the apogee of divine-human mutuality, the God encountered in prayer actually 'prays for us' (*yuṣallī ʿalaynā*)[88] as we pray to Him. 'Prayer', then, 'is from us and from Him'.[89] When God prays, He does so, says Ibn ʿArabī, 'by His name, the Last' (*al-Ākhir*).[90] This is because here 'God comes subsequent to the existence of the servant, for He is the very God whom the servant has created in his heart, through his discursive reasoning or through his fidelity to tradition. He is the God as object of belief'.[91] This 'God in the religious beliefs', as we have previously encountered it in Ibn ʿArabī's thought, is 'created' by man, as God created man and lives in a reciprocal and symmetrical relationship with him.[92] This symmetry for Ibn ʿArabī is so thoroughgoing that God and man occupy parallel positions in their respective roles as 'creator' of one another and in their respective places in worship. God even conforms in His manifestations to the individual spiritual propensities of the servant worshipping Him. This is best illustrated, says Ibn ʿArabī, in al-Junayd's words, 'when asked about *gnosis* of God and the *gnostic*: 'The colour of water is the colour of the vessel'''.[93] This is 'the matter as it really is',[94] says Ibn ʿArabī, and 'This is the God who prays for us'.[95] This God, then, is completely 'determined' by us, not just in our general collective 'creation' of Him in our religions, but, more specifically, in His actual nature and presence (the 'water'), *as these correspond to our various individual propensities (the 'vessel')*. We, too, when we pray, do so with the name *al-Ākhir*, for 'the one who prays lags behind the leader in the race'.[96] We and God are, then, perfectly symmetrical here;

88. *Fuṣūṣ*, p. 225.
89. *Ibid.*
90. *Ibid.*
91. *Ibid.*
92. See in particular the analysis here of Ibn ʿArabī's discussion of Zakariyyā.
93. *Fuṣūṣ*, p. 225.
94. *Ibid.*
95. *Ibid.*
96. *Ibid.*

when He prays to us, we have created Him and when we pray to Him it is possible only because He has created us and we thus 'lag' behind Him. Our 'creation' of Him may be *conceptual* and His creation of us may be *real*, but in the end He remains for us the God in our belief—our 'creation'.[97] As we have thus created Him in our own image, as it were, in praying to Him we really are praying to ourselves, for 'the believer's praise of the thing in which he believes is [really] his praise for himself'.[98]

Implied here is Ibn ᶜArabī's basic conundrum concerning the 'true God' in His essence and the 'created God in the beliefs'. Can we know the one ('true') God in our solipsism of 'self-worship' (of the God in the beliefs)? As is usual with Ibn ᶜArabī, the answer here must be both yes and no. For though on the one hand the God in the beliefs—our 'creation'—is just that, in its limitations, on the other, says Ibn ᶜArabī, if the believer would truly understand that God is present in all beliefs and in their objects—not just one's own—then 'he would know God in every form and every belief'.[99] Which God, again? As we know, Ibn ᶜArabī does not in his sufi metaphysics distinguish sharply between the remote God of essence and the revealed God of attribute, in the way of the theologians and the philosophers. On the contrary. For Ibn ᶜArabī the two Gods were both different and the same—*different,* according to our knowledge of the God in the beliefs, and *the same,* as the 'true God' who is *immanent* in all things, including the beliefs and their objects. However, in intense spiritual activity such as proper prayer, the 'true God' seems somehow to be 'more immanent' than elsewhere, as witnessed above in Ibn ᶜArabī's conception of the *mushāhada* and *ru'ya* in perfect prayer as being somewhat akin to *gnosis*. The truth with Ibn ᶜArabī, then, is always on both sides of the issue, but with *more emphasis* sometimes on one or

97. But as part of creation this 'created God' is also a manifestation of the 'true God', remote in His difference.

98. *Fuṣūṣ*, p. 226.

99. *Ibid.*

the other.[100] Thus in the case of prayer man's 'private God' in prayer seems more a reflection of the worshipper himself rather than a true God 'out there'—and of course the 'out there' for Ibn ᶜArabī is itself highly problematical. The ambiguity also remains, however, in typical Ibn ᶜArabī fashion:

> God said, "I am present in my servants' belief about me". God appears to His servant only in the form of the servant's belief. But God, if He wishes, may be absolute or qualified. Thus the God in the beliefs is [qualified], constrained by limitations. He is the God whom the servant's heart encompasses. But the absolute God is not encompassed by anything, for He *is* the things and He is the same as Himself. For this is something [*i.e.*, the absolute God] about which it cannot be said that it encompasses itself nor that it does not encompass itself. Understand! God indeed says the truth and guides on the path.[101]

The absolute God, then, is indeed ineffable.[102] Perfect prayer may be a very good way of encountering the created God and thereby achieving a scent of the absolute God, for in fact the absolute God '*is* the things' of this world in His immanence. But still, this side of death the best human channel to the ultimate for Ibn ᶜArabī is in man's relationship with woman. To reiterate:

> God essentially is totally divorced from all forms, so when in this way the issue [of seeing Him] becomes impossible, but [at the same time] seeing may only occur in material form, then seeing God in woman is the greatest and most perfect vision.[103]

Also, says Ibn ᶜArabī, the 'greatest union' (*wuṣla*), between God and man is to be found in the marital union of man and

100. Despite this shifting, I think the dominant idea throughout is on God immanent.

101. *Fuṣūṣ*, p. 226.

102. He is also, again, however, immanent.

103. *Fuṣūṣ*, p. 226.

woman (*nikāḥ*). Here, I think, lies the main difference between women and prayer as pathways to God: Prayer, even in its most perfect and highest forms, is ultimately *between man and himself* for Ibn ʿArabī. Wherever man turns in prayer and whichever aspect of 'God' he invokes, he is still 'praying to himself', in a hall of mirrors. Though the mirrors do also reflect transcendence through God's immanence in them, they mainly reflect the subject of prayer (man). The *wuṣla* is absent. True union is missing. The union of man and woman, for Ibn ʿArabī, in light of God's essential femininity (*ta'nīth al-dhāt*) and in view of all the other relevant aspects of interpretation, truly opens man outward toward his origin—within man's psychological, intellectual and metaphysical limitations in this world.

CHAPTER

11

A Lūṭian Epilogue

THE WISDOM OF DOMINATION IN THE WORD OF LŪṬ

Why a *Lūṭian* epilogue? Why not a final, summary statement recounting 'this book's main points', as an exposition of Ibn ʿArabī's Qur'ānic/ metaphysical outlook in the *Fuṣūṣ al-Ḥikam*? Indeed, as we know, each chapter of the *Fuṣūṣ* is representative of the whole, in any case. The most simple answer is that a summing-up does seem desirable and that this should be through Ibn ʿArabī himself. A concluding, polished gem from among the many treasures of the *Fuṣūṣ* would seem appropriate. The wisdom of Lūṭ (chapter thirteen) is well-suited to this purpose.

LOT/LŪṬ

The Biblical Lot, Abraham's nephew, was a mainly unsympathetic figure in the Bible, as well as in many post-Biblical Jewish sources, though sometimes seen as a righteous man. Identified with his compatriots, the sinners of Sodom, Lot had little to recommend him. In Christian literature, Lot's figure was somewhat rehabilitated, but in the Qur'ān and Islamic exegetical literature Lūṭ appears positively as a prophet of God's truth to an obdurate people from whom he ultimately separated.[1]

1. In the Hebrew Bible see: Genesis 11.31; 13.5–10; 14.1–16; 19.1–23; 19.14; 19.16; 19.30–38. For surveys, see, for example, *Encyclopaedia Judaica*, Vol. 11, pp. 507–508; *The Oxford Companion to the Bible*, p. 467; *Encyclopaedia of Islam*, new edition, Vol. 5, pp. 832–833; T. P. Hughes, *A Dictionary of Islam*, p. 299.

In all these traditions, however, he does not, or cannot, deter the people from their actions. The Qur'ānic point of Lūṭ's inability in this matter provides Ibn ʿArabī with a theme round which he develops his notion of Lūṭ's particular wisdom.

THE QUR'ĀNIC LŪṬ

The main framework story of Lūṭ in the Qur'ān is found in two places: 7:80–84 and 11:77–83. Here we see the struggle between Lūṭ and the miscreants. In both stories, Lūṭ's valiant efforts toward deterring them from their evil-doing come to nought—God destroys them while saving Lūṭ. In 7:81 their main sin is characterised as male homosexuality: 'Thus do you take men as the object of your desire, as opposed to women.' The Qur'ānic formulation here renders the people 'transgressors' (*musrifūn*) and their actions an 'abomination' (*fāḥisha*). In 11:77–83, the story does not explicitly report the nature of the people's misbehaviour, saying only that 'they would practice evil things'. IbnʿArabī's primary interest, however, is not in *the sort of sin* committed, but, rather, in Lūṭ's proclaimed anguish in not possessing the strength to deter the people from their sins. Ibn ʿArabī's main source here is found in 11:80, 'Would that I had the power to overcome you or that I had the recourse to some strong support'. This comes as Lūṭ's second cry of anguish in not having the strength to deal with the evil-doers. The first was in 11:77, at the beginning of this particular Lūṭ story-cycle, where God's angelic messengers came to Lūṭ, 'and he felt himself unable to protect them'. For Ibn ʿArabī, Lūṭ's inability is the defining characteristic of the *ḥikma* associated with this prophet. And this *ḥikma* will provide us our Lūṭian epilogue.

LŪṬ'S WISDOM

Lūṭ's *ḥikma* is that of 'power' and 'mastery', *ḥikma mulkiyya*,[2] or power exercised as *control*. But, as we have seen, the story of Lūṭ in the Qur'ān describes the very opposite: his total impotence in protecting the angels from the people and generally in curbing the people's evil acts and inclinations. As we now well know, such 'contradictions' or 'paradoxes' are the very stuff of Ibn ʿArabī's outlook, especially in his ascribing of various wisdoms to prophets. Here, then, Lūṭ's wisdom of power is that of his very impotence in preventing the unwanted behaviour. The wisdom of power here establishes this particular 'paradox', enabling Ibn ʿArabī to elaborate on his worldview in resolving the 'paradox'. This he does elegantly and succinctly, the better for our present purpose. From an initial statement of Lūṭ's lament in Qur'ān 11:80, 'Would that I had power over you or recourse to a strong support', and a Prophetic *ḥadīth*, 'May God be merciful to my brother Lūṭ who has indeed found a strong support',[3] Ibn ʿArabī derives an integrated statement of his general outlook round the issue of Lūṭ's inability to curb the people's bad behaviour.

POWERLESSNESS

For Ibn ʿArabī, Qur'ān 11:80, with Lūṭ's plaintive lament, is given final meaning in the cited *ḥadīth*. There it is made clear that Lūṭ *had* achieved the desired strong support (*rukn shadīd*) in the absence of the power he so desired. This support was 'strong', says Ibn ʿArabī, because God was with Lūṭ 'and He is strong'.[4] Additionally, 'strong support' here means Lūṭ's particular tribe (*qabīla*), and not his *larger* people (*qawm*) who would remain troublesome. Indeed, this would be the case for all

2. *Fuṣūṣ*, p. 126 and pp. 126–131 for the whole discussion of Lūṭ.
3. *Fuṣūṣ*, p. 127; al-Bukhārī, LX:11.
4. *Fuṣūṣ*, p. 127.

subsequent prophets after Lūṭ, says Ibn ʿArabī.[5] But again, the prophet's acquiring this sort of 'strong support' does not mean acquiring the power to deter the sinners. This, says Ibn ʿArabī, is because such worldly, active power is 'that effective determination (*himma*) so typical of humanity', but at the same time accidental to it and not essentially of it: 'an accidental power' (*quwwa ʿaraḍiyya*).[6] It is the concentrated human power and efficacy expressed in acting in this world (*al-himma bi'l-taṣarruf*), but it is ultimately futile as it cannot in fact change anything—notwithstanding the human agent's ideas to the contrary. This 'power' is what Lūṭ so lamented the absence of in himself, which might have helped him to stop the evildoers in their evil ways. But if this 'power' cannot really change anything, why does even a prophet such as Lūṭ seek it in order to use it in effecting worldly change? The answer for Ibn ʿArabī here incorporates much of his thinking on life's central problems: Lūṭ, as messenger/prophet, sought to curb these miscreants, as his prophetic nature, seeking the good, would impel him to do. But the prophet's nature, like that of the gnostic, is not essentially amenable to such activity; or, put another way, its mission is in other directions which remove it more from these practical works. Indeed, says Ibn ʿArabī, 'no prophet was sent until after [his] fortieth year—the time which sees him beginning in frailty and weakness'.[7] Ibn ʿArabī cites Qur'ānic words in support here, seeing in verses from two *sūras* the divinely-created pattern for human life: weakness, strength, weakness. Thus Qur'ān 30:54 gives the framework: 'It is God who created you in weakness, after weakness giving you strength and then after strength giving you again weakness and a grey head'; and Qur'ān 16:70 gives a particular construction to this framework: 'Some of you are returned to a feeble age, so they will then know nothing after having known much'.

5. *Ibid.*
6. *Ibid.*
7. *Ibid.*

This Qur'ānic paradigm of the child's weakness, the adult's relative strength and then the adult's 'grey' decline into a weakness involving loss of knowledge is for Ibn ʿArabī the proof that human power is 'accidental' rather than essential; for the Qur'ān says power is relevant only to one period of life and it cannot last. What is true for ordinary mortals is even more true for messenger/prophets who only begin their prophetic careers at the age of growing incapacity. For Ibn ʿArabī, though, this is exactly why the prophetic career begins in the twilight of the prophet's life rather than in the more vital middle period. The 'weakness' of later years is a strength. It is the strength of true knowledge and gnostic understanding, *maʿrifa*. Thus, says Ibn ʿArabī:

> If you ask what prevents the prophet having this effective power when spiritual aspirants more junior than he possess it, and, one might think, the messengers are even more worthy of it, we would answer, you are right, but another view counters you: that is that true knowledge does not allow concentrated human power (*himma*) free rein. Indeed, the greater one's *maʿrifa*, the less one's concentrated power and efficacy in this world.[8]

Possessors of gnosis, *maʿrifa*, then—messengers/prophets and sufi adepts alike—are actually restricted by their deeper knowledge from an active and efficacious participation in the world. *Maʿrifa* as passivity is a realisation of God's true sovereignty over His creation, the *ḥikma mulkiyya* which Ibn ʿArabī attributes to Lūṭ. There are 'two reasons' for this, says Ibn ʿArabī, first because the possessor of *maʿrifa* has realised 'the station of divine servitude' (*ʿubūdiyya*) and he looks toward his origins in God and, secondly, because of 'the unity of the one who is active in this way with the object of his activity'.[9] This person, consequently, 'does not see anything to which he might proffer his *himma* and

8. *Fuṣūṣ*, pp. 127–128.
9. *Fuṣūṣ*, p. 128.

that prevents him doing so. From this perspective, he sees that his opponent does not deviate from his true nature which he came to possess in the state of fixity of his essence and in the [concomitant] state of his non-being. Nothing will come into [conditional] being except as it was in the state of non-being and fixity [of essence]. Thus will he not infringe his true nature or violate his own way'.[10]

The deeper understanding provided by *maᶜrifa* for Ibn ᶜArabī, then, elucidates basic principles of his thought, as seen through Lūṭ's particular situation. These principles, here expressed so pithily, may already, in what has thus far been said, constitute a 'Lūṭian microcosm' of Ibn ᶜArabī's outlook. This microcosm is further elaborated in the remainder of the chapter. Lūṭ's 'inability' does in fact constitute a power, because it derives from his knowledge that all things—human actions included—are as they are in worldly existence from their particular fixity in pre-worldly non-being (*thubūt*). This is the 'paradoxical' power of powerlessness, where incapacity signals the power of esoteric understanding (*maᶜrifa*)—the power to do nothing effectual in the world, on the realisation that all is as it is in expression of the divine essence itself; and in the knowledge that ultimately all multiplicity is unity. Thus, in Ibn ᶜArabī's view, to the extent that one's *maᶜrifa* increases, likewise does one's effective action through concentration (*taṣarruf bi'l-himma*) decrease. *Apparent* contradiction or conflict—and it is that – in this world, for one who knows is a chimera derived from the ignorance which takes appearance for reality, as above. The gnostic, then, knows 'his opponent has not deviated from his true nature, which was his in the state of fixity of his essence and in his related state of non-being. For nothing could be manifest in the opponent's existence except what he had already possessed in that "prior" condition'.[11] There can be no true contradiction or conflict

10. *Ibid.*
11. *Ibid.*

for Ibn ʿArabī—alluding to the confrontation between Lūṭ and the people—as this is merely 'an accidental matter which the veil covering people's eyes creates'.[12] Ibn ʿArabī will provide Qur'ānic support for this, in juxtaposing elements from 30:7 and 2:88.

In this juxtaposition, Ibn ʿArabī practices his internal cross-referencing of the Qur'ān, seeing the Book, always, as a seamless document. Thus, 30:7, 'But most of them do not know—they know the externals of this worldly life and they are neglectful', is for Ibn ʿArabī to be explained by another verse from another *sūra*, 2:88, 'Our hearts are coverings'. His explanation is thus: '[The Qur'ānic words, "They are neglectful..."] in fact constitute a linguistic inversion (*maqlūb*) of God's words "Our hearts are coverings"'.[13] Ibn ʿArabī means that the word *ghāfilūn*, 'neglectful ones' in 30:7, really is to be seen as a letter-inversion of the word *ghulfun*, in 2:88, 'coverings,' the consonants of the root being the same but *in different order here*. In Ibn ʿArabī's understanding, the people described in 30:7 as not knowing and 'neglectful' are in fact impeded from knowing the deeper truth by a covering, *ghilāf*, which is 'a cover (*kann*) that keeps him from understanding the matter as it really is'.[14]

The picture is now clear: those who possess the deepest knowledge (*maʿrifa*) cannot—and, due to that knowledge, do not wish to—be very effective in this world. Lūṭ was obviously an *ʿārif* and, therefore, ineffectual. He was, however, also a prophet whose job it is to sway people and bring them over to the side of God—to make them believers. Ibn ʿArabī employs this *ʿārif*/prophet (*rasūl*) distinction to explain further his position and, in particular, to join it with his metaphysics, as the foundation of this exposition.

Thus, says Ibn ʿArabī: 'When the *ʿārif* acts effectively in the world through *himma*, it is from a divine injunction, not by

12. *Ibid.*
13. *Ibid.*
14. *Ibid.*

choice'.[15] As for the *rasūl/nabī*, then, 'There is no doubt that the station of messengership (*risāla*) demands action for reception of the message which the messenger brings. In this way does the messenger make manifest God's law'.[16] Here is the difference between *rasūl* and *walī*, for, says Ibn ʿArabī, 'The *walī* is not like that'.[17] The difference, though, lies not in their level of spiritual perfection which, it would seem, is equal with the two figures; it is, rather, *with their respective roles*. The *rasūl/nabī* must preach and disseminate his revelation and this obviously requires acting toward reception of that message, while the *ʿārif/walī* simply develops spiritually with no necessary practical involvements of this sort. However, Ibn ʿArabī expands on the role of the *rasūl/nabī*, emphasising that figure's abiding reluctance to attempt an efficacious worldly involvement, despite his obligation to preach God's truth. Ibn ʿArabī will also seek here to underscore a main metaphysical point.

The messenger, then, does not explicitly court worldly involvement, even when his role necessitates it, says Ibn ʿArabī; for the messenger is compassionate toward his people and 'he does not wish to be excessive in turning the argument against them. In that would lie their destruction. So he spares them.'[18] This gentle and reluctant messenger/prophet, so considerate of the sensibilities of his people in preaching God's truth to them (with its necessary demands) is circumspect also for other reasons. He knows that even his presumably most potent means of swaying an audience, miracles, are never widely effective. Indeed, he knows that when a miracle is manifested some will as a result become believers, some will understand it but reject it and refuse to confirm it out of evil, arrogance and envy, while still others will attribute it to magic and deception.[19] Messengers/

15. *Fuṣūṣ*, p. 129.
16. *Ibid.*
17. *Ibid.*
18. *Fuṣūṣ*, p. 130.
19. *Ibid.*

prophets thus know that, in any case, the only believer is 'one whose heart God illumines with the light of belief'.[20] Otherwise, miracles usually will *not* move people to accept revelation. Ibn ʿArabī sees this truth spelled out clearly in Qur'ān 28:56: 'You do not guide those whom you wish, but God does guide those whom He wishes'. This truth was exemplified in the clearest way, says Ibn ʿArabī, in the case of the Prophet's beloved uncle, Abū Ṭālib, whom the Prophet, to his great disappointment, could not persuade to accept Islam.[21] It was this incident, in fact, which occasioned the revelation of Qur'ān 28:56, enjoining prophetic modesty in these matters. For Ibn ʿArabī, all this is, in effect, God saying that for a messenger 'the only thing incumbent upon him is preaching the revelation'.[22] Qur'ān 2:272 for Ibn ʿArabī adds further scriptural substance to the argument: 'Guiding them is not incumbent upon you; rather does God guide those whom he wishes'.

Having made his point now so clearly, Ibn ʿArabī carries the argument to what is for him its very foundation: the metaphysical substrate. And here, again, he cites the Qur'ān as his point of departure, in the continuation of 2:272: 'He knows most about those who are guided'. This means, says Ibn ʿArabī, 'those who give to God knowledge concerning their guidance in their state of non-being, in their fixed essences'.[23] Thus: 'Those who are believers, in the [state of the] fixity of their essence and in the state of their non-being, will [likewise] appear in that form in the state of their [conditional] existence. God had known that they would then consequently be [believers]'.[24] For this reason,

20. *Ibid.*

21. *Ibid.* Tradition reports that Abū Ṭālib remained loyal to the Prophet until his death, but that, to Muḥammad's great disappointment, his uncle never did accept Islam. Standard accounts of this relationship can be found in the main biographies of the Prophet and in histories of early Islam.

22. *Ibid.*

23. *Ibid.*

24. *Ibid.*

says Ibn ʿArabī, 'God said, "He knows most about those who are guided"'.[25]

God's knowledge, however, seems not that of an omnipotent God who, as Qur'ān 2:272 says, 'guides those whom He wishes', but rather only that of an omniscient God whose knowledge here derives from the nature of His 'servants' in their pre-existent state. His servants 'give Him' His knowledge of their 'future' status as believers (or not), according to Ibn ʿArabī. But for Ibn ʿArabī, the *rasūl*/prophet could not truly guide anyone—as Lūṭ's situation made clear—for only God does that. What, then, is God's role here with respect to His servants and their belief (or unbelief) and what is His servants' moral status with respect to their own belief, with Lūṭ as the immediate background to the issue?

Solely on the Qur'ānic grounds of 2:272, as Ibn ʿArabī has cited it, the picture is very clear: God guides his creatures as He wishes and He knows who is guided and who is not. Lūṭ, and other *rusul*, might just as well minimise their efforts at dramatic and forceful persuasion and stick to disseminating the revelation. Though there are obvious problems of 'free-will' and 'determinism' lurking in such Qur'ānic ideas, later mainstream Islamic theological thought elegantly and easily accommodated itself: the 'excluded middle' between 'freedom' and 'coercion' was, in effect, *included* and installed as a 'pivot', enabling one to see the issue from either side. Thus God as absolute sovereign and as the only source of causal efficacy *did* determine and empower human actions but, at the same time, human beings were considered responsible for what they did and God's justice *was* complete and absolute.[26] Ibn ʿArabī here adheres with

25. *Ibid.*

26. Though the theological argumentation around this issue was certainly not uniform and monolithic in its conclusions, this compromise was central to the doctrine of much of Sunnī Ashʿarī theology. The early Ashʿarī notion of *kasb*, acquisition, may be seen as the focal point in the doctrine. See *Encyclopaedia of Islam*, new edition, article *kasb*, Vol. IV, pp. 690–694. Even, for example, the later 'philosophical theologian', Fakhr al-Dīn al-Rāzī, who rejected and went beyond the early notion of acquisition, arrived at essentially the same conclusions by other means. See al-Rāzī's *Muḥaṣṣal Afkār al-Mutaqaddimīn wa'l-Muta'akhkhirīn, passim.*

fidelity to the explicit notion in this Qur'ānic verse (and others like it) and the central traditional theological gloss on the issue. However, one serious difference remains: the fixed essences (*aʿyān thābita*) would still appear to detract from both God's status and power and man's free will, as it is on their foundation that God's servants 'give' to God the knowledge of who they irrevocably are—believers or not, among other things. And God, it seems, cannot then 'guide' as He might wish, *e.g.*, to belief rather than unbelief, 'those whom He wishes', as all of His creatures appear to be what they are according to their fixed nature in their fixed essences.

This difference is telling: in Qur'ānic and related theological terms, human freedom of action is 'freedom' in the usual understanding of that term. For Ibn ʿArabī, however, human freedom of choice and efficacy are *determined* by the fixed essences. Thus one's 'free' choice of belief or unbelief—the behaviour pertinent to Lūṭ's story—is also *determined.* Even when we 'choose freely', our 'choice' was ineluctable and remains irrevocable, an unfolding of our *aʿyān thābita.* In this context, even God's attempt to change the situation, should He so desire, is inconceivable.

This is a finely focused expression of Ibn ʿArabī's sufi metaphysics in its integration with the Qur'ān. The metaphysical, the ethical and the scriptural are layered and overlapped in a seamless integration. The 'determinism' introduced with the *aʿyān thābita* is metaphysical, not personal. Its ineluctable nature in this sense does not detract from or diminish the moral agency and accountability of the individual or God's authoritative power. The structure of divine injunction and human response, with the assumption of human choice and responsibility, remains rock-solid, *as one dimension* within a cosmology of timeless fixed essences in a universal unity of absolute being. The phenomenal world as it is, in its multiplicity and division, contains a central component of revelational ethics, where divine power, human freedom of choice and divine responses (in reward or punishment) constitute the core. Ibn ʿArabī sincerely speaks this language. However, he also speaks the language of his metaphysics in clear association with the other language, as we know. The Qur'ān, as source and text of the first language, here ensures the permanency and immutability of the ethical truths spoken in that tongue, while also, more deeply, indicating for Ibn ʿArabī the metaphysical truths emanating from that text, for those who understand. Thus the miscreants whom Lūṭ could not separate from their unbelief *are* guilty of wrongdoing out of choice, as that choice of wrongdoing is implicit in revelation itself; and God *is* capable of allowing them that choice. But equally, there is the metaphysical fact that the choice itself, God's and man's, in its very freedom, is *compelled* and *ordained* in the very order of things. The divine and human 'free' choices and their results are subsumed within the larger universe of metaphysical order and determination—and the choices are then fixed *in their own domain.*[28]

Ibn ʿArabī's 'two languages', ultimately, are necessarily subsumed within the larger category of God's very nature in his own essence. The realities designated in the 'two languages' are for Ibn ʿArabī manifestations of the divine essence; this is the source and meaning of their reciprocality. The metaphysical language takes pride of place, though not greater 'importance', in this scheme, as it is the most 'universal' and 'comprehensive', most truly reflecting God's own nature. Ibn ʿArabī makes this clear toward the end of his discussion of Lūṭ, saying, in God's name: '[Just as We are not unjust to our servants], likewise we say to them only what Our essence gives us to say to them. Our essence in fact makes known to us in its very nature that We will say this and not that. We say, then, only what We know we will say'.[29] If God is 'compelled', it is His own nature which 'compels'. His words to His servants—commandments and

27. 'Choice', however, here loses its ordinary meaning.
28. *Fuṣūṣ*, pp. 130–131.
29. *Fuṣūṣ*, p. 131.

prohibitions—must be as they are for this reason, as must everything. In this view, the *aʿyān thābita*, like all else, are a reflection of the divine essence which represents Ibn ʿArabī's unitive absolute being. Unknowable in itself, this divine unity/absolute being is 'known' only in its guise as conditional being, every aspect of which is as it is for that reason. Lūṭ's preaching of God's message to the sinners, their recalcitrance and God's destroying them, here constitute an ineluctable 'foreordained' drama, played to the fixed script of the true God's own essential nature. 'God' here, of course, is both Ibn ʿArabī's 'created God in the religious beliefs' and the divine essence/absolute being, the former being 'directed' by the latter. Lūṭ, as prophet, was aware of this, but his role of one who warns in the drama (a 'losing' part) remained incumbent upon him, despite the inevitability of his 'failure'. Here, again, absolute unitive being in the divine essence is manifested in the multiplicity of phenomenal being, this 'intersection of realms' reflected in the words of the Qur'ān. Ibn ʿArabī sums up these reciprocal relationships in a closing message of Lūṭian truth:

> Everything is from us and from them.
> The exchange is between us and them
> Even if they are not from us, then we are no doubt from them.
> So realise, Oh friend, this wisdom of domination in the word of Lūṭ.
> For it is the quintessential esoteric knowledge.
> Thus has the secret become clear to you and the matter lucid.
> And that which is called odd is indeed implicit in the even.[30]

Here the 'paradox' of the reciprocality—God and man, the One and the many, the odd and the even—as it has been resolved in Ibn ʿArabī's telling of Lūṭ's tale, is 'the quintessential esoteric knowledge' (*lubāb al-maʿrifa*).

30. *Ibid.*

Bibliography

ʿAbdur Rabb, Muḥammad, *The Life, Thought and Historical Importance of Abū Yazīd al-Bisṭāmī*, Dacca, 1971.

Aberbach M. and Smolar, L., 'The Golden Calf Episode in post-Biblical Literature', *Hebrew Union College Annual*, 39, 1968.

Addas, Claude, *Quest for the Red Sulphur: The Life of Ibn ʿArabī*, translated from the French by P. Kingsley, Cambridge, The Islamic Texts Society, 1993.

Allard, Michel, *Le Problème des attributs divins dans la doctrine d'al-Ashʿarī et de ses premiers grands disciples*, Beirut, 1965.

al-Anṣārī, Abū Muḥammad ʿAbdullāh Jamāl al-Dīn b. Hishām, *Sharḥ Qaṭr al-Nadā wa-Ball al-Ṣadā*, Cairo, 1963.

Avery-Peck, A.J. and Neusner, J. (eds.), *The Blackwell Companion to Judaism*, Oxford, Blackwell Publishers, 2000.

Bori, Pier Cesare, *The Golden Calf*, trans. D. Ward, University of South Florida, 1990.

al-Bukhārī, Muḥammad b. Ismāʿīl, *Ṣaḥiḥ*, 3 volumes, ed., L. Krehl, Leiden, 1862–1868, Volume IV, ed. T. Juynboll, 1907–1908.

Burrell D. and Daher N., *Al-Ghazālī on the Ninety-nine Beautiful Names of God*, Cambridge, The Islamic Texts Society, 1992

Chittick, William, *Imaginal Worlds: Ibn al-ʿArabī and the Problem of Religious Diversity*, Albany, SUNY, 1994.

——*The Ṣūfī Path of Knowledge*, Albany, SUNY, 1989.

Chodkiewicz, Michel, *The Seal of the Saints: Prophethood and Sainthood in the Doctrine of Ibn ʿArabī*, trans. L. Sherrard, Cambridge, The Islamic Texts Society, 1993.

Corbin, Henri, *Creative Imagination in the Sufism of Ibn ʿArabī*, trans. R. Manheim, Princeton, 1969.

The Encyclopaedia of Islam, new edition, Leiden, E.J. Brill, 1960–.

The Encyclopaedia of Islam, old edition, Leiden, E.J. Brill, 1913–1938.

Encyclopaedia Judaica, Jerusalem, Keter, 1971.

The Encyclopedia of Religion, ed., M. Eliade, New York, Collier Macmillan, 1987.

Evstatiev, Simeon, 'The Khātam al-Nabiyyīn Doctrine in Arabic Historical Thought' in *Studies in Arabic and Islam*, proceedings of the 19th Congress, Union Européenne des Arabisants et Islamisants, Halle, 1998, eds. S. Leder, H. Kilpatrick, B. M. Jartel-Thoumian, H. Schonig, Uitgeverij Peeters, Leuven, Paris, Sterling, VA, 2002, pp. 455–467.

Firestone, Reuven, *Journeys in Holy Lands*, Albany, SUNY, 1990.

Frank, Richard, M., *Beings and their Attributes: The Teachings of the Baṣrian School of the Muʿtazila in the Classical Period*, Albany, SUNY, 1978.

al-Ghazālī, Abū Ḥāmid, *al-Maqṣad al-Asnā fī Sharḥ Maʿānī Asmā' Allāh al-Ḥusnā*, ed. F. Shehadi, Beirut, 1971.

Graham, William, *Divine Word and Prophetic Word in Early Islam*, Mouton, The Hague, 1987.

Al-Ḥakīm, Suʿād, *al-Muʿjam al-Ṣūfī*, Beirut, Dandara, 1981.

Hughes, Thomas P., *A Dictionary of Islam*, London, 1885.

Ibn ʿArabī, *Fuṣūṣ al-Ḥikam*, ed. A. ʿAfīfī, Beirut, n.d..

Ibn Ḥanbal, Aḥmad, *Musnad*, 11 volumes, Cairo, 1949–1953.

Ibn Kathīr, *Tafsīr*, Cairo, n.d.

Izutsu, Toshihiko, *God and Man in the Koran*, The Keio Institute of Cultural and Linguistic Studies, 1964.

——*Sufism and Taoism*, Berkeley, University of California, 1984.

——*The Structure of the Ethical Terms in the Qur'ān*, Tokyo, Keio University, 1959.

al-Kisā'ī, *Qiṣaṣ al-Anbiyā'*, trans. M. Thackston, Wheeler as *Tales of the Prophets*, Boston, Twayne Publishers, 1978.

Lazarus-Yafeh, Hava, *Intertwined Worlds, Medieval Islam and Biblical Criticism*, Princeton, Princeton University Press, 1992.

al-Maḥallī, Jamāl al-Dīn Muḥammad b. Aḥmad and al-Ṣuyūtī, Jamāl al-Dīn ʿAbd al-Raḥmān b. Abū Bakr, *Tafsīr al-Imāmayn al-Jalālayn*, Beirut, n.d..

Muslim, b. al-Ḥajjāj, *Ṣaḥiḥ*, 6 volumes, Cairo, n.d..

Nasā'ī, Abū ʿAbd al-Raḥmān, *Sunan*, Cairo, 1964.

Nicholson, Reynold, *Studies in Islamic Mysticism*, Cambridge, 1921.

The Oxford Companion to the Bible, New York, Oxford University Press, 1971.

Qāshānī, ʿAbd al-Razzāq, *Sharḥ ʿala Fuṣūṣ al-Ḥikam*, Cairo, n.d.

Rahbar, Da'ūd, *God of Justice: A Study of the Ethical Doctrine of the Qur'ān*, E.J. Leiden, Brill, 1960.

al-Razi, Fakhr al-Dīn, *Muḥaṣṣal Afkār al-Mutaqaddimīn wa'l-Muta'akhkhirīn*, ed. T. Saʿd, Cairo, n.d..

The Shorter Encyclopaedia of Islam, Leiden, E. J. Brill, 1953.

Schimmel, Annemarie, *As Through a Veil: Mystical Poetry in Islam*, New York, Columbia University, 1982.

——*Mystical Dimensions of Islam*, Chapel Hill, University of North Carolina, 1975.

al-Suyuṭī, see al-Maḥallī.

Watt, William M., *Free Will and Predestination in Early Islam*, Luzac, London, 1948.

al-Zamakhsharī, Abū'l-Qāsim, *al-Kashshāf*, Beirut, 1977.

Index

ᶜAbd Allāh b. Ubayy, 194
ᶜAbdur Rabb, M., 162
Aberbach, M., 40
Absolute Being, 9–10, 19, 117, 146, 167, 169–171
Abū Ṭālib, 212
Ādam (Adam), 17–18, 22–24, 27, 29, 176–177, 179, 181, 185
Addas, C., 2
ᶜAfīfī, A., 3, 5
ᶜĀ'isha, 194
Ali, A. Yusuf, 13
Allard, M., 18
Anbiyā', Nabiyyūn (see also Prophets), 142
al-Anbiyā' al- ᶜĀmiyyūn (see also General Prophets), 143
al-Anbiyā' al-Musharriᶜūn, Nabī Musharriᶜ (see also Legislating Prophets), 143, 148
al-Anṣārī, ᶜAbdullāh Jamāl al-Dīn, 191
ᶜĀrif (ᶜĀrifūn), 84, 91, 112, 134, 143, 171, 210
ᶜĀrif / Walī, 211
Avery-Peck, A. J., 137
ᶜAyn Thābita, Aᶜyān Thābita, (see also Fixed Essences), 11–12, 19, 80, 85, 87, 93, 98, 159, 214
al-Bisṭāmī, Abū Yazīd, 123, 162
Breath, Divine, 118, 120 ,135
Bori, P. C., 39
al-Bukhārī, 36, 128, 184, 206
Chittick, W., 126
Chodkiewicz, M., 13
Conditional Being, 9–10, 19, 117, 146, 171
Corbin, H., 2, 10
Exodus, 39
Fātiḥa, 105, 107–108, 196–198
Firestone, R., 69
Fixed Essences, 11–12, 19, 159, 212
Frank, R. M., 167
Friend of God (God's Friend), 69, 71–72
General Prophets, 143
Genesis, 17, 70, 204
al-Ghazālī, Abū Ḥāmid, 72, 78–79
God created in the Religious Doctrines, 10
God's Mercy, 46, 106, 116, 156–158, 163–166, 169–174
Graham, W., 196
al-Ḥakīm, S., 10–12, 20, 126, 159
al-Ḥaqq al-Makhlūq fī al-Iᶜtiqādāt (see also God created in the religious doctrines), 10, 121, 126
Hārūn (Aaron), 11–12, 25, 30, 38–45, 47–48, 50–51, 53–54, 56, 58, 64, 66, 106
Ḥikma Aḥadiyya (see also Wisdom of Divine Unity), 104

Ḥikma Fardiyya (see also Wisdom of Singularity), 176
Ḥikma Ilāhiyya (see also Wisdom of Divinity), 18
Ḥikma Imāmiyya (see also Wisdom of Leadership), 44
Ḥikma Mālikiyya (see also Wisdom of Divine Sovereignty), 155–156
Ḥikma Muhayyamiyya (see also Wisdom of Ecstatic Love), 71–72
Ḥikma Mulkiyya (see also Wisdom of Domination), 206
Ḥikma Qadariyya (see also Wisdom of Divine Decree), 138, 142, 152
Ḥikma ʿUluwiyya (see also Wisdom of Exaltedness), 26
Hūd, 102–104, 107–108, 114, 164
Hughes, T. P., 104, 154, 204
Ḥukm, 21, 75, 82, 93, 95, 117, 168–169
Iblīs, 23
Ibn Kathīr, 181
Ibrāhīm (Abraham), 69–71, 73–75, 77, 81, 96, 99, 101, 169, 170
al-Insān al-Kāmil (see also Perfect Man), 18, 21, 109, 177
Isaiah, 70
Izutsu, T., 103, 156, 161
Jesus, 52
al-Junayd, Abū'l-Qāsim, 123
Kawn Jāmiʿ, 18–21
Khalīl, Khalīl Allāh (see also Friend of God), 69, 71, 73–75, 99–100
al-Khiḍr, 150
al-Kisā'ī, 152
Lazarus-Yafeh, H., 137
Legislating Prophets, 143
Lubāb al-Maʿrifa, 216
Lūṭ (Lot), 204–207, 209–210, 216
Majālin, 10, 59
Majālin Ilāhiyya, 60
Maʿrifa, 84, 90, 134, 208–210
Maryam, 175
Matthew, 52
Muḥammad, 176–177, 179–183
Mūsā (Moses), 25–30, 32–33, 35–48, 50–51, 53–54, 56, 58–59, 64, 66, 173
Nafas (*Anfās, Nafas al-Raḥmān, al-Nafas al-Raḥmānī*; see also Breath, Divine), 118, 120, 135, 186
Neusner, V., 137
Nicholson, R., 162
Nisba (Nisab), 79, 159, 167
The One and the many, 7–11, 60, 122
Parat, R., 69
Perfect Man, 18, 21, 36
Perfume, 181, 190–193, 195, 199
Prayer, 181, 190, 196–203
Prophets, 142
al-Qaḍā' wa'l-Qadar, 138–144, 146–147, 149, 151
al-Qāshānī, ʿAbd al-Razzāq, 3
Qasī, Abū'l-Qāsim, 169
Rahbar, D., 103, 106, 161
Raḥma (see also God's Mercy), 46, 116, 118, 157, 166, 168
al-Rāzī, Fakhr al-Dīn, 213
Ṣalāt (see also Prayer), 181, 190, 196–200
Sāliḥ, 114
Schimmel, A., 4–5, 161
Sermon on the Mount, 52
Shehadi, Fadlou A., 72
Shuʿayb, 106, 114, 122, 129, 136
Ṣirāṭ Mustaqīm (see also Straight Path), 105–106, 110
Smolar, L., 40
Straight Path, 106, 111–112

Subjugation, 54–59
Sufi Metaphysics (metaphysics, metaphysical), 3, 5–9, 11–15, 20, 22, 24, 34, 49, 50, 53, 64, 66, 72, 75, 82–84, 97–99, 101, 112–113, 132–133, 142–146, 149, 151, 153, 156–160, 162–164, 166–167, 170, 172–173, 178, 201, 203, 214
Tajallin, 68, 79–80
Takhallul, 70–72, 74–75, 77–78, 81, 96, 98, 100
Ta'nīth Dhāt, 193, 203
Taskhīr (see also Subjugation), 54
Thackston, W. M., 152–153
Ṭīb (see also Perfume), 190, 195
ʿUzayr (Ezra), 137–139, 142, 146, 148–153
Watt, W. M., 140
Wisdom of Divine Decree, 137–138
Wisdom of Divine Sovereignty, 154–155
Wisdom of Divine Unity, 104
Wisdom of Divinity, 17–18
Wisdom of Domination, 216
Wisdom of Ecstatic Love, 69, 71
Wisdom of Exaltedness, 25–26
Wisdom of Leadership, 38, 44
Wisdom of Singularity, 176
Woman (Women), 181–183, 186–188, 191–193, 196
Wujūd Muqayyad (see also Conditional Being), 9, 17, 19, 92–93, 99, 117, 122, 146
Wujūd Muṭlaq (see also Absolute Being), 9, 92, 99, 117, 122, 146, 167, 169, 171
Wuṣla, 189, 202
Zakariyyā (Zachariah), 18, 75, 106, 121, 154, 156, 158, 170, 175, 200
al-Zamakhsharī, Abū'l-Qāsim, 150
Ẓill, 10–11